IMAGES
of America

MARSHALL

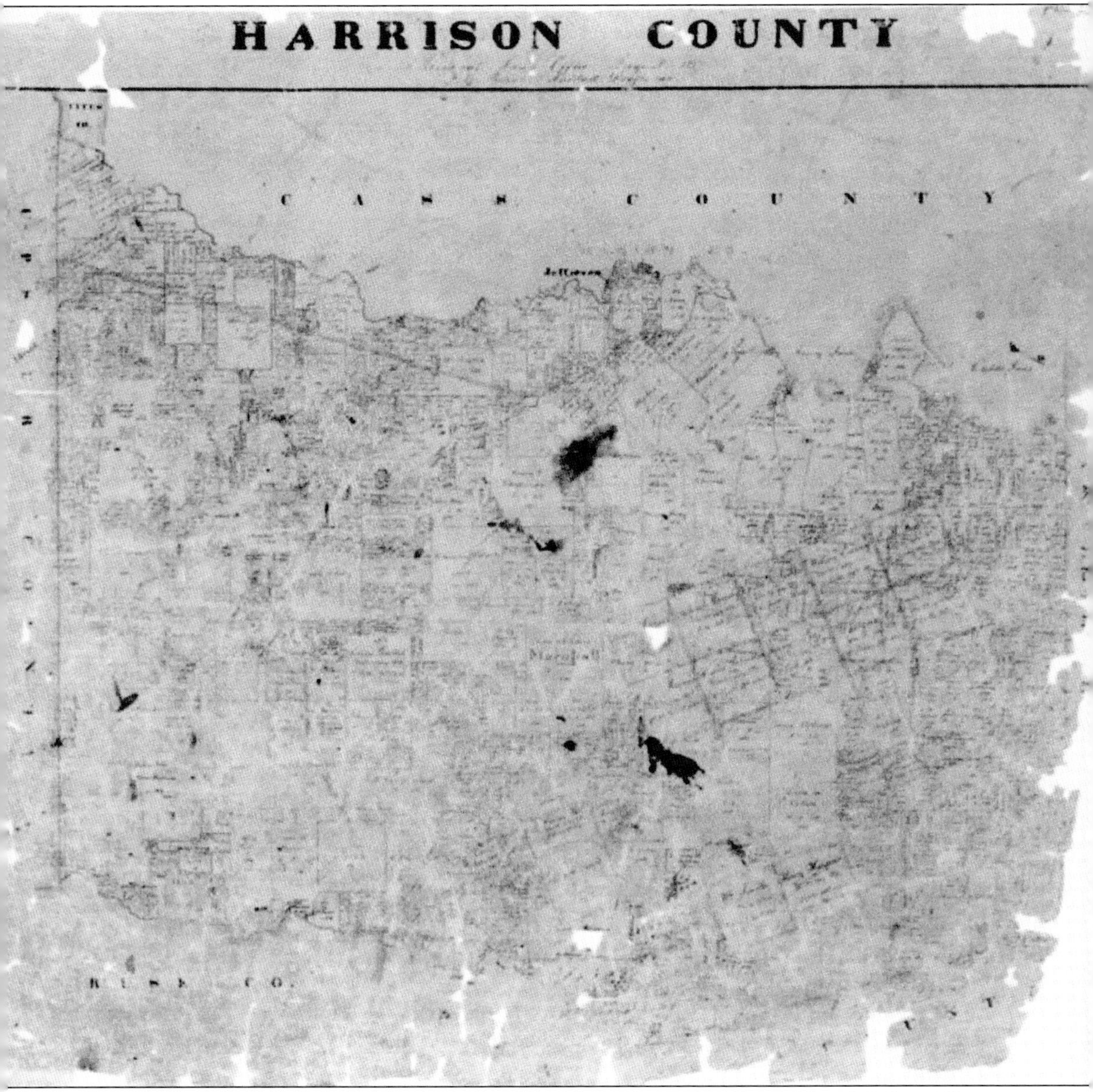

This early map of Harrison County was acquired from the Texas General Land Office. (Courtesy of Texas General Land Office, Archives and Records, Austin.)

ON THE COVER: Harrison County was created in 1839. It has had three county seats and five courthouses since that time. The structure shown on the cover was completed in 1901. It is the third courthouse to be located on Peter Whetstone Square. The architect in charge of this construction was C. B. Lancaster, a resident of Harrison County, and the design architect was James Riely Gordon. The building now houses the Harrison County Historical Museum, the offices of the county commissioners, and the office of the county judge. (Courtesy of the Harrison County Historical Museum.)

IMAGES
of America

MARSHALL

Joyce Williamson,
Pat Smith-Gasperson, Lucile Estell,
and the Harrison County Historical Museum

ARCADIA
PUBLISHING

ISBN 978-0-7385-7903-0

Published by Arcadia Publishing
Charleston, South Carolina

Printed in the United States of America

Library of Congress Control Number: 2010920202

For all general information, please contact Arcadia Publishing:
Telephone 843-853-2070
Fax 843-853-0044
E-mail sales@arcadiapublishing.com
For customer service and orders:
Toll-Free 1-888-313-2665

Visit us on the Internet at www.arcadiapublishing.com

This book is dedicated to Mr. and Mrs. Hugh Estell, Rockdale, Texas; Mr. and Mrs. Fred G. Smith, Norphlet, Arkansas; Adrian Gasperson, Marshall, Texas; Mr. and Mrs. Dallas Rawlinson, Jacksonville, Texas; and T. J. Williamson, Marshall, Texas.

Contents

Acknowledgments		6
Introduction		7
1.	Influence of the French and Spanish	9
2.	Colonization, Mexican Rule, and Texas Independence	17
3.	The Harrison County Courthouse	23
4.	Economic Development of Marshall	35
5.	Railroads in Marshall	57
6.	Marshall during the Civil War	69
7.	Education in Marshall	77
8.	Historic Churches in Marshall	87
9.	More about Marshall	93
10.	The Bright and Shining Future of Marshall	111

Foreword

For more than a century and a half, Marshall, Texas, has stood as a towering symbol of American pride and ingenuity. Beginning with the rumble of the 1811 earthquake, which created Caddo Lake and ultimately the land that Marshall, Texas, occupies, it has developed into a place that is as rich and fertile and varied as the people who have inhabited it, tilled it, loved it, and died for it when necessary. Most important of all, it has been preserved to be loved by generations yet unborn.

This book is important because it reminds us of our past. It tells us who we are and why we are the way we are. It is necessary for us to connect ourselves to this past if we are to continue our heritage of faithfulness to God, integrity, and freedom. It is to those brave souls who have brought us thus far and to those who will guide us in the years to come that this book is dedicated.

The Harrison County Museum has been extremely supportive of this project. Special thanks is expressed to Janet Cook, executive director of the Harrison County Historical Museum; Gwen Warren, collections coordinator for the museum; and Peggy Riddle, special consultant responsible for the design and preparation of exhibits in the museum.

The three of us who prepared this book are longtime friends and longtime educators. Each of us was, at some point in our careers, a teacher. It is our hope that within these pages lies the essence of what we thought and taught. This book is a salute to Marshall, now working toward the completion of its second century as a thriving community laced with American values. It is a salute to our schools, which have worked so diligently to preserve our history and to pass it forward to the next generation. Most of all, it is a salute to the students who challenged us and inspired us and whom we love dearly!

—Pat Smith-Gasperson, Retired
Superintendent of Schools
Marshall, Texas (1984–1994)

ACKNOWLEDGMENTS

The majority of photographs in this book are the property of the Harrison County Historical Museum, and unless otherwise noted, they came from that collection. Photographs were scanned by Gwen Warren, the collections coordinator for the museum, and Ben Hughes, a professional photographer from Marshall, Texas. Henry Bradbury permitted the use of postcards from his extensive collection of Marshall scenes, and he also provided technical advice. Leta Kay with the Caddo Lake National Wildlife Refuge also assisted with the acquisition of both photographs and information.

Janet Cook, the executive director of the Harrison County Historical Museum, provided invaluable consultative assistance with research and editing the book. Also assisting in providing information was Peggy Riddle, the museum consultant from Dallas, Texas.

Anyone who loves Marshall and its rich heritage will recognize immediately the contribution and foresight of the late Vivian Hackney as he arranged with Marshall artist Max Cole to paint highlights in the city's history. These paintings are now the property of the Harrison County Historical Museum. Their existence and the narrative that accompanies each painting enrich and clarify the history of Marshall. They exist because of the efforts of one of Marshall's strongest historians, Vivian Hackney. Photographs of the paintings are found throughout this book, compliments of museum consultant Peggy Riddle. The original photographs are owned by the Harrison County Historical Museum.

Hannah Carney, editor for Arcadia Publishing, provided valuable assistance in the production of the book.

INTRODUCTION

Nestled among the towering pines of East Texas is the city of Marshall, located on seven hills, as was the ancient city of Rome. First there was the land, and then overnight, 25,000 acres of that land became mystical, magical Caddo Lake. Americans native to this area, the Caddo Indians, say that this lake was formed as a result of the earthquake, which occurred in New Madrid, Texas, in 1811. Others attribute it to a mass of trees, which fell into and blocked the Red River, resulting in the upheaval of the land that formed Caddo Lake. Regardless of which account is true and accurate, Caddo Lake is there—it is real and lends to the area a mystique, which radiates from it, giving the entire East Texas area a compelling and distinct atmosphere. The rich land first existed and then came the people. It is from this equally rich heritage of the land, and the people who inhabited it, that there arises a history, which is brave, undaunted, and inspiring. It is a history that epitomizes a people filled with courage and valor, citizens dedicated to American ideals with a history worthy of its preservation.

Seven flags have flown over the land that is now Marshall, Texas—the flags of France, Spain, Mexico, the Republic of Texas, the Confederate States of America, the State of Missouri (government in exile), and the United States.

Through the years the economy of Marshall has varied. It was a cotton-producing area until the 1930s. Cotton and other agriculture-related industries have been prominent since Marshall became a railroad town early in its history, thereby guaranteeing its dominance over its sister city of Jefferson, which the railroad bypassed. Education has been, and continues to be, a major emphasis. Marshall is now the home of East Texas Baptist University, Wiley College, and Texas State Technical College. Bishop College was formerly located in Marshall.

Marshall is the county seat of Harrison County. The city of Marshall has always operated around a square with the courthouse in the middle. Two men were of special importance in U.S. history at this time. Isaac Van Zandt suggested the name of Marshall after Chief Justice John Marshall. Van Zandt is buried in Greenwood Cemetery. Jonas Harrison suggested the name for the county. Today county business is conducted in a courthouse constructed adjacent to the square, and the restored 1901 courthouse houses the Harrison County Historical Museum and the offices of the county commissioners and county judge.

Marshall was laid out using a 64 block plan. A public square was placed in the center of the grid. Each of the boundary streets was named Border. North Border is now Grand Avenue, East Border is now Alamo Boulevard, South Border is now Travis Street, and West Border is now Grove Street.

The Caddo Indians were a prelude to the founding and growth of the city itself. Before Marshall was established as a city, the land on which Marshall stands was occupied by Tejas or Adais Caddo Indians. These were friendly people who were farmers and who did not move about very often. Their houses were much more permanent than most Native American dwellings throughout Texas. One reason that the Caddoes occupied this area was the fact that it had a wonderful climate, plenty of rainfall and land suitable for farming. They were friendly to both French and Spanish explorers as they came into East Texas.

The Caddo Indians are no longer found in large numbers in East Texas. In nearby Robeline, Louisiana, there is a tribe of Adais Caddo Indians led by Chief Rufus Davis. In addition to being the leader of these Native Americans, Chief Davis is a very successful businessman. Also, he was recently honored for working out successful solutions for some of today's energy problems. He has recently been awarded patents for two of his solutions for two of today's energy problems. Many of the traditions that are observed today by Native Americans were also observed by their ancestors that were living on the land where Marshall is now located.

Many of the features that drew the Caddo Indians to this area also attracted settlers coming in from other areas in the United States to seek a new life. The ample wood, the game, the rainfall, and the abundance of fresh water also attracted newcomers to stay in the area.

One

Influence of the French and Spanish

During the early years of exploration in East Texas, adventurers from both France and Spain evidenced an interest in what is now Texas. As had many before them, they were looking for a passage to the Orient. First was Spanish leader Hernando Cortes in 1519, although his concern was more with other parts of Texas rather than the area that now is Marshall. Others were to follow, venturing into the unknown, which included the part of East Texas that Marshall is now located.

In 1542, Luis de Moscoso attempted to lead Spanish explorers through Arkansas to Mexico. They headed through Caddo Lake and then southward through the land where Marshall was to be founded some centuries later. Moscoso and his entourage moved southwestward, probably about as far as Mineral Wells. They found it increasingly difficult to obtain food and eventually headed back toward East Texas.

In 1679, approximately 300 Spanish troops moved northward through East Texas in an effort to stop French encroachment. They were unable to find a way to cross Caddo Lake. Encouraged by the presence of the friendly Native Americans, they began a settlement at Port Caddo, but they were unable to maintain it because of the remoteness and scarcity of resources.

The Native Americans living in the area that was to become Marshall interacted with these early visitors, usually in a positive way. The Caddo Indians were peaceful farmers and home builders. The French and Spanish both learned much from them.

However, inroads of the French and Spanish were brief and had little direct influence on Marshall, which reflects neither strong French or Spanish influences today. But they did have a significant influence on Texas as a whole, an influence seen today in both architecture and language. The first two flags, the Spanish and the French, were to set the stage for the rich and colorful history that is embedded in Marshall. During this time, both France and Spain gained favor with the Caddo Indians, which assisted both nations as they continued their search for the riches reported to abound in the New World.

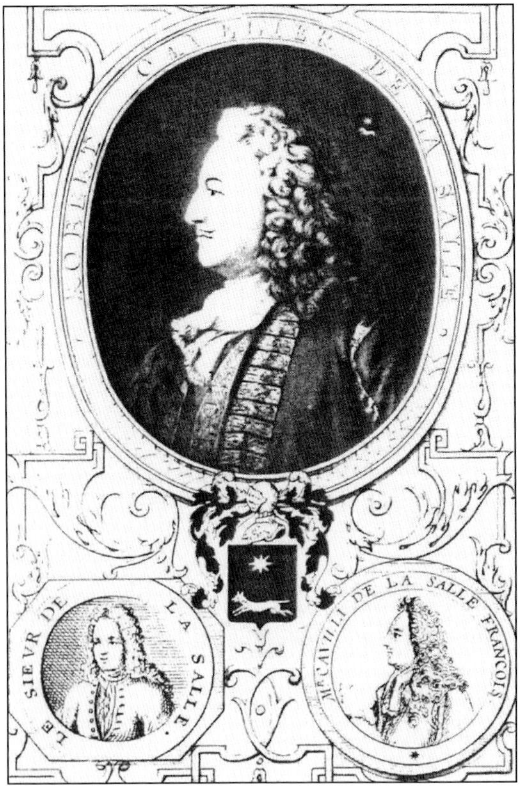

Robert Cavelier Sieur de la Salle was extremely influential in the exploration and colonization of the New World by the French. (Courtesy of Institute of Texan Culture, University of Texas at San Antonio, No. 072–0681.)

The rivers in Texas were extremely important to early settlers and Native Americans alike. They were dependent upon them not only for water, but also for transportation. This map indicates the location of Native Americans and rivers in Texas. (Reprinted with permission from the *Atlas of Texas*, Austin: Bureau of Business Research, 1976. Copyright held by the University of Texas Board of Regents.)

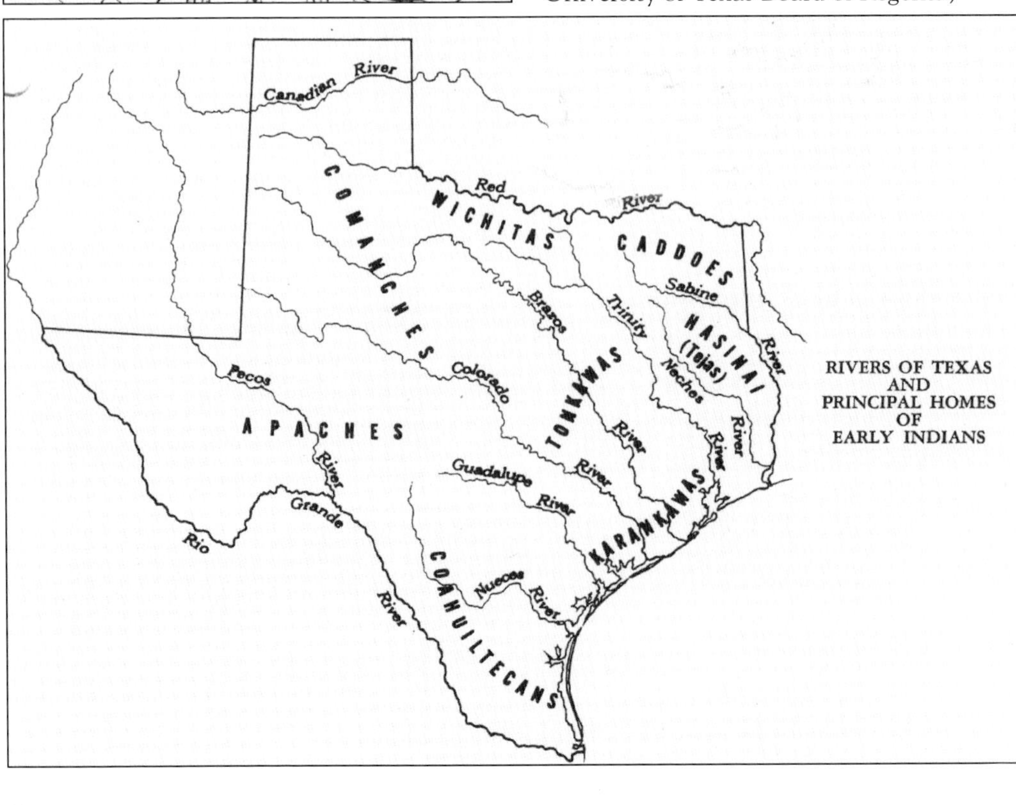

Caddoes were among the Native Americans who inhabited East Texas. They were farmers who lived in thatched huts and were generally a peace-loving people. (Courtesy of W. S. Benson Publishing Company, Austin.)

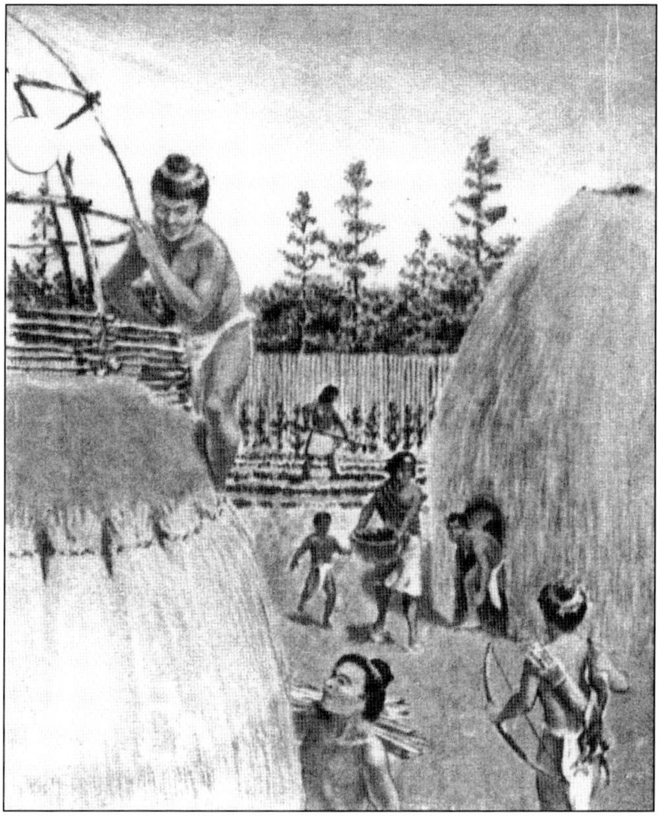

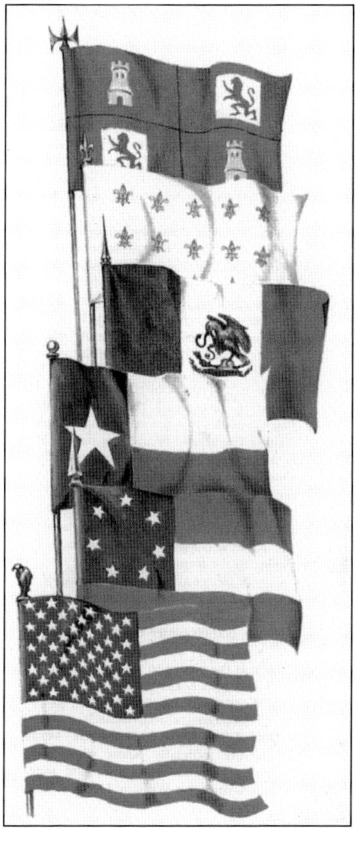

Seven flags have flown over Marshall; six of them are shown here. From top to bottom are the flags of Spain, France, Mexico, Republic of Texas, Confederate, and the United States. (Courtesy of W. S. Benson Publishing, Austin.)

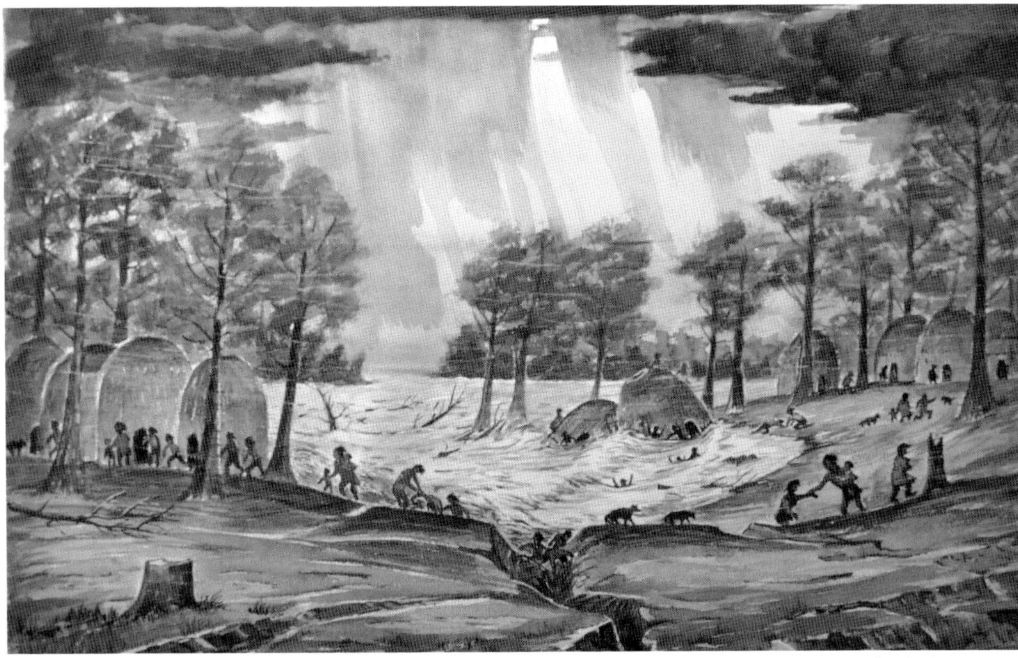

December 16, 1811, was the first of a series of major earthquakes near New Madrid, Louisiana Territory (now Missouri). Legend has it that Caddo Lake was formed during this time. The Caddo Indians told settlers stories of big noises and water flowing over the land. The story was interpreted to mean that an earthquake formed Caddo Lake. It is now generally accepted that the land that would become Caddo Lake was flooded by a log jam on the Red River, known as the "Great Raft."

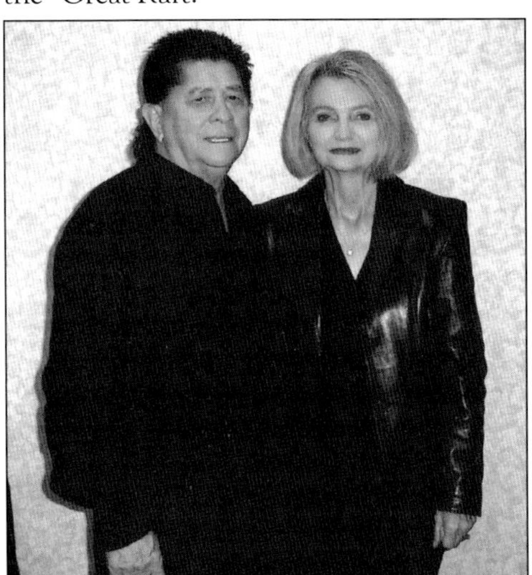

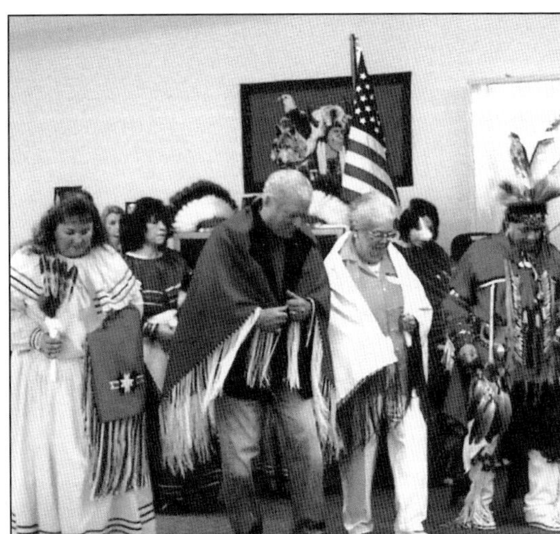

Above left are Chief Rufus Davis and his wife, Ann, who live on the reservation located near Robeline, Louisiana. The Indian Culture Center there, seen above right, preserves the colorful history of the Caddo Indians. Members of the Adai Caddo Indians join board members from the National Historic Trail El Camino Real de los Tejas in a welcome dance for visitors to the Adai Reservation near Robeline, Louisiana. (Above left, courtesy of Chief Rufus Davis and Ann Davis; above right, courtesy of Lucile Estell.)

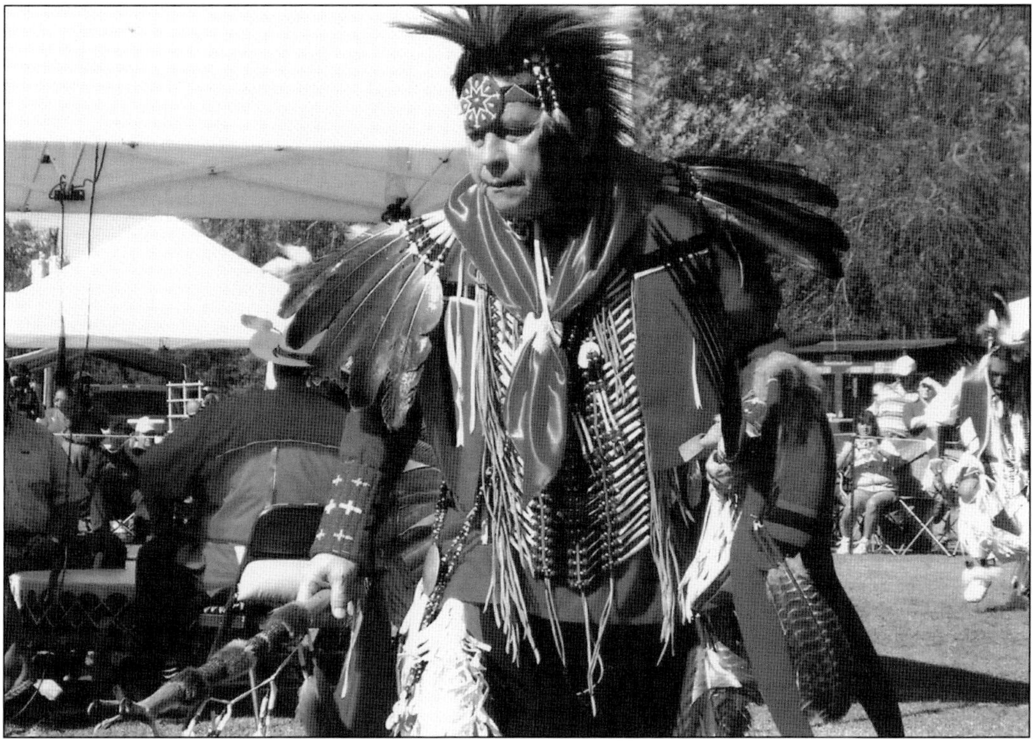

A powwow is held each October at the Indian Cultural Center near Robeline. Chief Davis is shown in this picture wearing traditional regalia for the dances. (Courtesy of Chief Rufus Davis.)

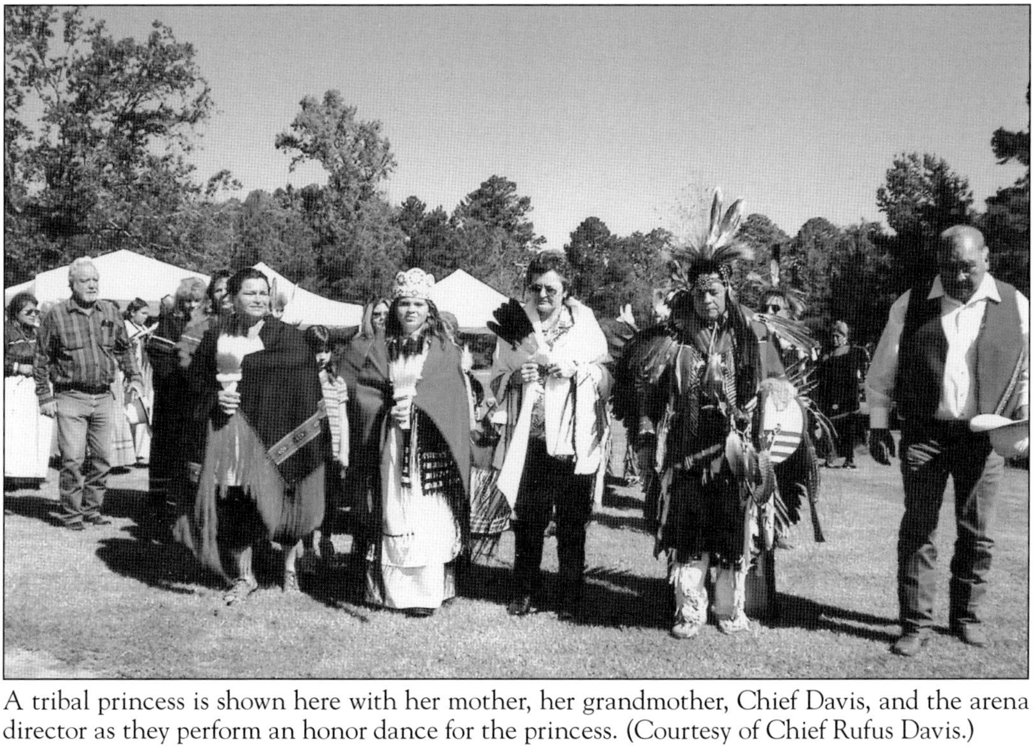

A tribal princess is shown here with her mother, her grandmother, Chief Davis, and the arena director as they perform an honor dance for the princess. (Courtesy of Chief Rufus Davis.)

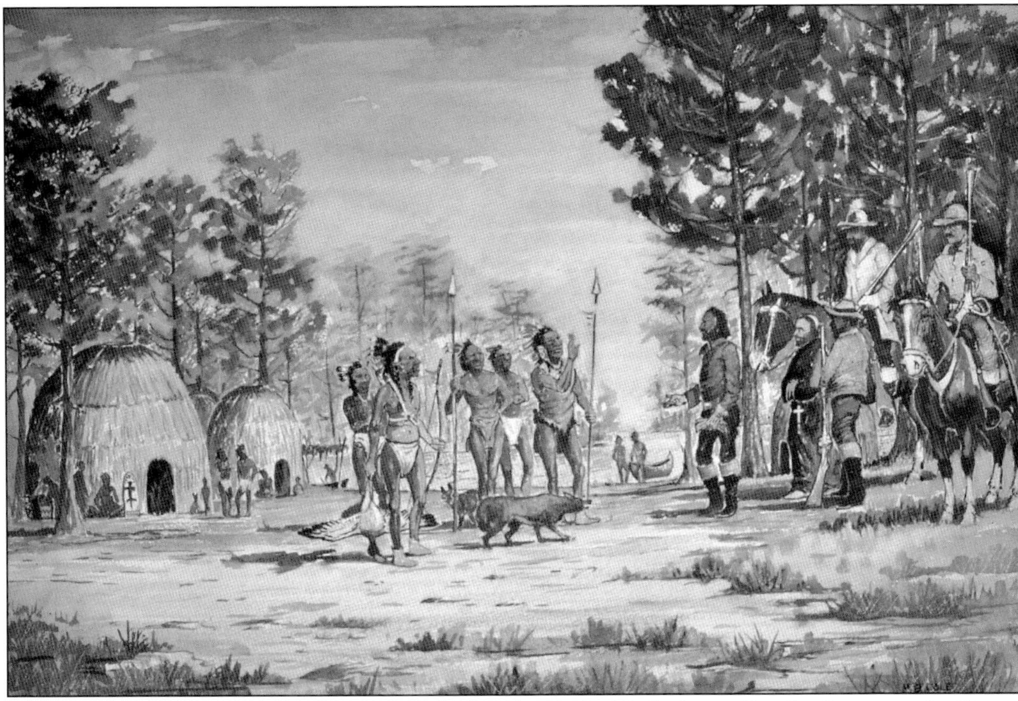

Both French and Spanish explorers trafficked with the Caddo Indians. Rivalry between the French and Spanish eventually led to the creation of a buffer zone called the Neutral Ground. It was disputed until 1839. Excavation of Native American burial grounds in Harrison County indicates that both the French and the Spanish traded with the Caddo Indians. Dr. Herbert Bolton, in his book *Texas in the Middle of the Eighteenth Century*, places both French and Spanish in the area. Note the thatched hut on the left side of the picture. This is typical of the Caddo dwellings.

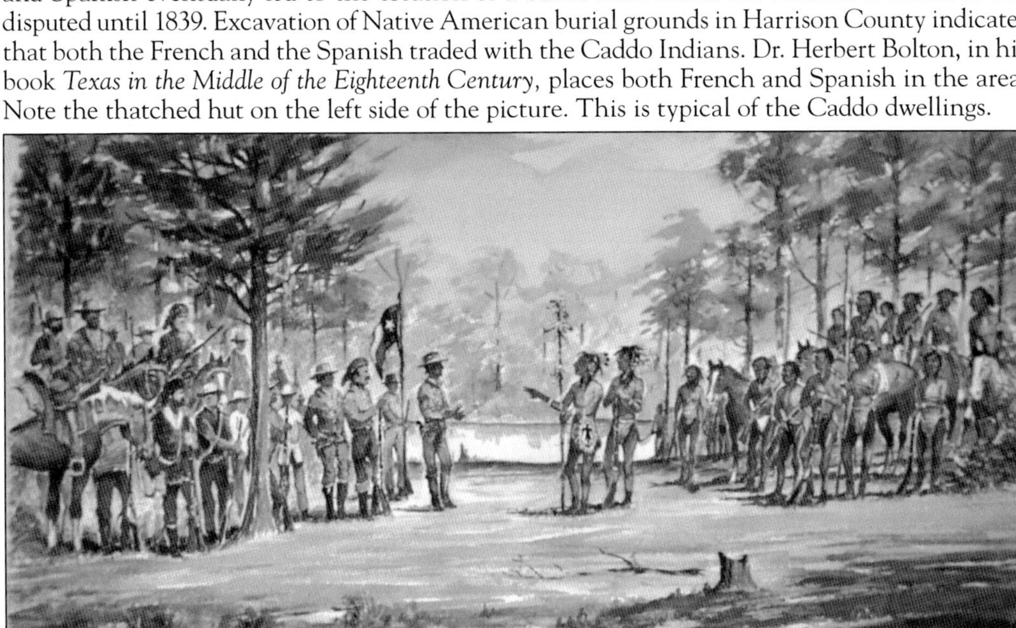

A large number of Caddo Indians lived in what is now Harrison County and also to the east near Shreveport. When the Louisiana Purchase was made, immigration to Texas increased. Thus Indian agents were authorized to buy land from the Native Americans, who had little choice but to sell. The Caddo Indians eventually left Harrison County, some heading for Shreveport and some farther south.

Both French and Spanish explorers exerted influence over the geographic area where Marshall is located. They both wanted to establish trade with the Native Americans and set up trading posts. Missions were established in many places to strengthen their hold on the area. However, no missions were located in Marshall. (Courtesy of W. S. Benson Publishing Company, Austin.)

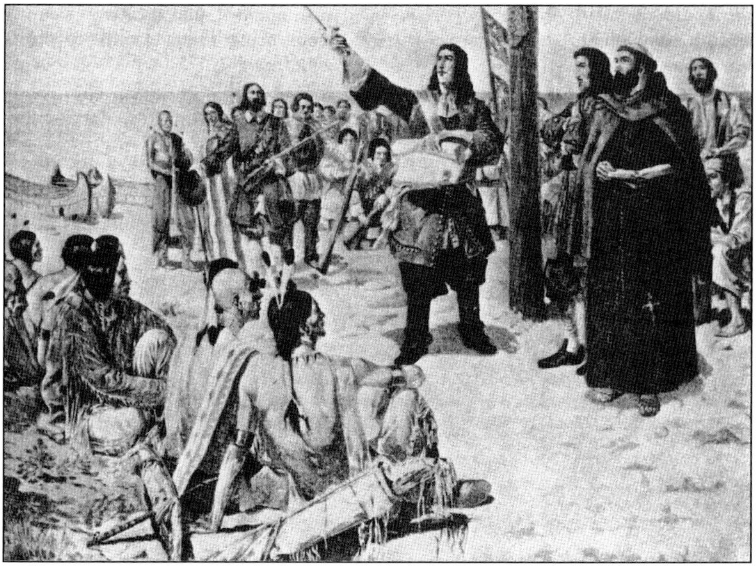

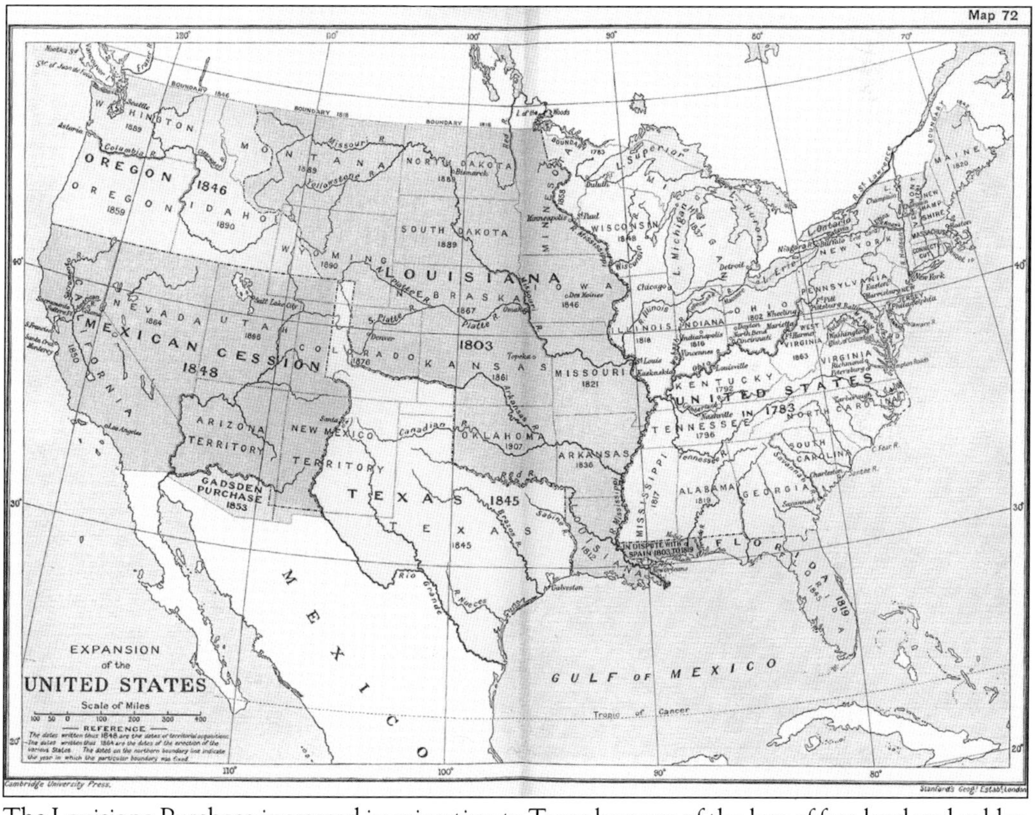

The Louisiana Purchase increased immigration to Texas because of the lure of free land and golden opportunities. It also accentuated a strip of ground shown on this map as Neutral Ground. This ground was claimed by both the United States and Spain. The city of Marshall was located inside this neutral ground, resulting in a conflict within the county commonly called the Regulator/ Moderator War. This map indicates the close proximity of Marshall to land that was included in the Louisiana Purchase, a fact that made Marshall subject to some effects from it.

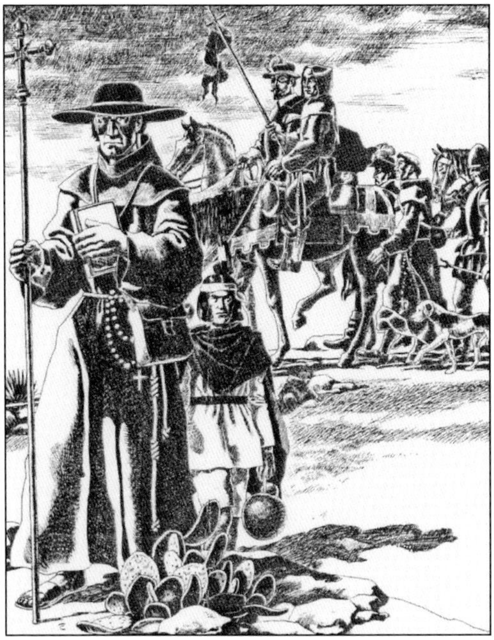

This is a pen-and-ink drawing by Jose Cisneros of a Franciscan missionary, a Native American, and Spanish soldiers. A major objective of the Spanish was to convert the Native Americans. (Courtesy of Institute of Texan Culture, University of Texas at San Antonio, courtesy of Cieofas Calleros Estate.)

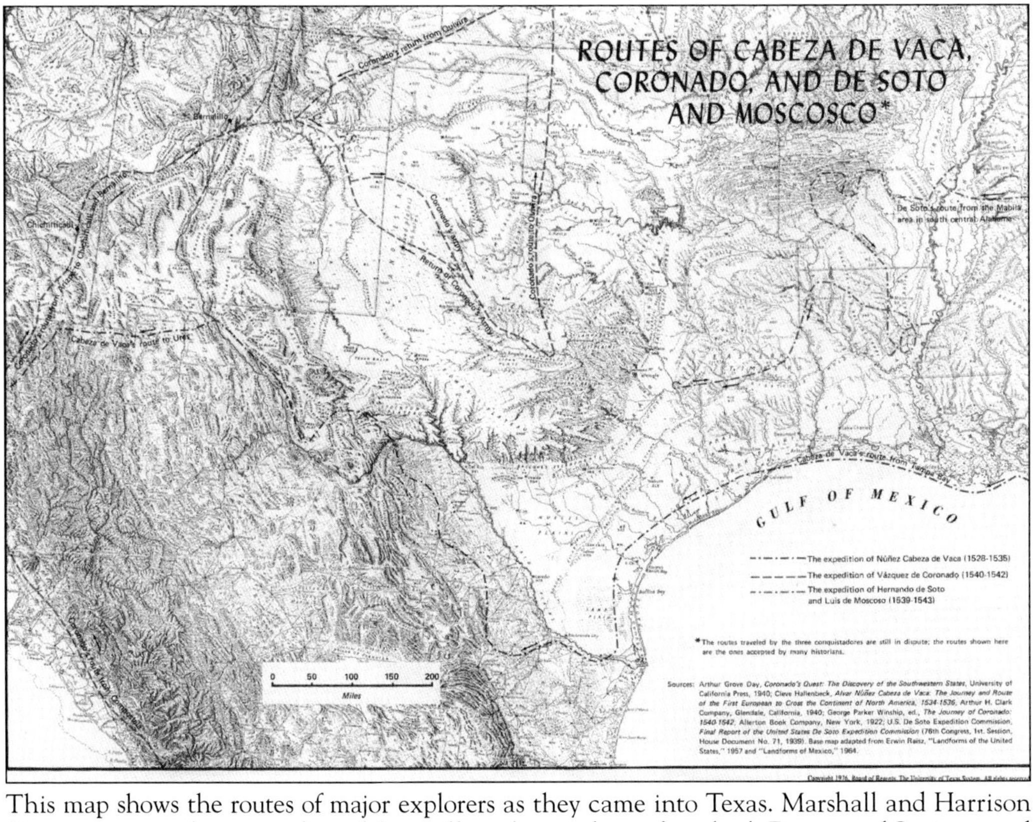

This map shows the routes of major explorers as they came into Texas. Marshall and Harrison County were on the outer edges of these efforts, but explorers from both France and Spain passed through Marshall. (Reprinted with permission from the *Atlas of Texas,* Austin: Bureau of Business Research, 1976, page 44. Copyright held by University of Texas Board of Regents.)

Two

Colonization, Mexican Rule, and Texas Independence

Settlers began moving into present-day Harrison County in the 1830s. The first settlers recorded in the area were John Beaty and his wife. They settled near Fern Lake and were befriended by a man named Amaryllis until they could build their own log cabin. It was in this log cabin that Beaty's wife gave birth to Sara Amaryllis Beaty, the first white child born in Harrison County.

It became increasingly clear that Texas would not be content to stay under Mexican rule and become citizens of Mexico. These were citizens of the United States who were taking advantage of the plentiful, fertile land that existed in Texas. They brought with them their desire for freedom. The situation became critical as citizens in Gonzales defied the Mexican Army to "Come and Take It," referring to the cannon that they had for their protection. The Texas Revolution continued as the Alamo fell and as settlers fled from the Mexican Army in what was known as the Runaway Scrape. The Battle of San Jacinto spelled freedom for the settlers. One outstanding citizen of Marshall at this time was Walter Paye Lane, an Irishman who came to the area in 1836. He also fought in the Civil War. He returned to Marshall where he served as a deputy federal marshal and later as treasurer of Harrison County.

As these important events occurred all over the rapidly developing Texas frontier, Marshall began to take shape and grow in concert with the rest of the state. Six years after the founding of Harrison County in 1839, and four years after the founding of Marshall in 1841, Texas became a republic. The republic lasted until 1845, at which time Texas joined the United States as the 28th state.

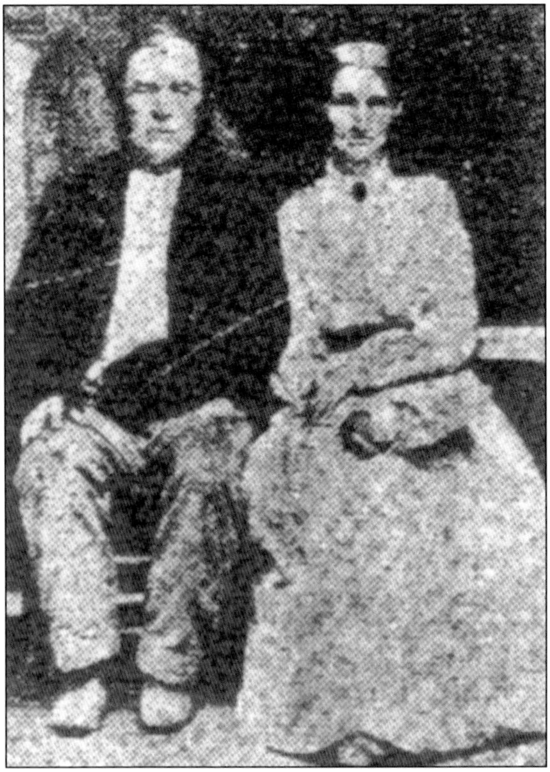

James and Emily Cellum were among the early settlers who came to Marshall. Cellum was present at San Jacinto when Santa Anna surrendered. They settled on 160 acres, 9 miles east of Marshall. They built a cabin with no windows and only one door. Once when Emily was at home with only one female servant, they spotted a bear about to abscond with their only pig. They pursued the bear, killed the pig and the bear, and ate well, at least for a short time.

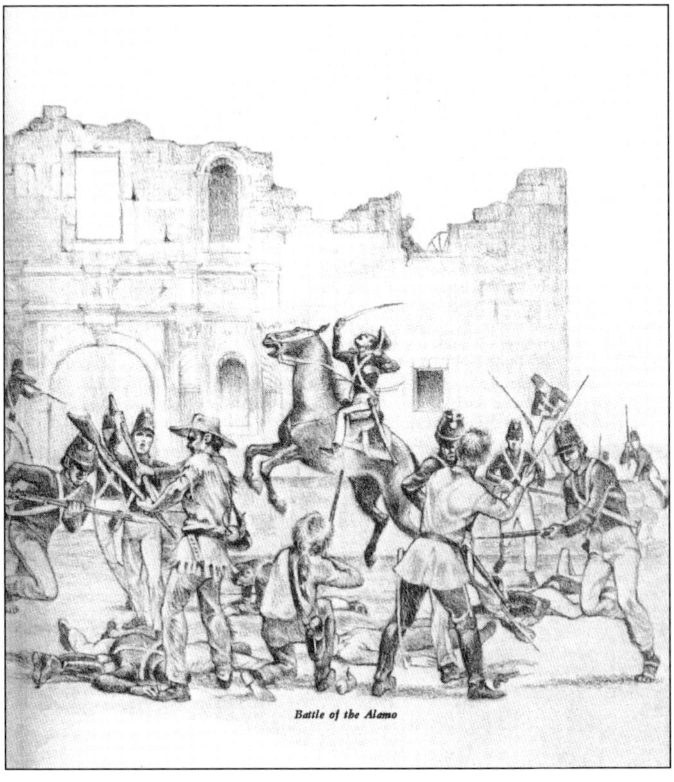

Battle of the Alamo

During this time, Texas was able to win its independence from Mexico and become a republic. This encouraged immigration. It was clear that Marshall was to become a leading city in the new republic. Leaders such as Peter Whetstone guided its growth. (Courtesy of W. S. Benson Publishing Company, Austin.)

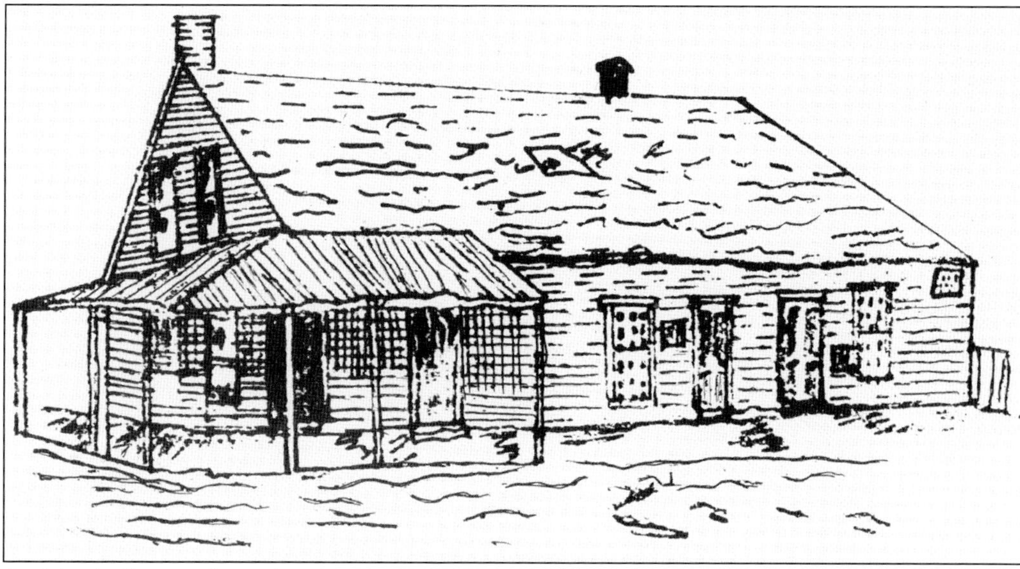

As Marshall was taking shape, so was the new republic. The capitol was to be in Houston, and Sam Houston was elected president of the republic by a vote of 5,119 out of 6,640 votes cast. The executive mansion, seen above in a drawing, was located in Houston.

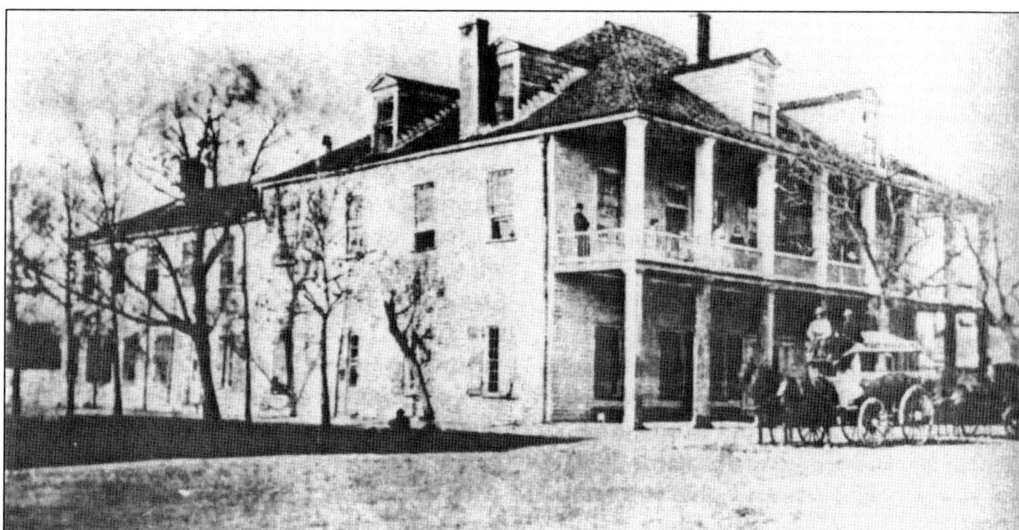

Capitol of the Republic, Houston **Barker Texas History Library**

The capitol of the republic was also located in Houston. Mirabeau B. Lamar was elected vice president. Also, a vote taken on annexation in this election showed a large number of Texans expressing the desire to become a state.

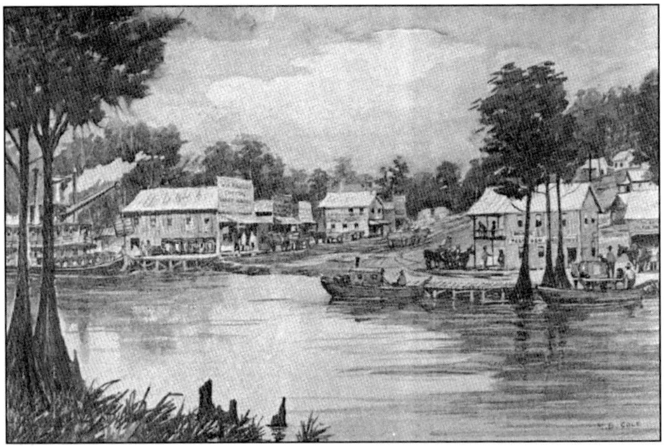

Port Caddo was once a thriving city near Marshall. It played an important part in the shipping of cotton. However, its location made it difficult to navigate to it, and eventually all traces of the city vanished.

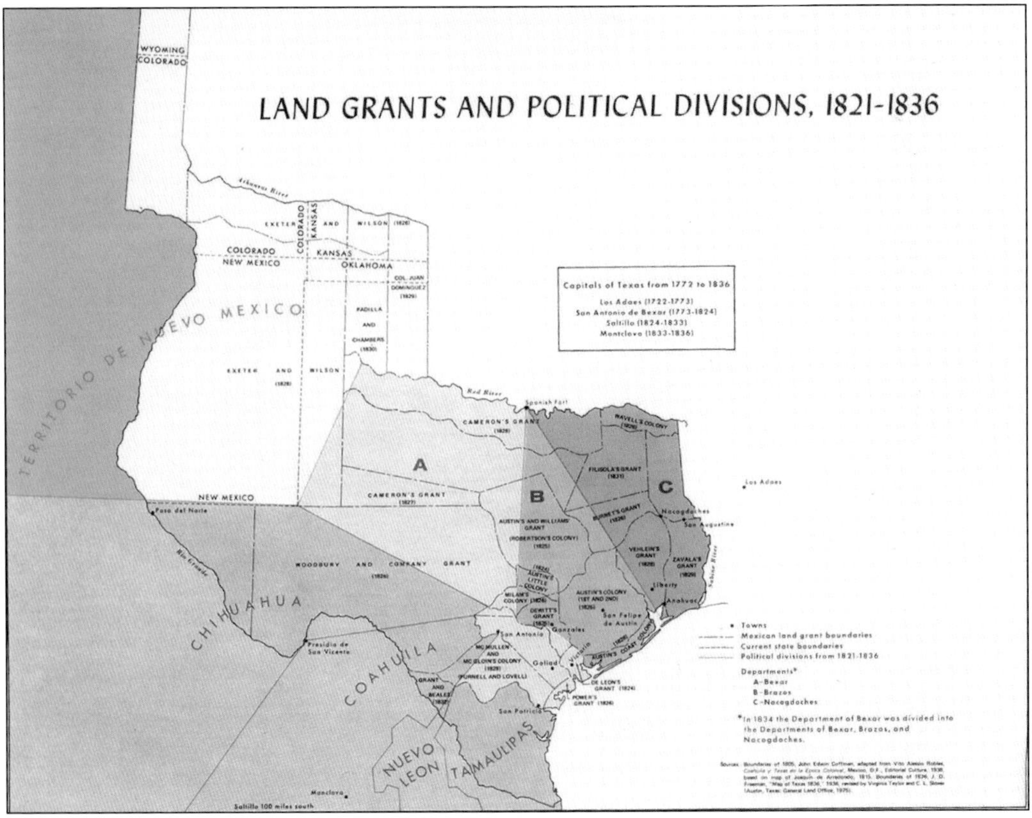

This map shows major land grants as they existed in the days of the Republic of Texas. Cheap land was a major incentive in encouraging settlers to travel to Texas. Peter Whetstone, one of the founders of Marshall, received a land grant in 1838. When it became known that the county seat of Harrison County was to be moved from Pulaski, there was much rivalry over where it was to be located. Peter Whetstone was anxious for the county seat to be on his land. He offered land for a courthouse, churches, and schools. He courted leaders to get his land selected, sweetening the pot with a drink of whiskey from a jug which he had secured in the trunk of a tree. He was successful, and the town of Marshall was laid out on 150 acres. Whetstone donated 80 acres, the eastern half of his survey. (Reprinted with permission from the *Atlas of Texas*, Austin: Bureau of Business Research, 1976, page 46. Copyright held by University of Texas Board of Regents.)

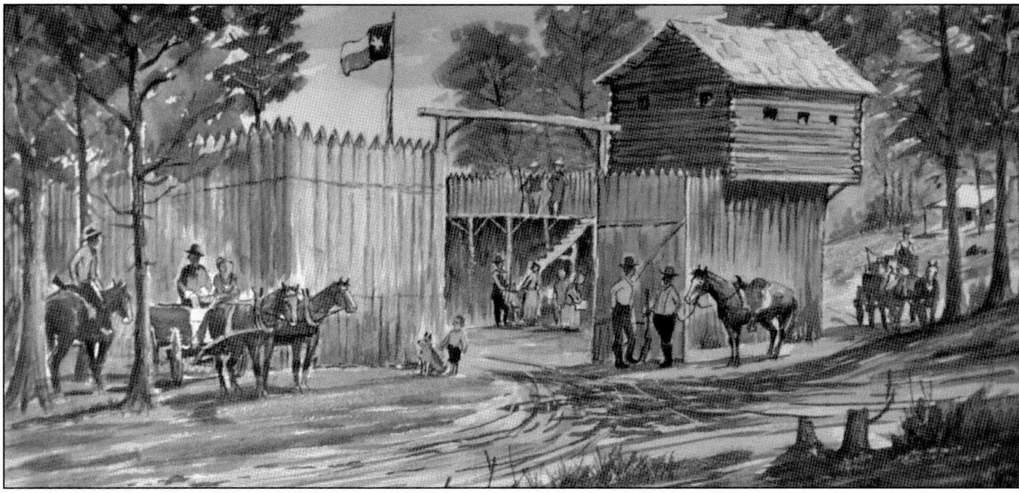

Fort Crawford was established near Hallsville as one means of protection against the Native Americans. It was one of several forts that Pres. Sam Houston ordered to be built. It did provide some protection for the early settlers.

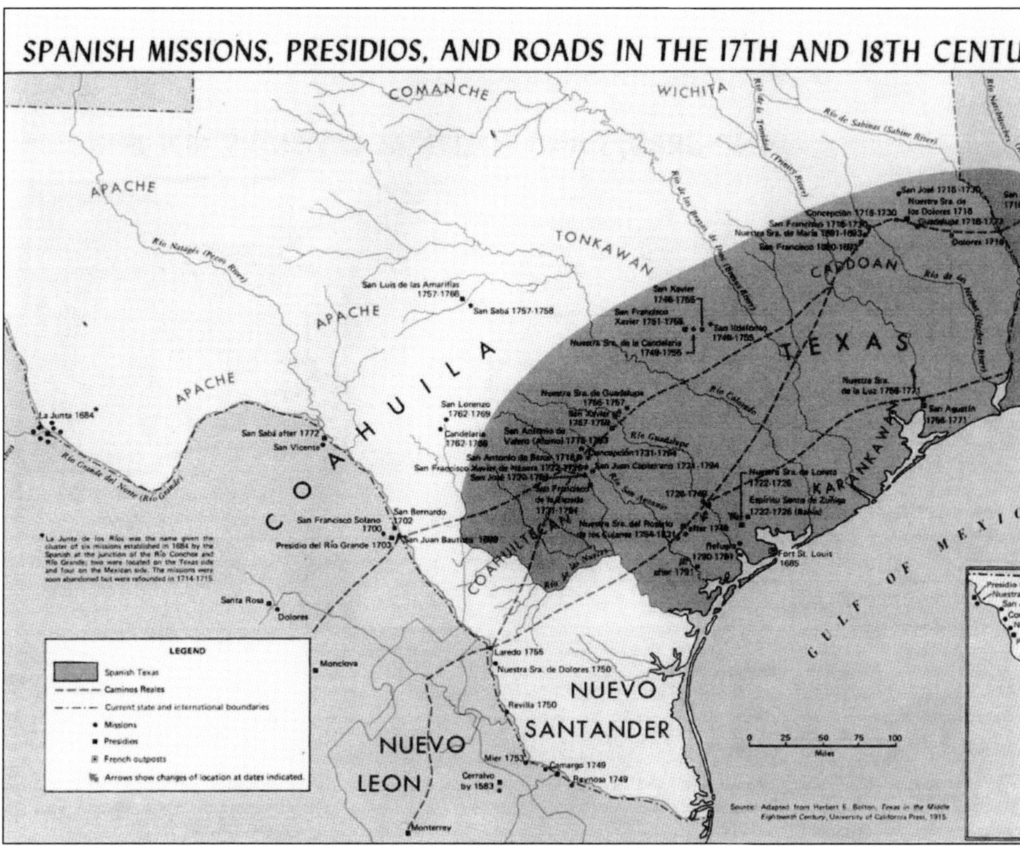

Spanish inroads were made into Texas. Presidios were set up, and a road system was in place. These early inroads carried forth to impact the history of all of Texas, including Marshall and Harrison County. (Reprinted with permission from the *Atlas of Texas*, Austin: Bureau of Business Research, 1976, page 44. Copyright held by University of Texas Board of Regents.)

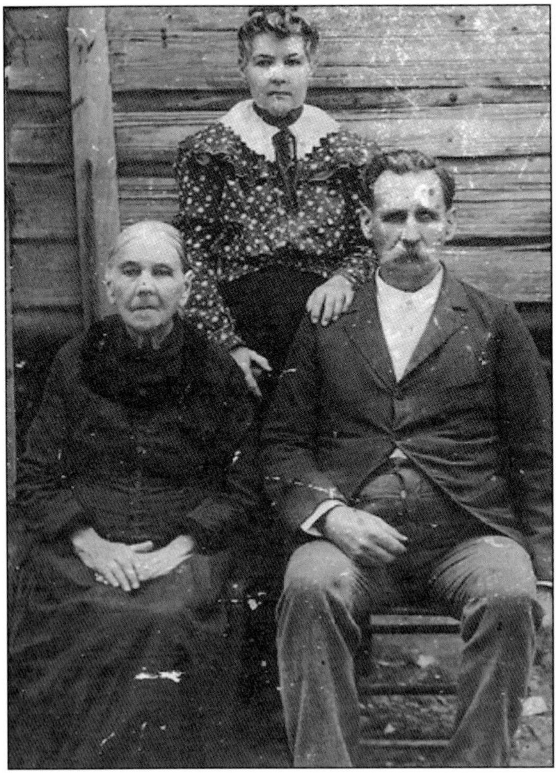

Early settlers in the area included the McPhail family. They settled in the Harleton area in 1853, building a log cabin for their shelter and protection.

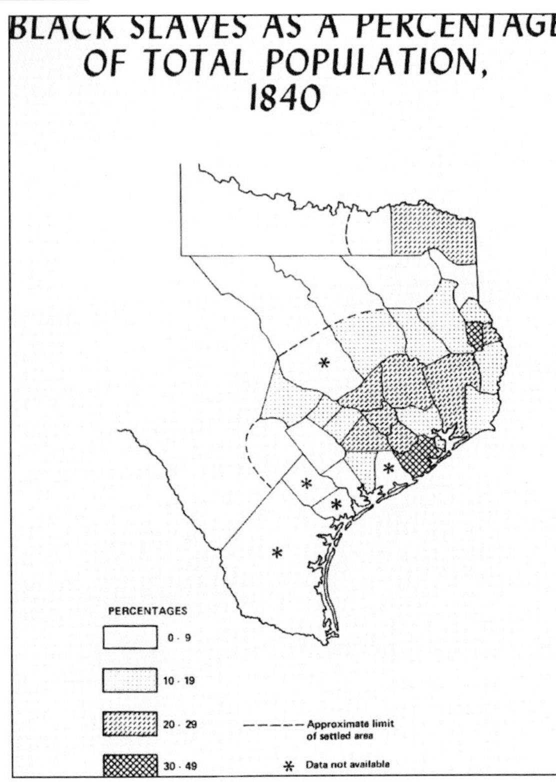

Slavery existed during the early days of the republic, but as this map indicates, the percent of slaves in Marshall was much less than in other parts of the state in 1840. (Reprinted with permission, Austin: Bureau of Business Research, 1976, page 52. Copyright held by University of Texas Board of Regents.)

Three

The Harrison County Courthouse

In 1839, Harrison County was created from Shelby County, and Greensboro was selected as the county seat. Next, Pulaski became the county seat. Finally the county assumed its present boundaries and began to seek a county seat, because the first two places named had been declared "unsanitary."

A committee was appointed by the Republic of Texas in 1841 to survey the county and select another county seat. One member of the committee, Peter Whetstone, was anxious for the county seat to be located on his land. As they discussed the possibilities, one person remarked that the land was nice but too dry. Whetstone responded to this by taking them to the corner of Houston and West Franklin where there was a spring. They drank water from the spring. Whetstone then reached into a large oak tree that stood nearby, took out a jug of whiskey, and passed it around several times. The site was then accepted as the county seat. Isaac Van Zandt suggested that the city be named Marshall in honor of Chief Justice John Marshall. Marshall retains its position as county seat today.

The present courthouse is the third courthouse built in the center of Marshall's town square. The first courthouse was a log cabin adjacent to the square. As a larger structure was needed, a new building called the Little Virginia Courthouse was constructed. It fell into disrepair and was replaced by a larger, grander courthouse constructed in 1888. This courthouse burned, and the commissioners authorized a new building. In 1900, the present building was started. This original building was expanded in 1924 and again in 1927, adding east and west wings to the structure.

A new Harrison County Courthouse was built in 1964. The 1901 structure was preserved and now houses the Harrison County Historical Museum as well as the offices of the county commissioners and the county judge. It is one of Texas's famed restored courthouses, and it is the focal point for Marshall's Wonderland of Lights celebration each Christmas.

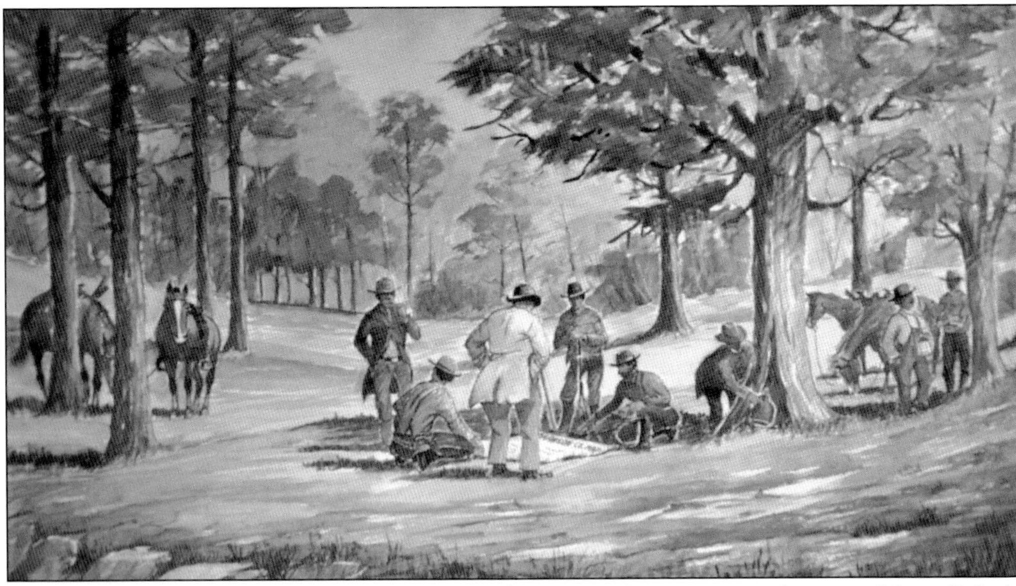

When it became known that the county seat of Harrison County was to be moved from Pulaski, there was much rivalry over where it was to be located. Peter Whetstone was anxious for Marshall to be the county seat. He offered land for the courthouse as well as for churches and schools. He courted leaders to get Marshall so designated, sweetening the pot with a drink from a jug of whiskey that he had secured in the trunk of a tree. He was successful, and the town of Marshall was laid out on 150 acres. Whetstone donated 80 acres, the eastern half of the survey. He also donated 10 acres for Marshall University.

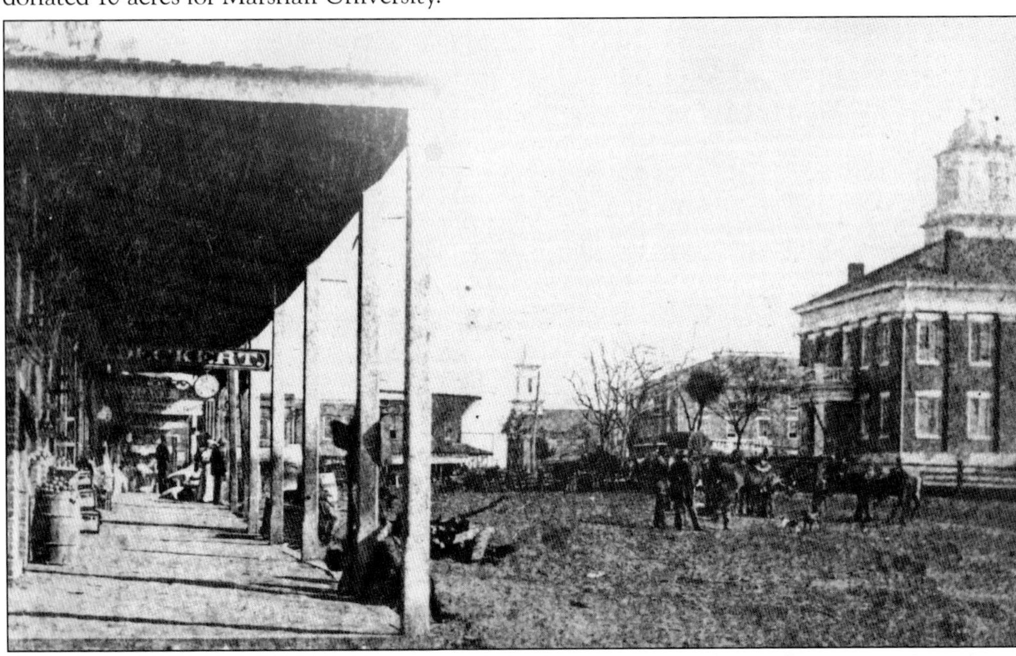

The date of this early photograph of the square is not known, but the Little Virginia Courthouse is shown on the right. It was patterned after courthouses in Virginia, hence the name Little Virginia Courthouse. This structure replaced earlier log buildings that served as courthouses and were in no way as elaborate as this one.

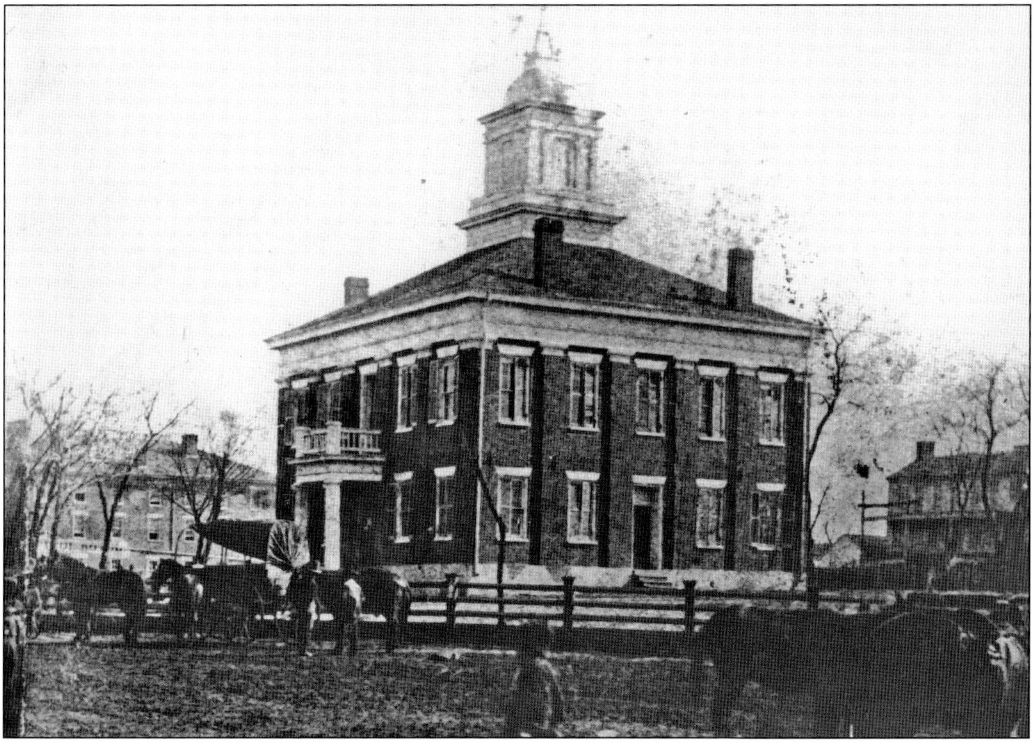

This courthouse, the Little Virginia Courthouse, was completed in 1848 on a corner of Peter Whetstone Square. Whetstone donated the land for the structure as well as land for other public buildings in Marshall.

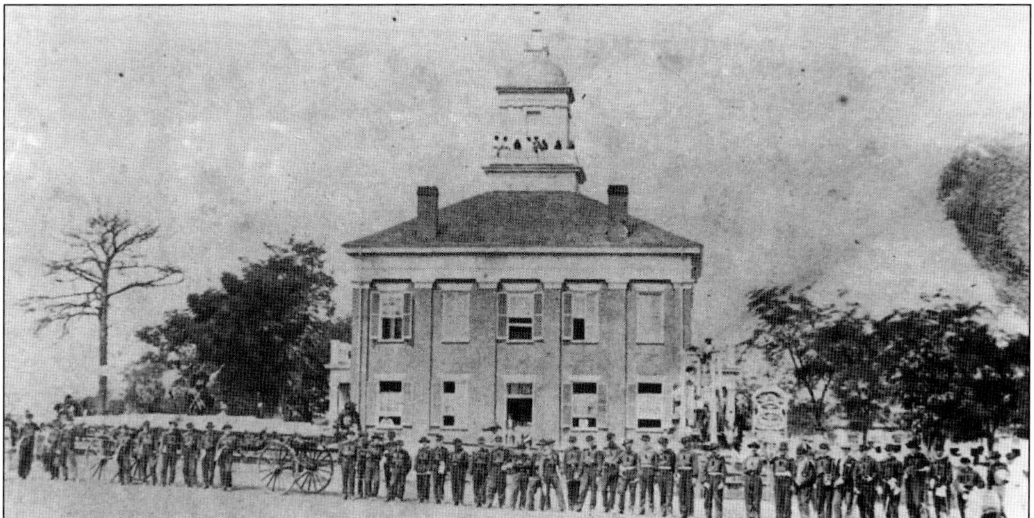

This early courthouse was called the Little Virginia Courthouse because of its resemblance to courthouses in Virginia. It was a source of pride for citizens. Eventually there arose some safety issues, and a committee composed of T. W. Winston, J. S. Wagamon, and A. P. Starr was appointed to examine the building and make a recommendation. It was condemned in 1888 for safety reasons. This photograph, taken about 1852, shows a line of volunteer firefighters posing in front of the courthouse.

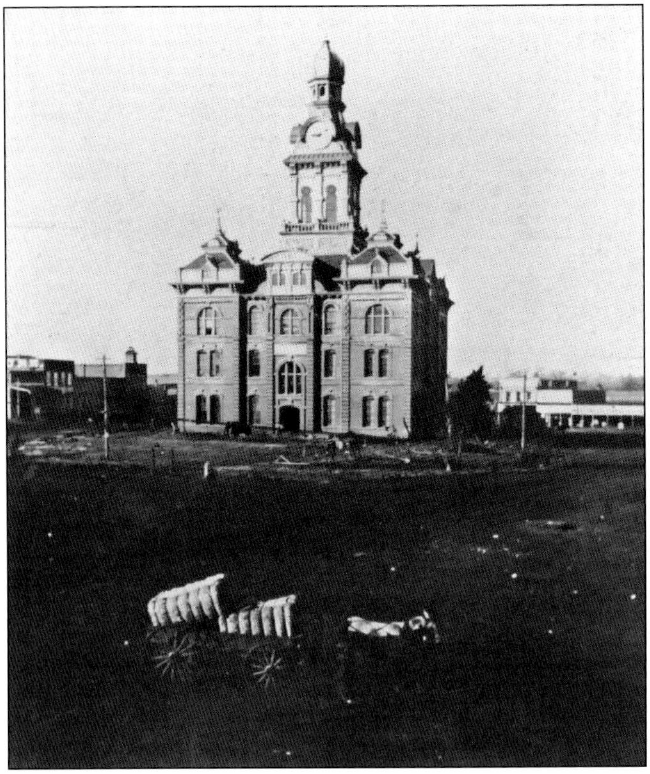

A larger structure built to replace the first Little Virginia Courthouse had a newer Gothic design. James Higgins was given a contract for $42,000 plus a $1,000 fee for tearing down the old building. A large cat was a resident of this second Little Virginia Courthouse. Each morning, someone could give him a nickel that he would carry in his mouth to the butcher shop. He would return with a little package of meat, get in his favorite chair, and eat it. He refused to be rescued and perished in the fire of 1899.

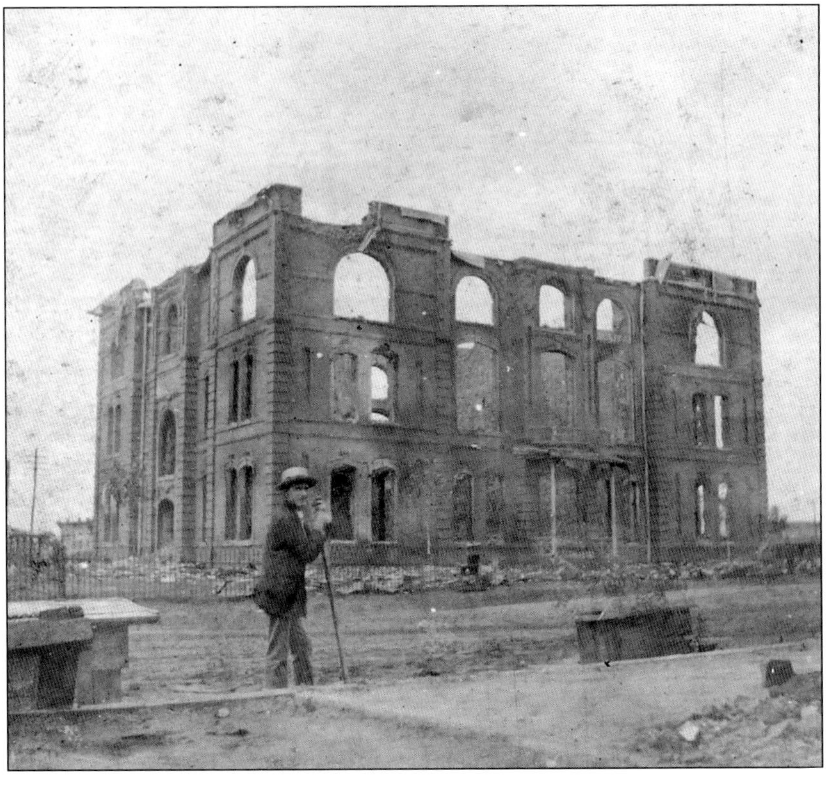

Fire destroyed the second Little Virginia Courthouse on June 8, 1899, and most of the county records were lost. The fire began as work was being completed on the courthouse, but the exact cause was not known.

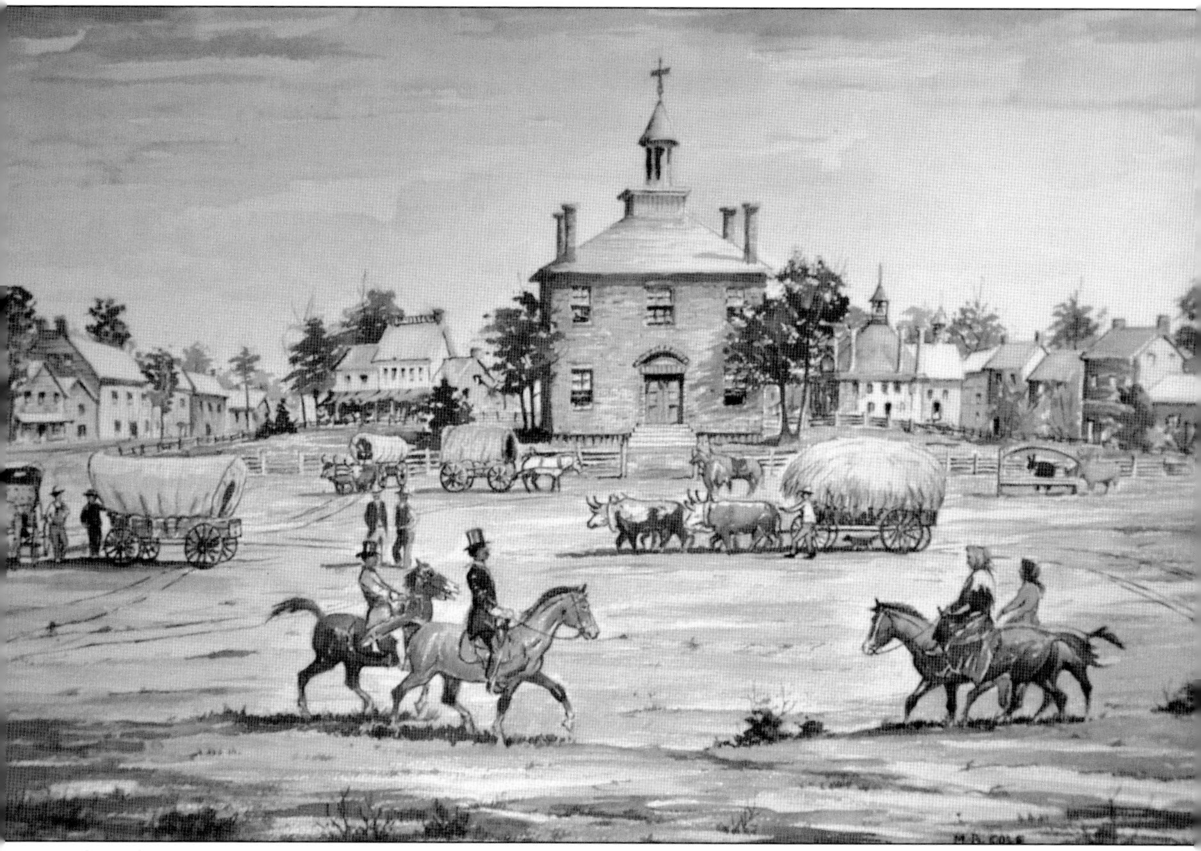

The Little Virginia Courthouse was a source of great pride in Harrison County. When the first one was deemed unsafe by a special committee appointed to examine that issue, officials immediately authorized the construction of a replacement building with the cost to not exceed $50,000. The committee examining the safety of the building had three members: T. W. Winston, J. S. Wagnon, and A. P. Starr. James Higgins was the low bidder on the second Little Virginia Courthouse. Commissioners also agreed to use the old courthouse for a time, thus giving Harrison County the distinction of having two county courthouses.

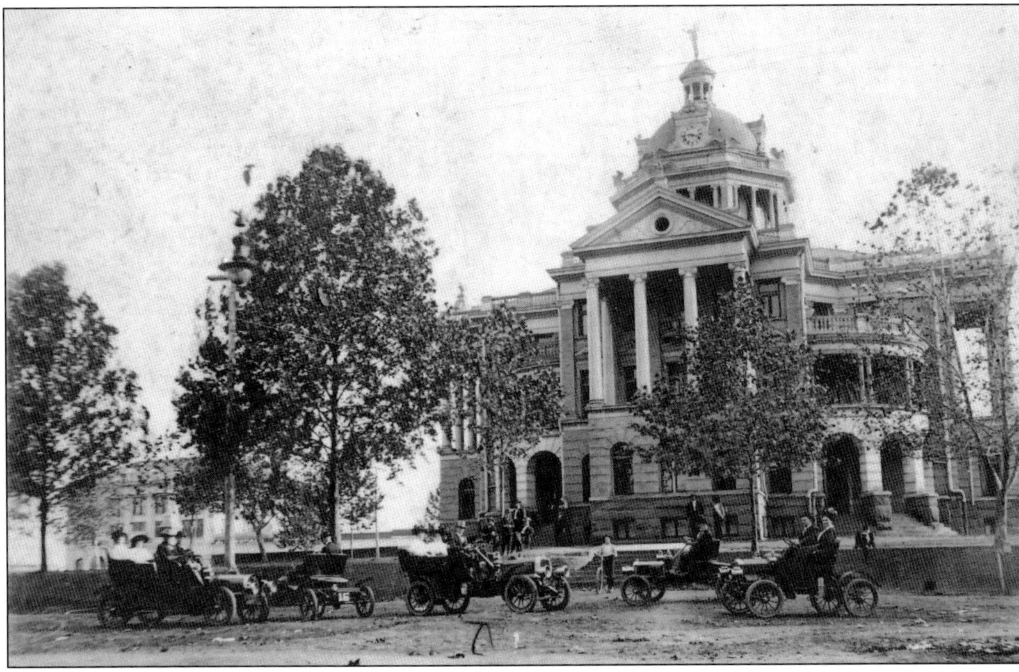

On August 16, 1899, the commissioner's court authorized the issuance of bonds to build a new courthouse. It was to have three stories and a basement. This new courthouse was to be erected on Peter Whetstone Square in the same location as the burned courthouse.

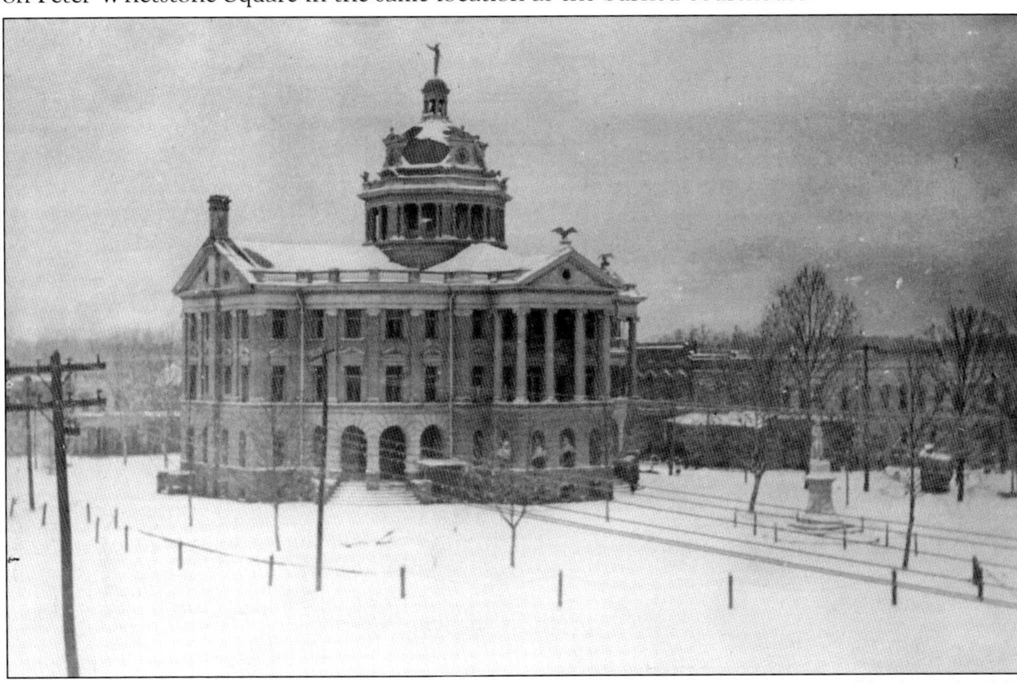

The newly authorized courthouse was to use Roman Cross architecture. Granite blocks to build it came by railroad from Burnet, Texas. A lifelong Harrison County resident, C. G. Lancaster, was the architect in charge of construction. The design architect was J. Reily Gordon, a well-known architect of the day. The style is Renaissance Revival.

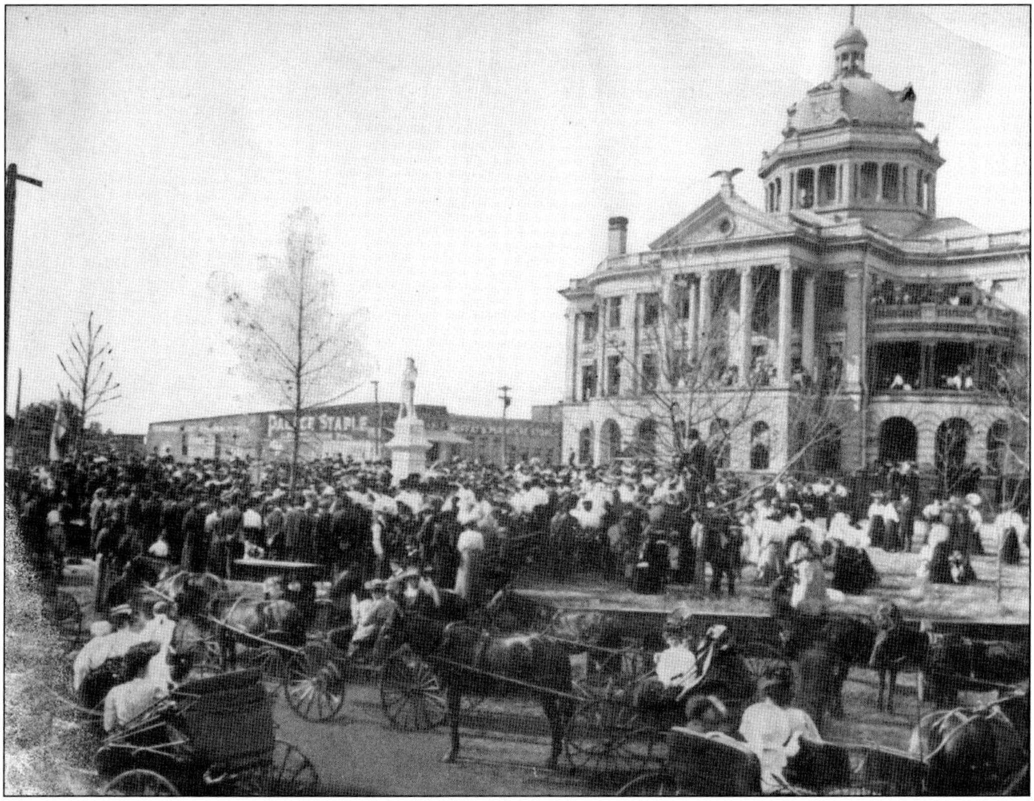

The cost of this new structure was $62,000. There is a Big Ben clock on top of the courthouse. E. Howard Clock Company of Wortham, Massachusetts, manufactured it, although there are no records on the actual cost of the clock. The bell in the courthouse measures 3 feet in diameter. Engraved on the bell are these words: "Erected in 1900, H. L. Littlejohn, County Judge; J. D. Jimpsey, Commissioner pct. 2 and 5; T. A. Whaley, Commissioner, precinct 3; Lee Killingsworth, Commissioner, precincts 4 and 6, E. T. Rosborough, clerk, J. W. Muncen, sheriff. Gordon and Lancaster, architects and Sonnefield and Ermens, contractors."

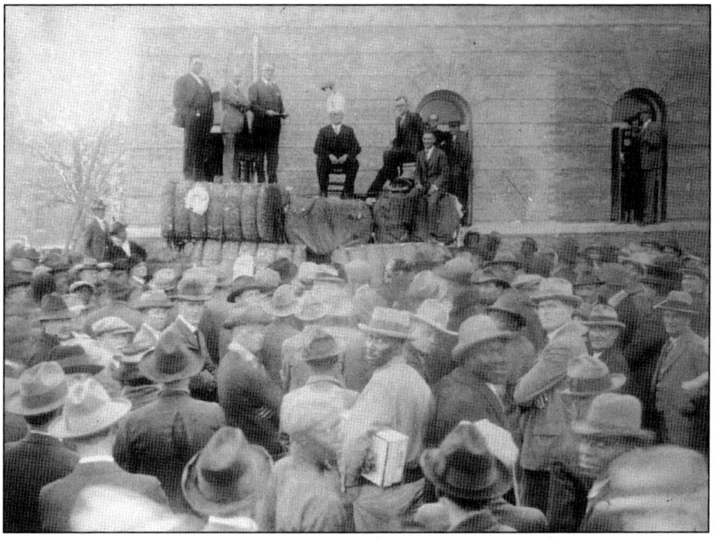

This photograph shows the first bale of cotton being sold at the northeast corner of the courthouse. Cotton flourished in Marshall for a time. Records indicate that 9,353 bales were produced in a period beginning September 1, 1880, and ending late in the year 1881.

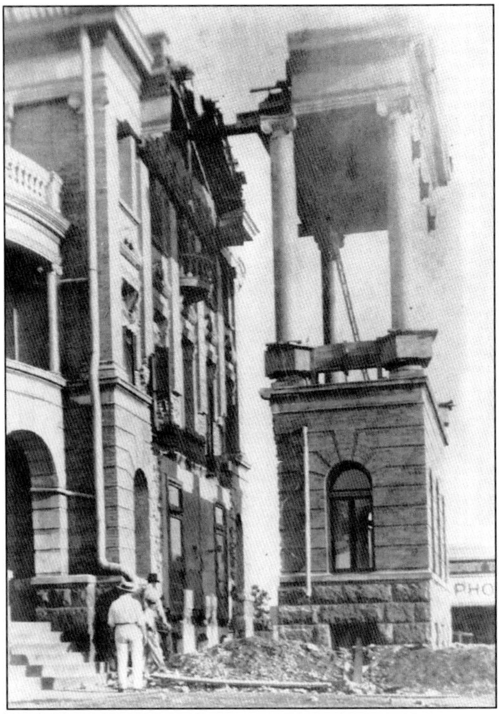

A courthouse expansion took place in 1924 and again in 1927, as east and west wings were added to the structure. Lancaster was the architect for the additions, thus assuring the continuity of style in the building. This photograph shows the east expansion.

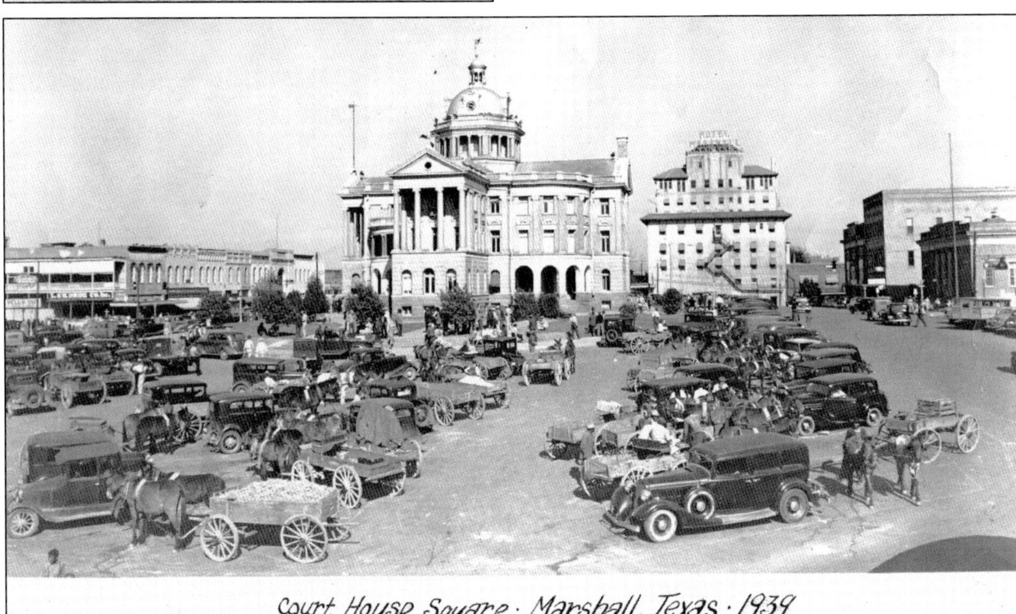

This photograph shows the courthouse square in 1939 during somewhat prosperous times. World War II was on the horizon, but it had not yet begun. Marshall had taken an active part in the Texas Centennial celebration in Dallas, providing two days of entertainment at Texas Centennial's Dallas Fair Park under the direction of Marshall mayor Louis Kariel, who traveled to Dallas to share the history of Marshall with the world! Among those going to Dallas were the College of Marshall band and choir. The number of vehicles shown in this 1939 photograph of the square indicates the extent of activity present in the town at that time.

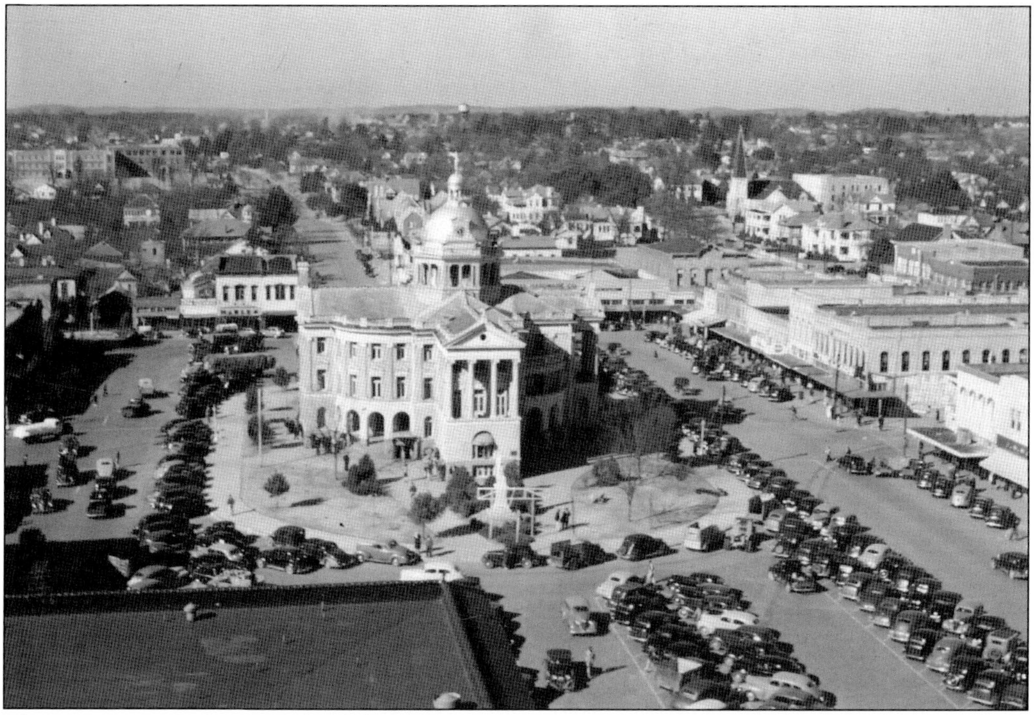

This is an aerial photograph of the square, taken in 1942. By this time, World War II was in progress, and Marshall was affected, as was the rest of the world. Shown in this scene is the growth that was taking place in Marshall as it expanded in all directions from the courthouse.

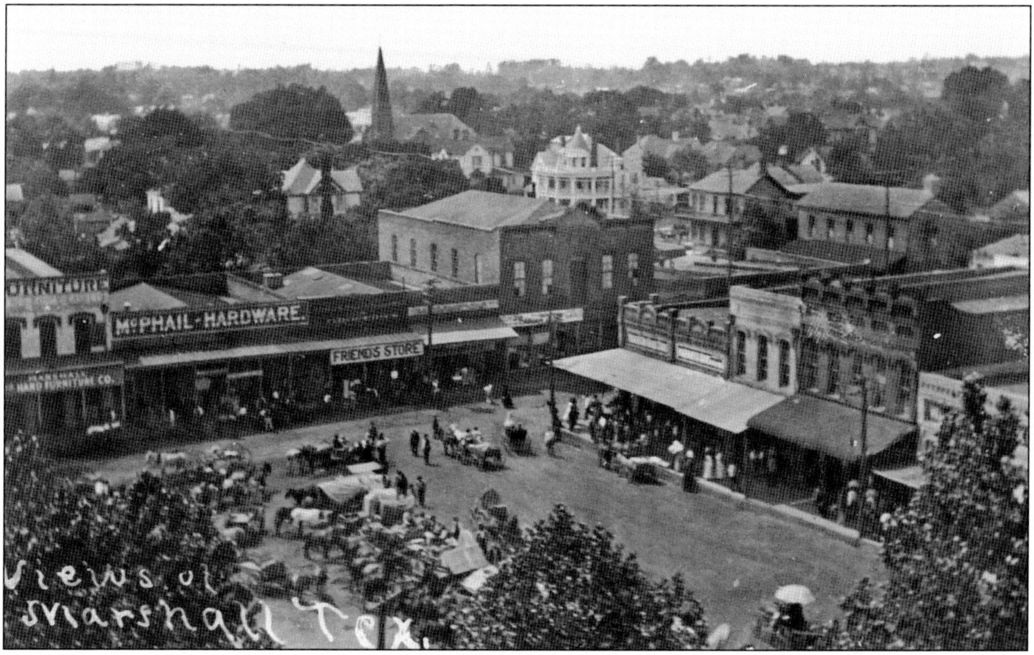

The northwest corner of Peter Whetstone Square is shown here. A date for this photograph is not available. However, activity around the buildings indicates that it is an early photograph. Horses appear to be the major means of transportation.

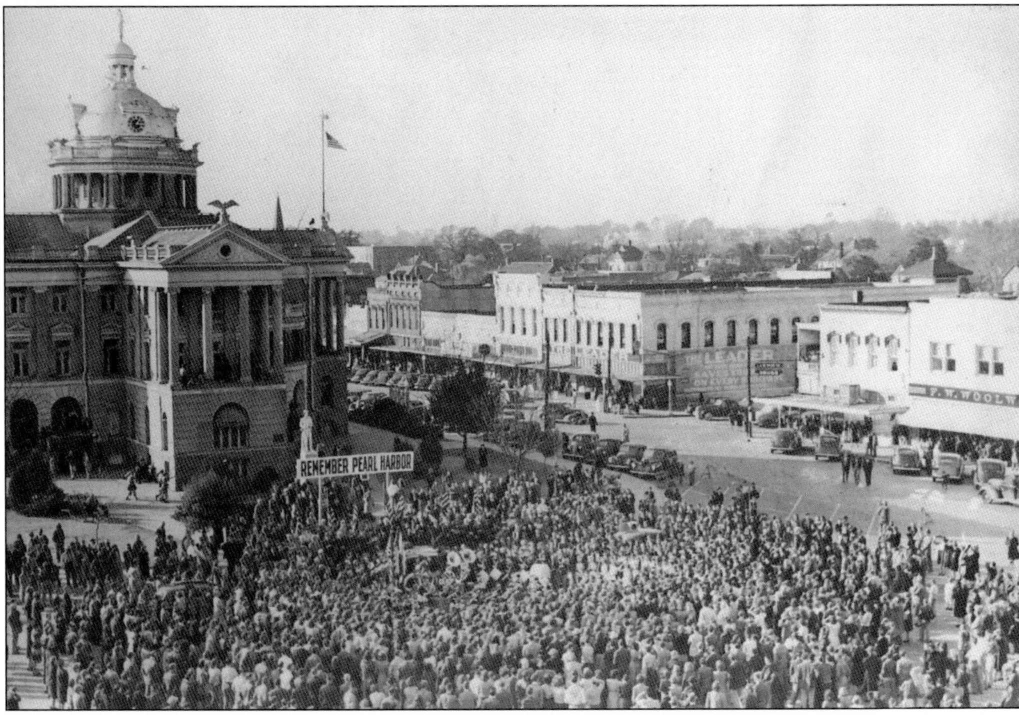

This is a bond rally held on the square in 1942. By this time, a $23-million plant, Longhorn Ordnance Works, was in full operation in Karnack. This encouraged growth in Marshall as well. The plant operated until 1945 and was reactivated during the Korean War. It was also used during the Vietnam War to build motors for Pershing missiles. It is now a wildlife preserve.

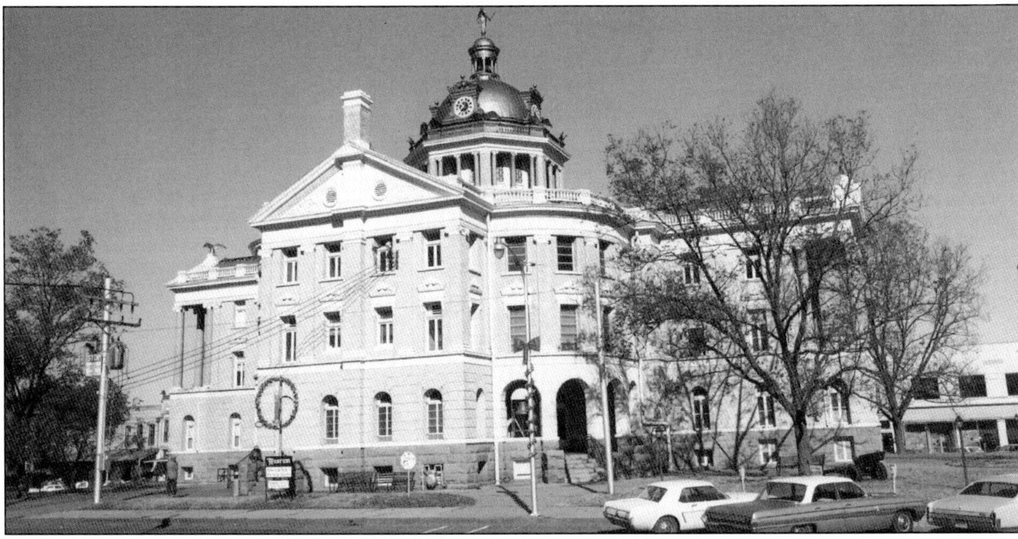

This postcard view of the courthouse reflects the majesty of its history. The first two buildings to serve as the Harrison County Courthouse were log structures. These were replaced by two Little Virginia Courthouses, both patterned after courthouses located in the Old Dominion State. Finally there was the majestic structure shown on this postcard. It continues to dominate Peter Whetstone Square today, although the official courthouse is located across the street. (Courtesy of Henry Bradbury.)

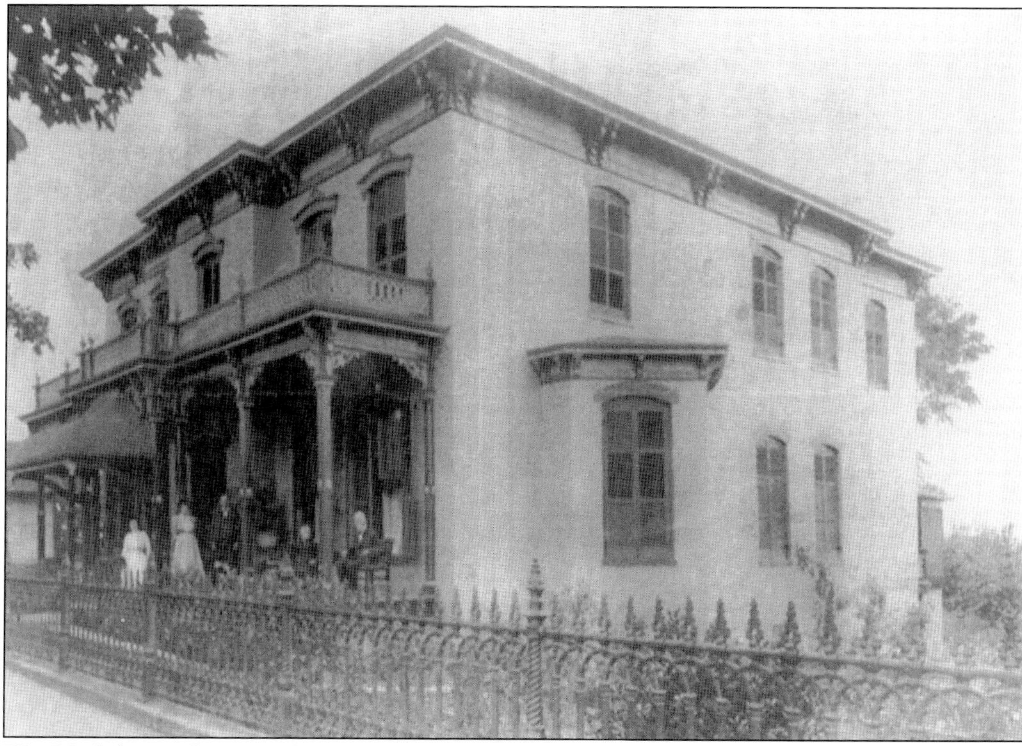

The Umbdenstock House, located on Peter Whetstone Square, was built in 1879. It was razed in 1954 to make room for the new courthouse.

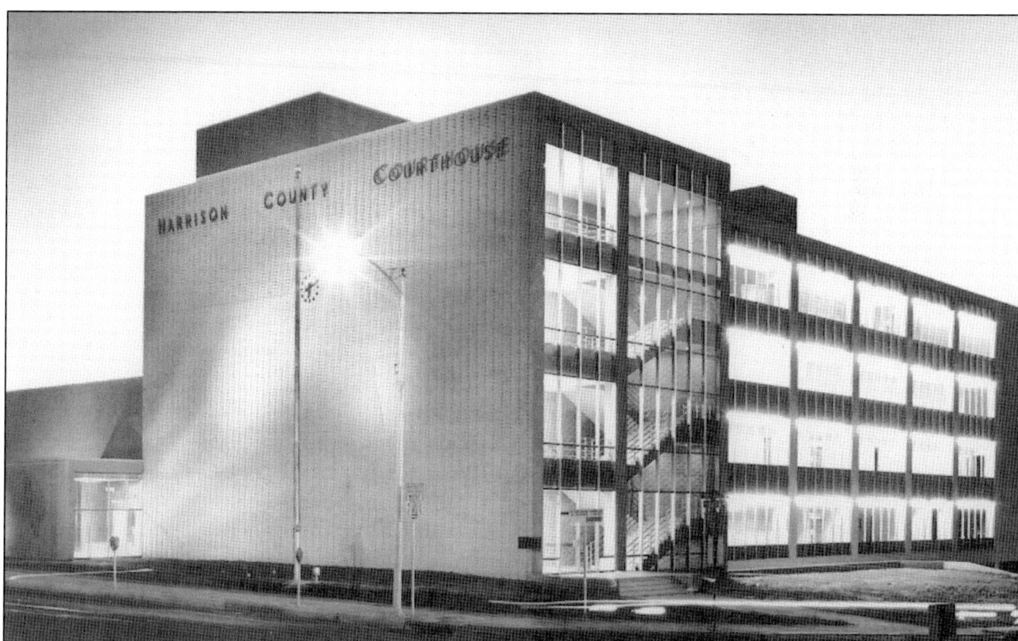

Voters approved the construction of a new courthouse in 1963, resulting in the building of this structure. The 1901 courthouse became the Harrison County Historical Museum.

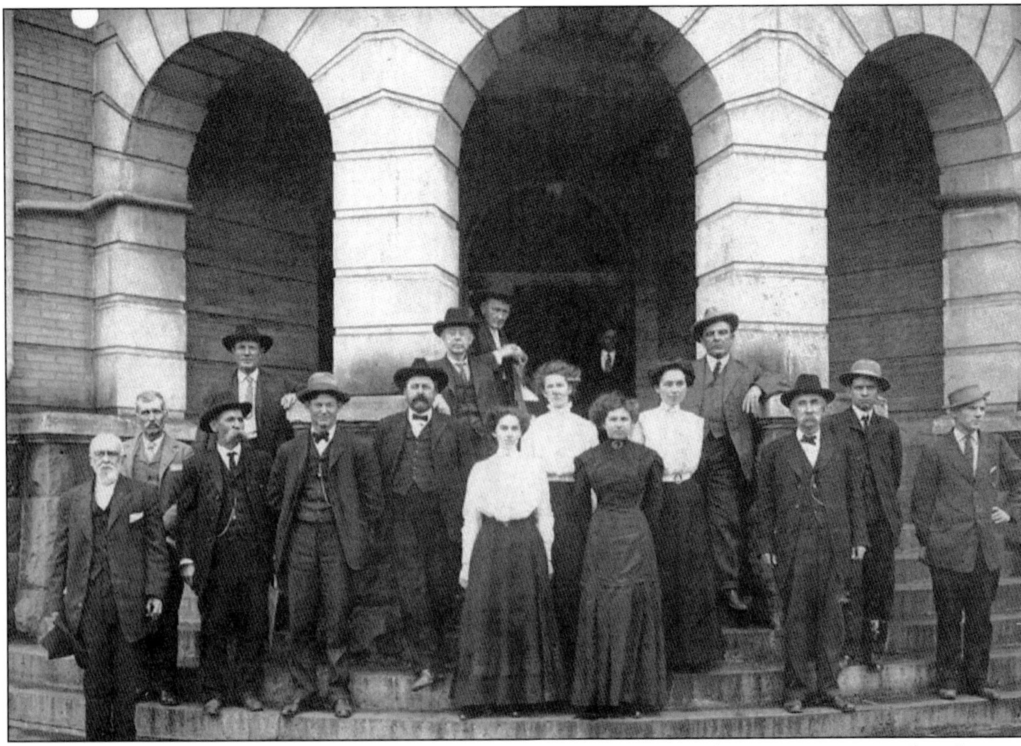

This photograph is of the Harrison County Courthouse staff. The picture is not dated nor is anyone in the photograph identified.

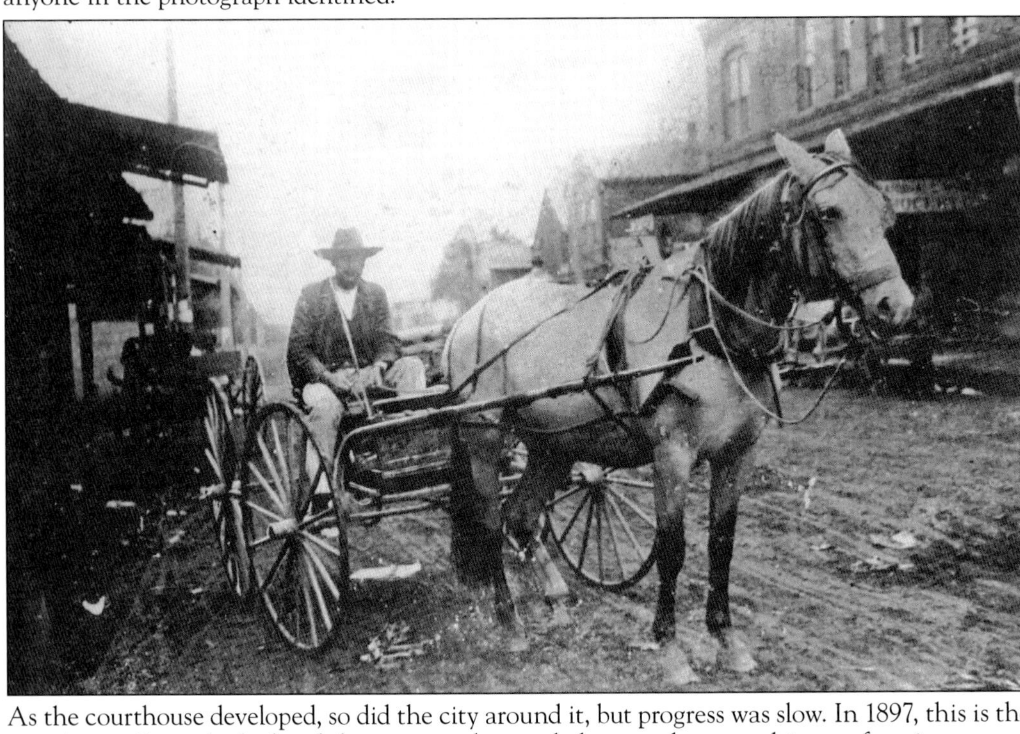

As the courthouse developed, so did the city around it, but progress was slow. In 1897, this is the way Austin Street looked and the way people traveled to get about on this new frontier.

Four

Economic Development of Marshall

The influx of settlers into Marshall brought about the need for stores and services designed to meet their needs. Edmund Key opened a dry goods store. It was located on the square where the Federal Court Building now stands. A second dry goods store was opened by G. Gregg.

In 1845, Charles Deckert opened a shoe store at the corner of West Houston and South Wellington Streets. George Satter came to Marshall to work for Deckert and ultimately purchased the store. Eventually, he sold the building to Joe Black. It was used by Black until 1947.

The first candy store in Marshall was owned by the Dopplemeyers. Also, during these early days, several saloons were established, one by Mr. Longenetti. An undertaking parlor was owned by George Rains. There were no grocery stores in the beginning, so groceries were shipped to Marshall from New Orleans, Louisiana.

As Marshall grew, it expanded around the square. This was the center of all activity, and it was around this square that businesses grew and flourished. Later businesses developed out from the square. But the square still remains the center of activity and the heart of the daily life in Marshall. Early photographs of the square reveal the changes in transportation that were occurring during this time. Model T Fords and teams of mules mixed and mingled freely.

Marshall had one of the first post offices in Texas. It was established on May 22, 1845. Two other post offices were established in Harrison County at this same time. The first telegraph office in Texas opened in Marshall in 1894.

According to the 1850 census, Marshall was the fourth largest city in Texas. The population was 1,150, of whom 121 were slaves. Only San Antonio, Houston, and New Braunfels were larger.

In 1857, Judge George Adkins established the Capitol Hotel. This was later called Hotel Marshall. For many years it was the largest hotel between New Orleans and San Francisco. The structure was built by slave labor. Slaves made the bricks and built the walls. Two of these men, Dick Lane and Green Hill, were expert bricklayers. Adkins owned the building for about 30 years until it was purchased by Sam B. Perkins, who later established Perkins Department store on the lower floor.

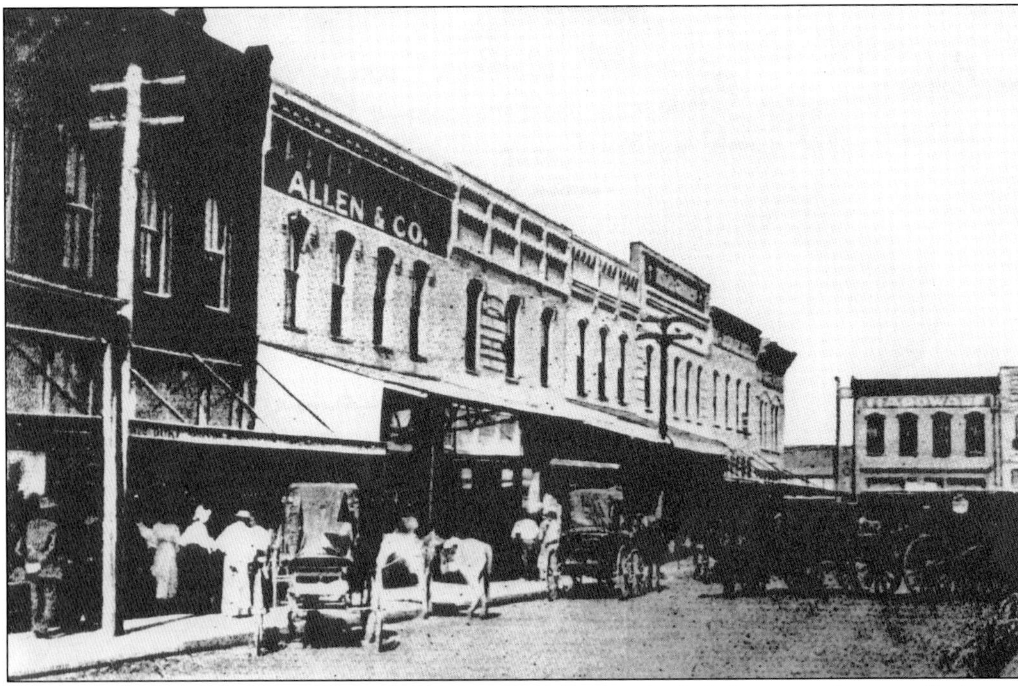

Pictured are several stores in Marshall during its early days. Included among these are Duke and Ayers Nickel Store. Note the variety of transportation modes available. Allen and Company was a haberdasher and located near this store was a millinery shop owned by Mrs. W. B. Allen. A second haberdasher, Dreyfuss, was also located in this general area, although this photograph is not clear enough to determine the exact location.

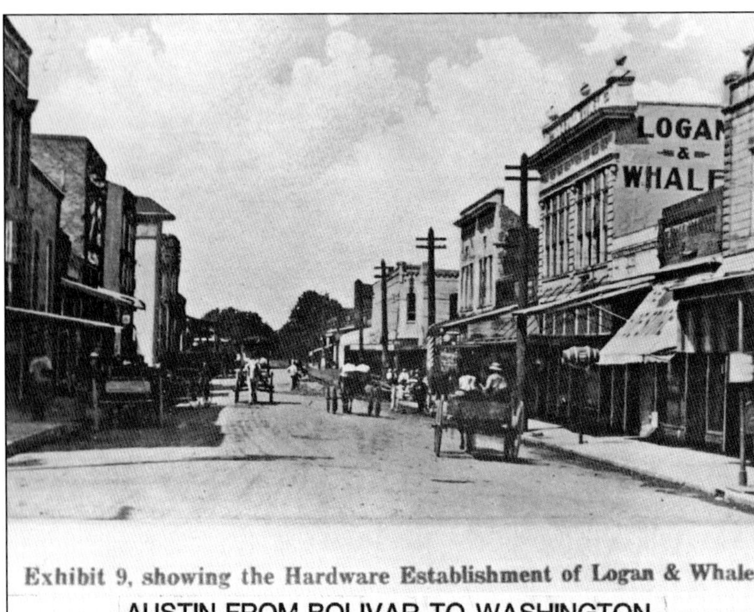

Austin Street is pictured during the early 1900s. The Logan and Whaley Hardware store was established in Marshall by L. R. Logan in 1884. Later Paul G. Whaley became a partner in the firm. In 1890, two of his brothers, E. C. and Tom, joined the firm. In 1907, a two-story building was erected at the corner of East Austin and North Bolivar. Logan and Whaley is still in operation in Marshall.

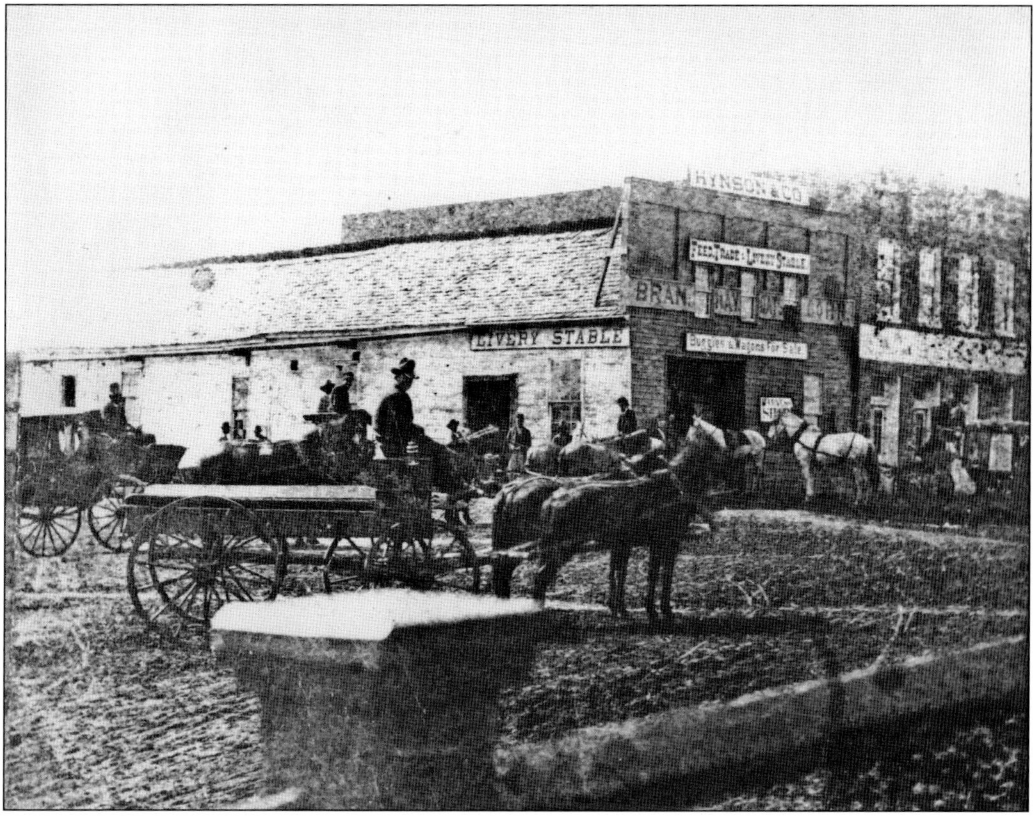

The exact location of this livery stable, probably pictured in the early 1900s, is not known. A livery stable was an important part of any community because of the heavy dependence on horses for transportation.

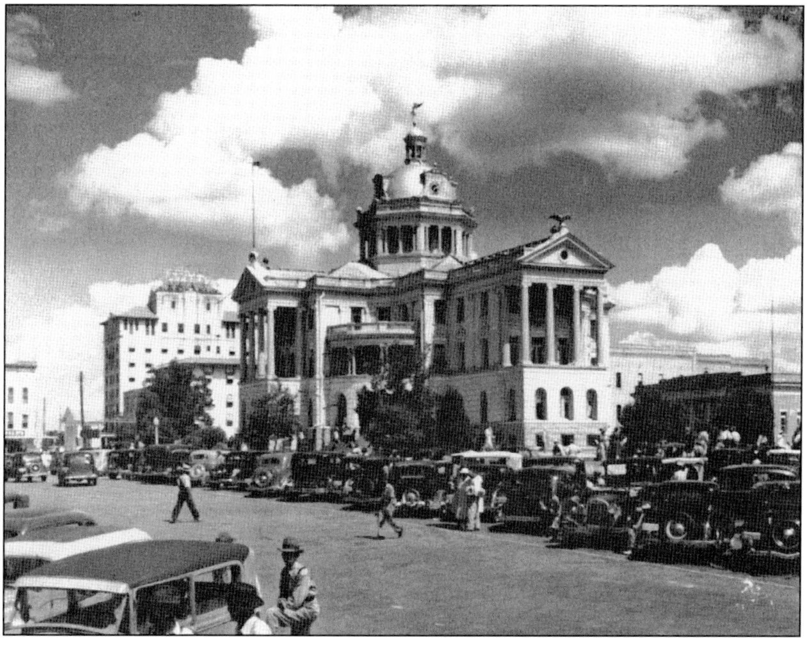

The northeast side of the square shows the activity and industry present in early Marshall. Hotel Marshall and the cupola of the First United Methodist Church are in the background.

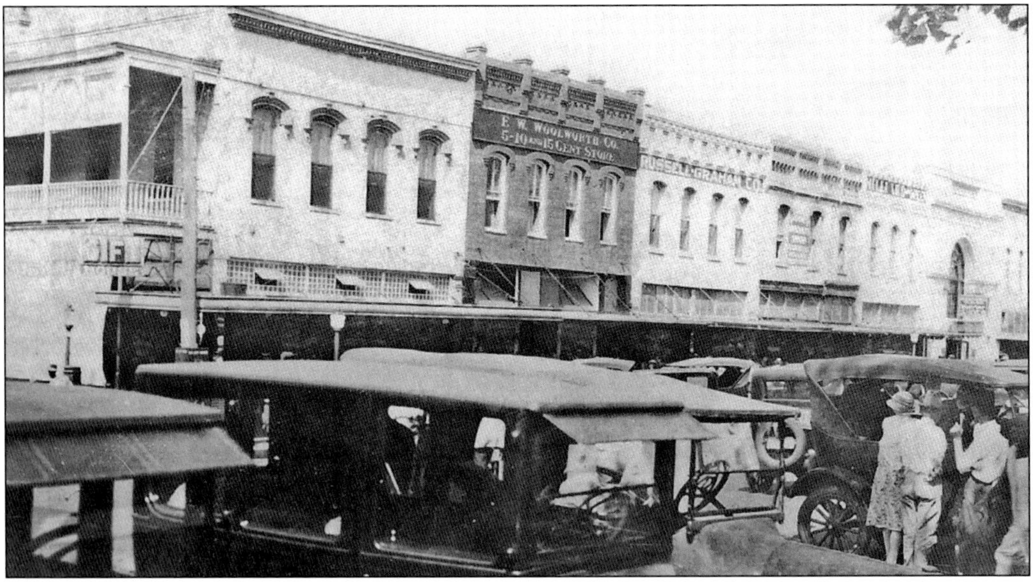

This photograph shows the northeast corner of the square. Styles and automobile models indicate an early-1900s date. There are many people in almost any photograph of the square, and life in Marshall continues to operate around Peter Whetstone Square.

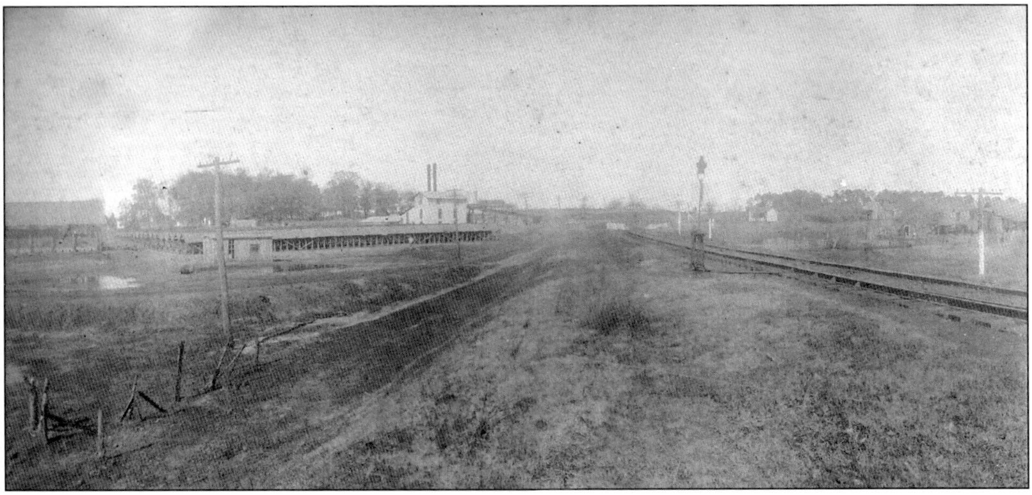

Marshall Brick and Manufacturing was organized in 1911. There was an initial investment of $40,000. By 1918, eight million bricks were made each year. By 1947, this number had risen to 15 million. Raw materials (clay and sand) present in Harrison County encouraged the growth of this industry.

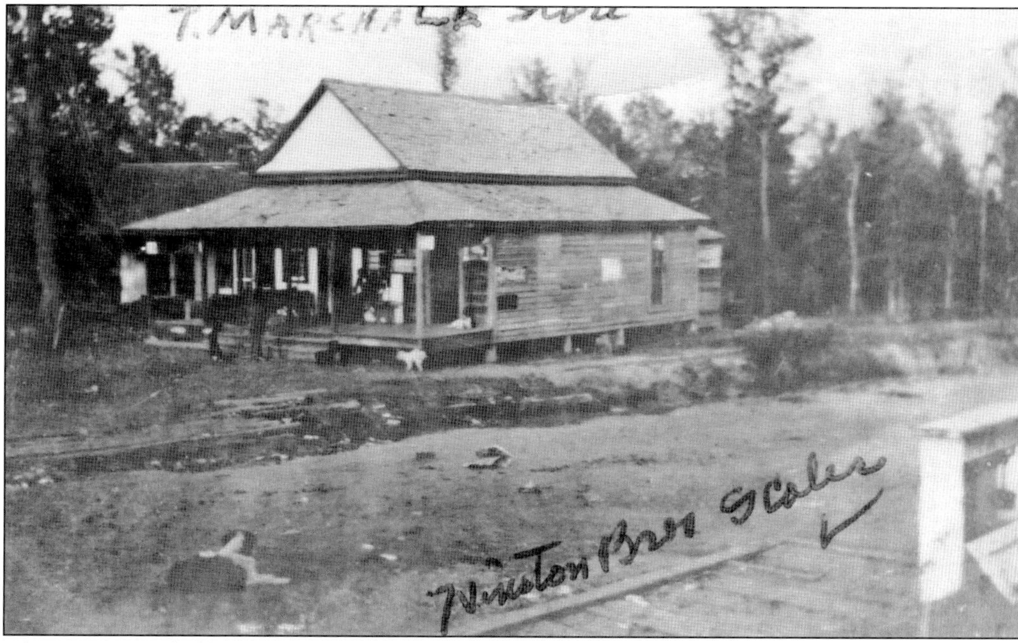

This is T. Marshall's store. Little is known about it, although Winston Brothers Scales can be seen in the lower right hand corner, indicating that it was used to receive agricultural products. (Courtesy of *Marshall News-Messenger.*)

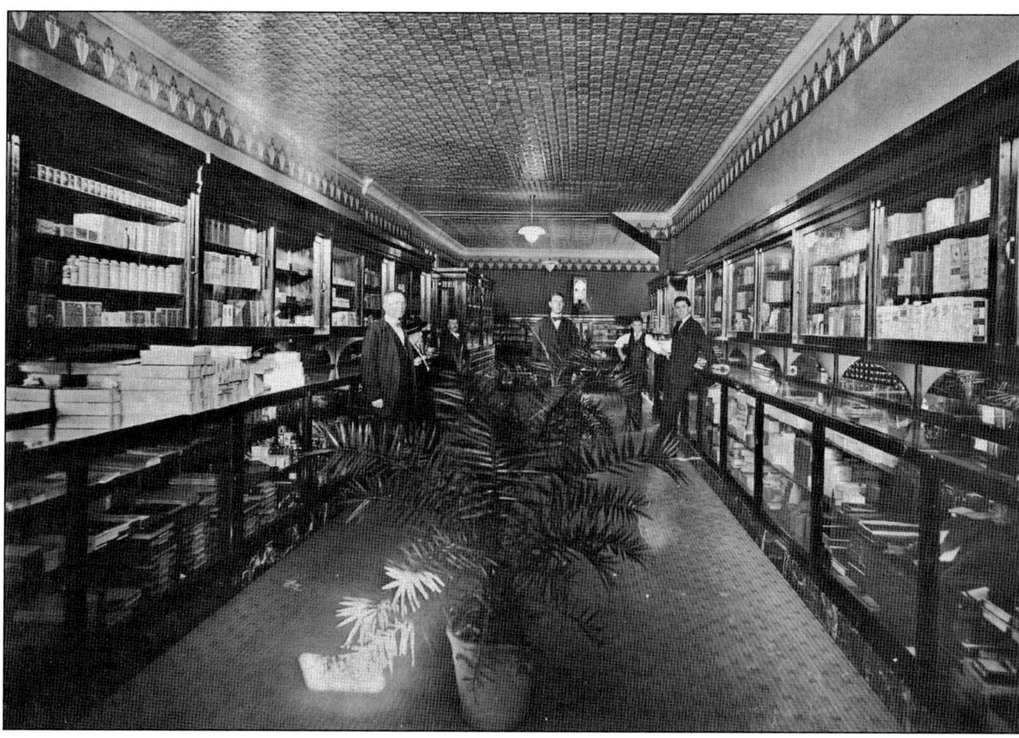

The owners of Matthewson Drug, H. W. Brown and George Recknagel, are pictured in the store around 1900. (Courtesy of *Marshall News-Messenger.*)

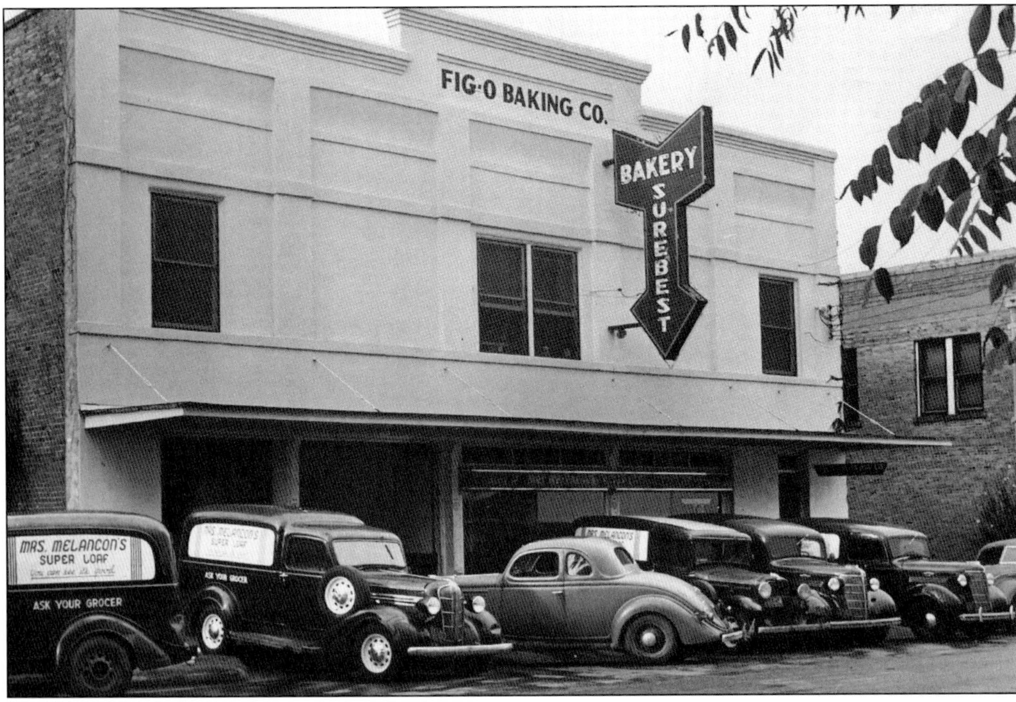

Fig O' Baking Company was established in Marshall in 1930 and located on Burleson Street. Later it became Mrs. Melancon's Bakery. It was well known for the wonderful smell of baking bread, which permeated the area. It was on a direct path for students walking to East Texas Baptist University from downtown Marshall. Many a loaf of hot bread was consumed on the way home!

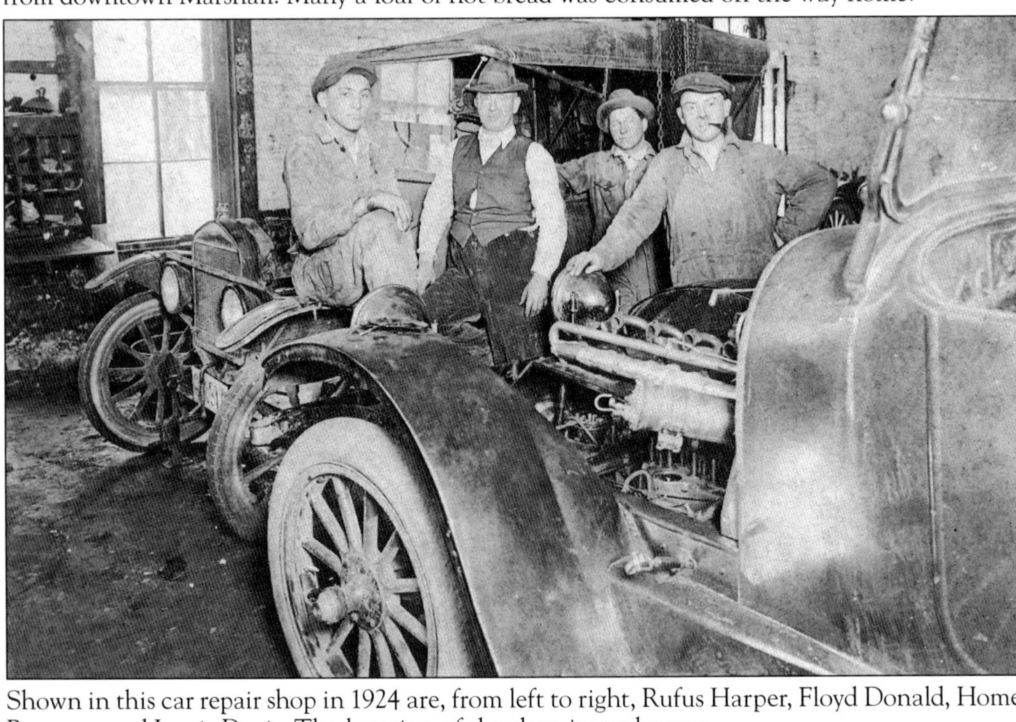

Shown in this car repair shop in 1924 are, from left to right, Rufus Harper, Floyd Donald, Homer Ransom, and Lewis Davis. The location of the shop is not known.

Baird Brothers Delivery Services worked in Marshall during the early 1900s. Delivery services such as this were popular in many early cities in Texas. It was a needed service because of the lack of other public transportation.

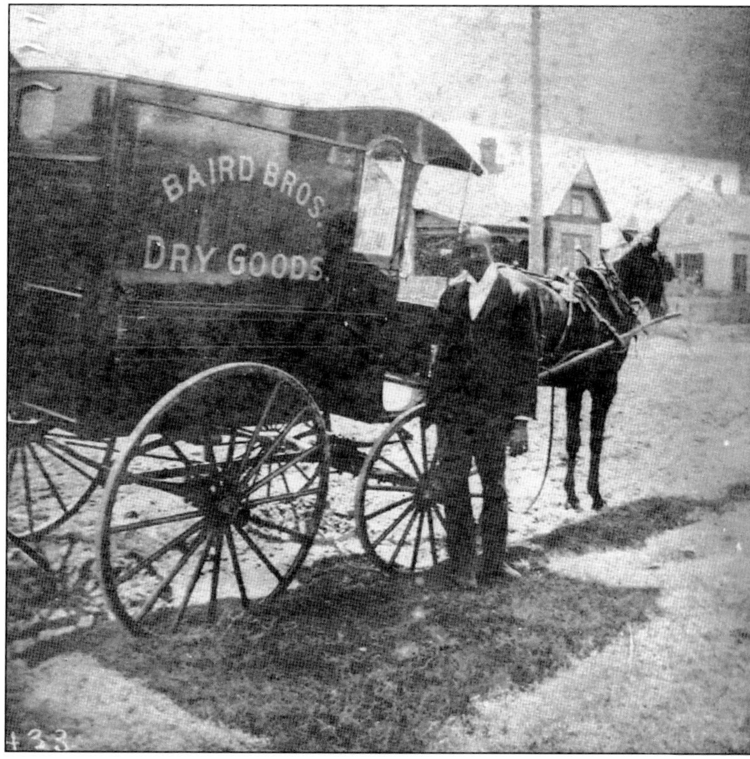

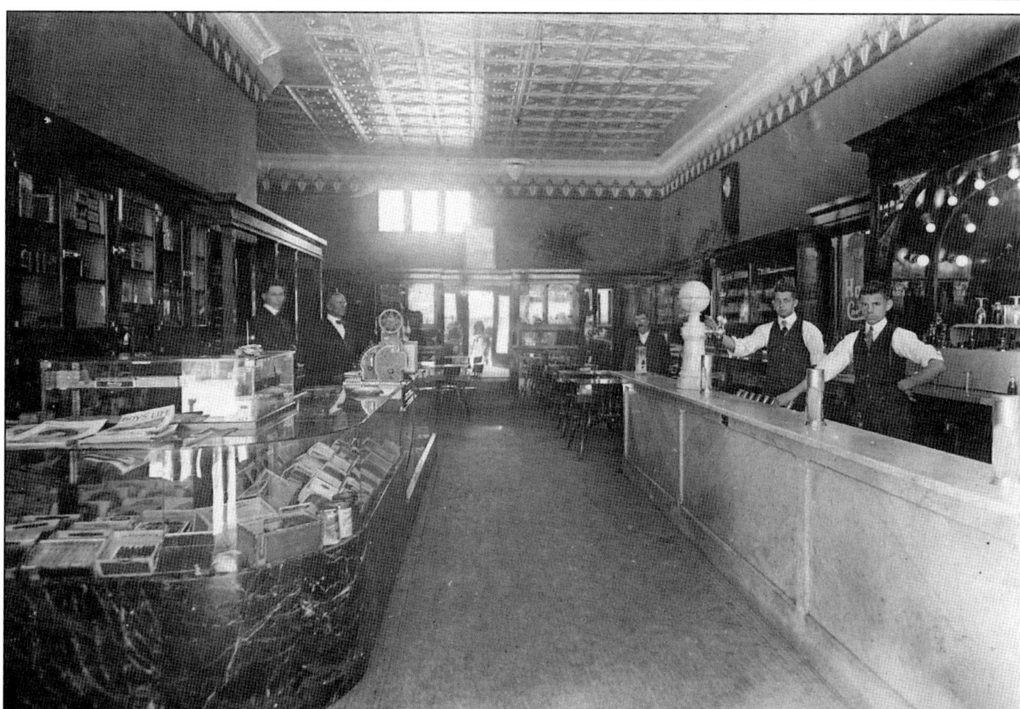

Jenkins Drugstore operated in Marshall in the early 1900s. Several other drugstores operated in the city at the same time. Little information is available about this one.

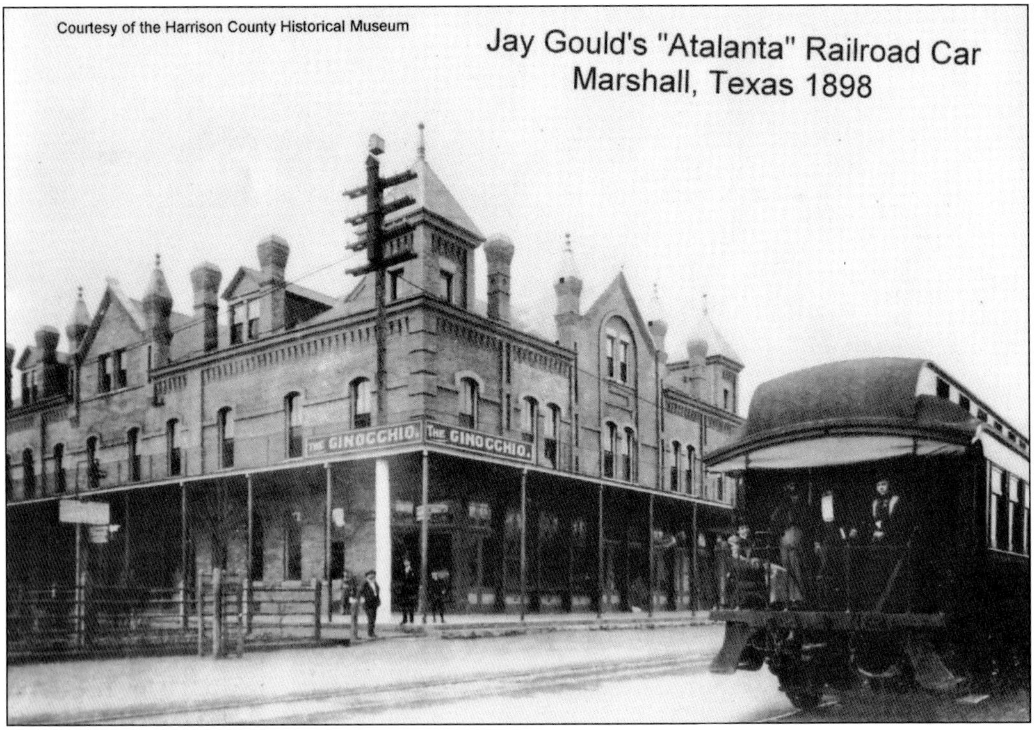

In the 1890s, Charles Ginocchio began construction on a building, which was to become a Marshall landmark. This is the Ginocchio Hotel as it appeared in 1898. Jay Gould's railroad car is shown in front of the hotel. This railroad car is now located in Jefferson.

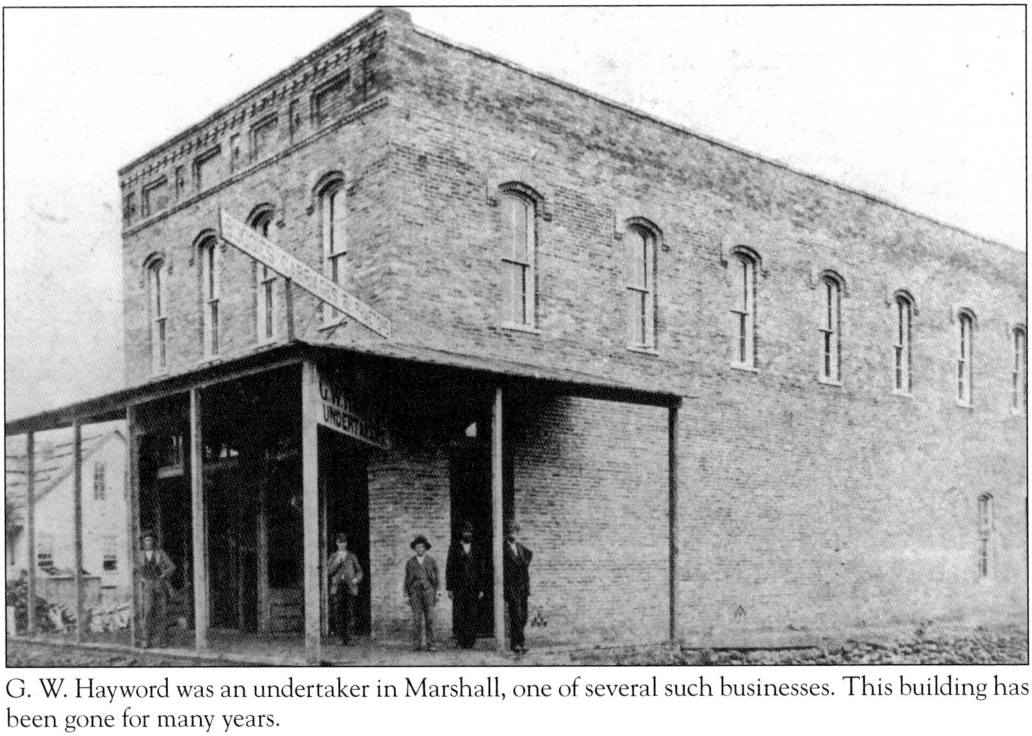

G. W. Hayword was an undertaker in Marshall, one of several such businesses. This building has been gone for many years.

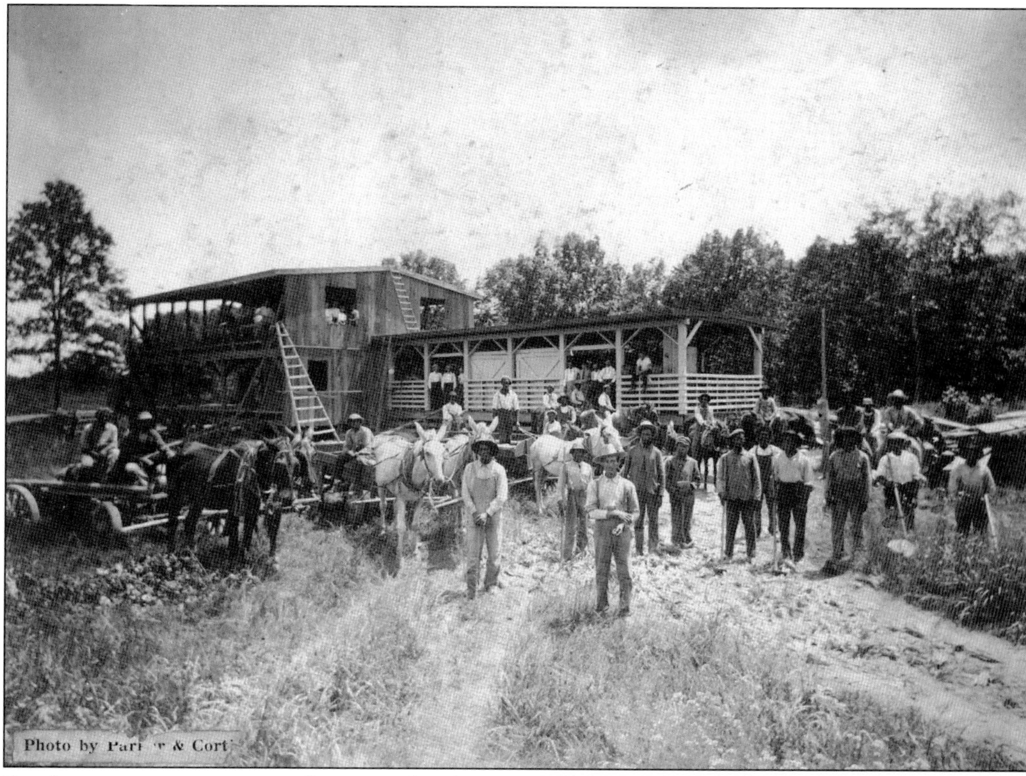

Peaches were an important business for the area. Above is the Caddo Peach Packing Shed in 1911. It occupied 1,500 acres and had 70,000 peach trees on the property.

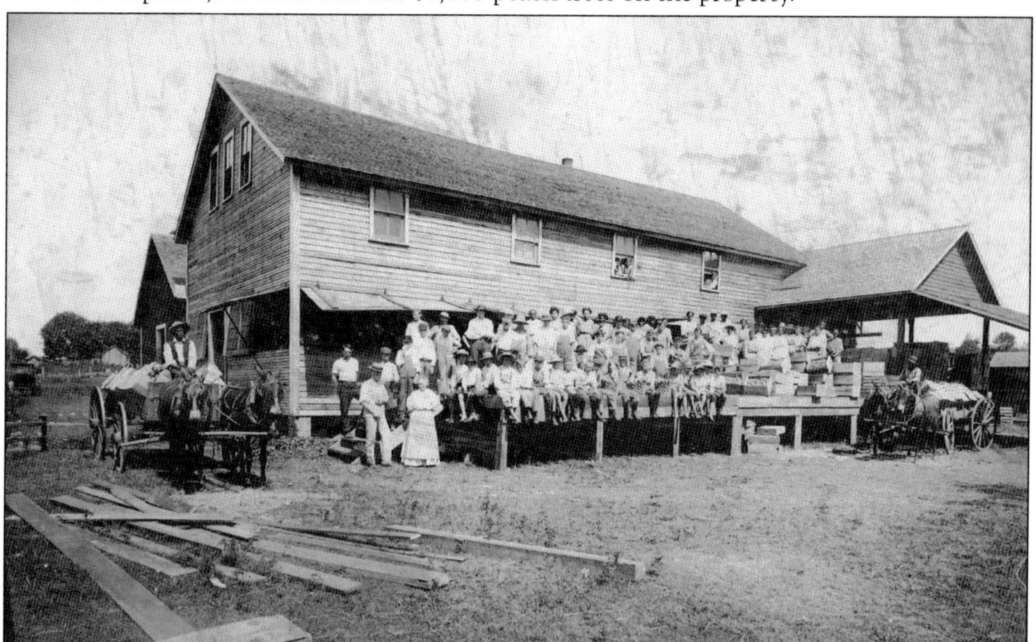

The Standard Orchard Company of Marshall owned the largest peach orchard in the south. This is the Verhalen Packing Shed, which was located in Scottsville.

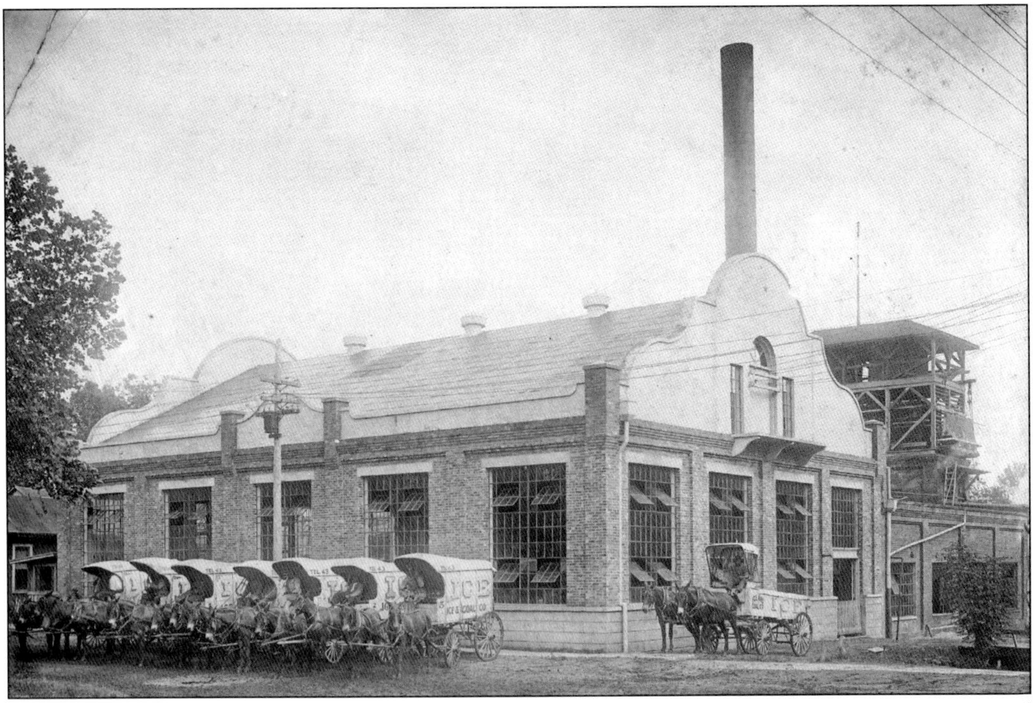

This Marshall branch of the Arkansas and Texas Consolidated Ice and Coal Company operated from the building shown in this photograph possibly as early as 1887. M. Israelson operated an electric-power generating plant at the same site as early as 1882. The operation of one contributed to the efficiency of the other. The electric department generated power that ran the machinery making ice. Blocks of ice were delivered to Marshall residents using horse-drawn ice wagons. In 1897, the electric company had more than 20 miles of wire and most downtown businesses were using electricity as their only source of light. An 1897 company pamphlet states, "The electric light has grown wonderfully in popularity among the owners of homes in this city, and the past two years show a rapid increase in this branch of the business." The building still stands at the southeast corner of Fannin and Fulton Streets.

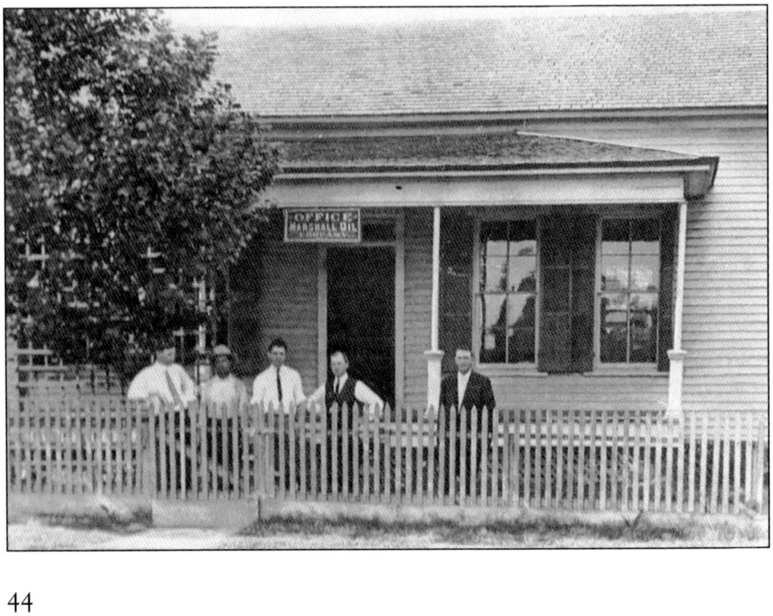

Marshall Oil Company was located at 110 Grand Avenue. It was founded in 1903 and in 1913 became the Cotton Oil Company.

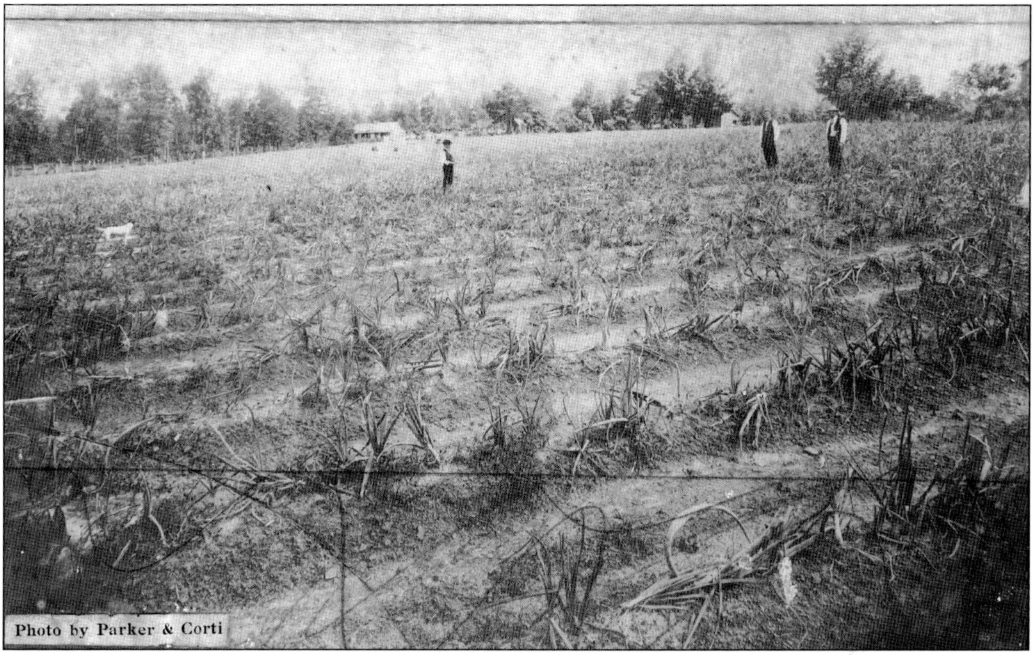

Marshall served as the marketing and shipping center for Harrison County's farmers. The primary cash crop was cotton, but others such as corn and peaches were also successful. A Harrison County farmer grows a field of onions in this photograph.

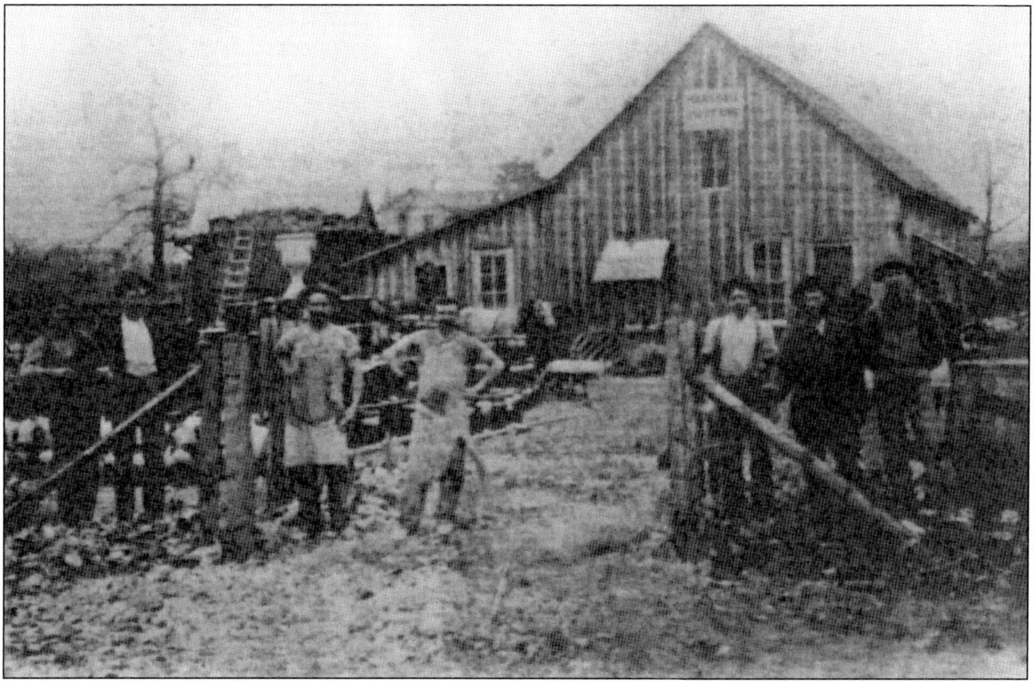

This is the original Lake Street location of Marshall Pottery. The first pottery in Marshall was organized in 1891 by Mr. Rocker. S. B. Ellis and his sons acquired the pottery in 1904. It is still in operation and continues to produce churns, flowerpots, stoneware, and gift items. (Courtesy of Dana Harris.)

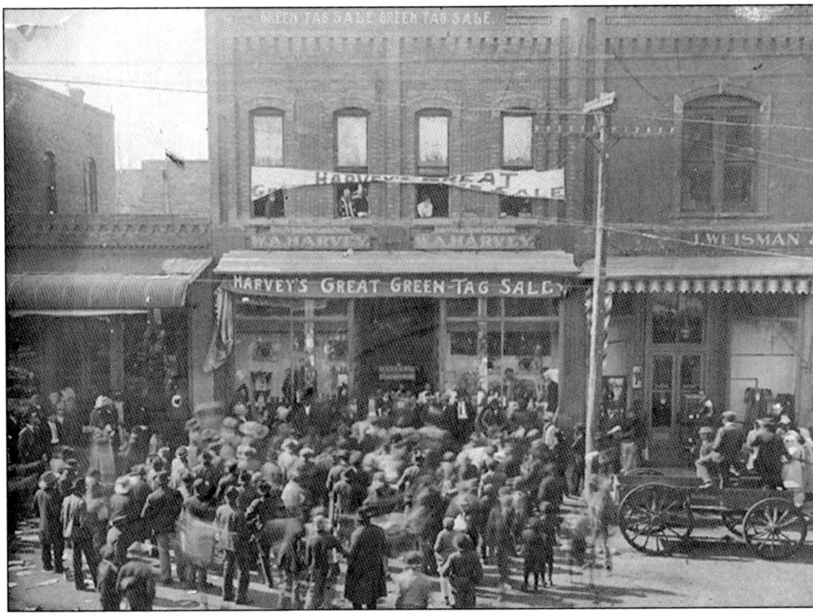

W. A. Harvey Clothing Store in 1900 is indicative of the growth of Marshall. As the population increased, so did the need for a place to shop. (Courtesy of *Marshall News Messenger.*)

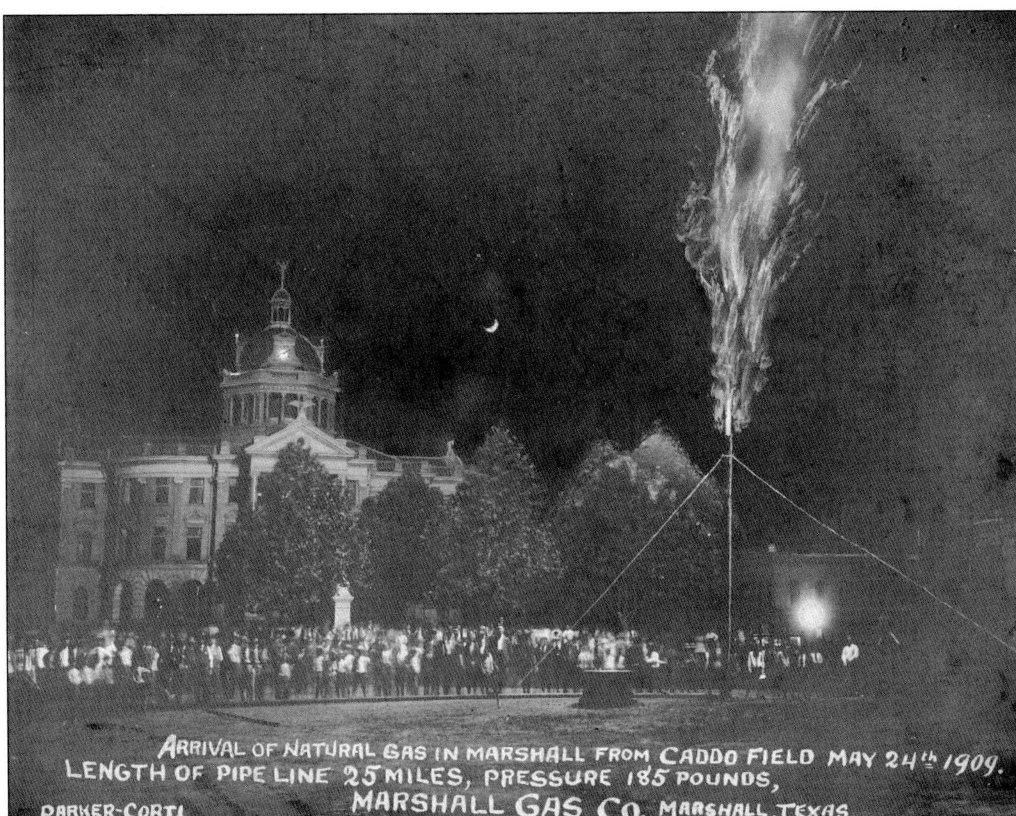

This photograph shows the arrival of natural gas in Marshall from Caddo Field, May 24, 1909. (Courtesy of *Marshall News Messenger.*)

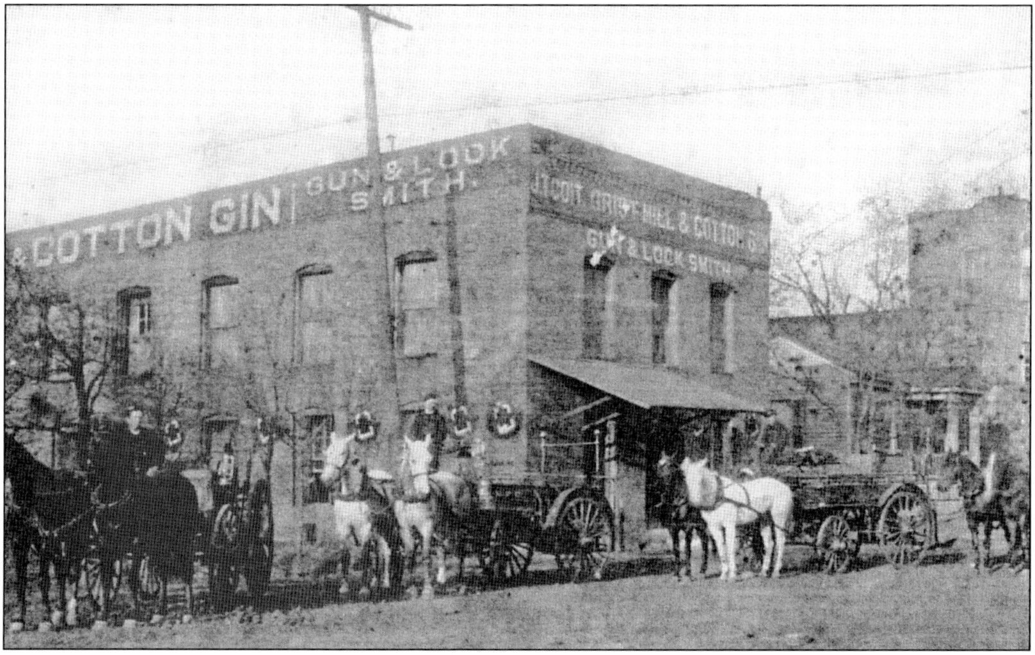

J. T. Colt Gristmill and Cotton Gin at West Houston Street and the square are pictured here in 1910. (Courtesy of *Marshall News Messenger.*)

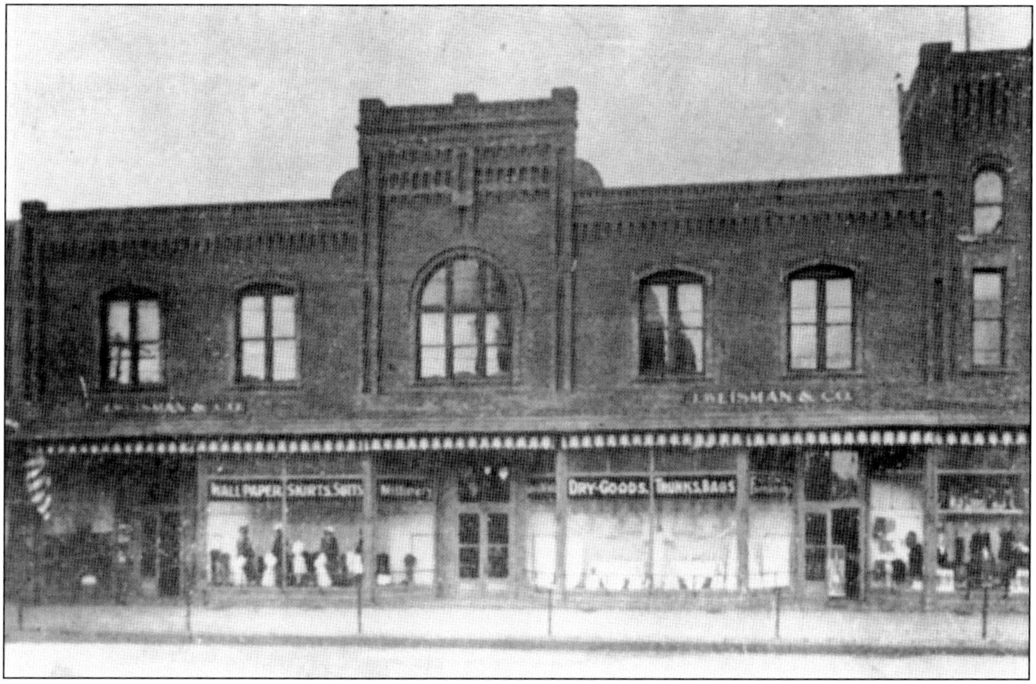

Jewish merchant Joe Weisman came to Marshall in 1868. In 1878, he formed the Joe Weisman and Company mercantile store, located on the north side of the square. Joe and his wife, Lena, were active at Temple Moses Montefiore and contributed greatly to the community. In 1900, he moved his growing department store into the newly constructed building shown in this photograph. It was operated by subsequent owners until 1990.

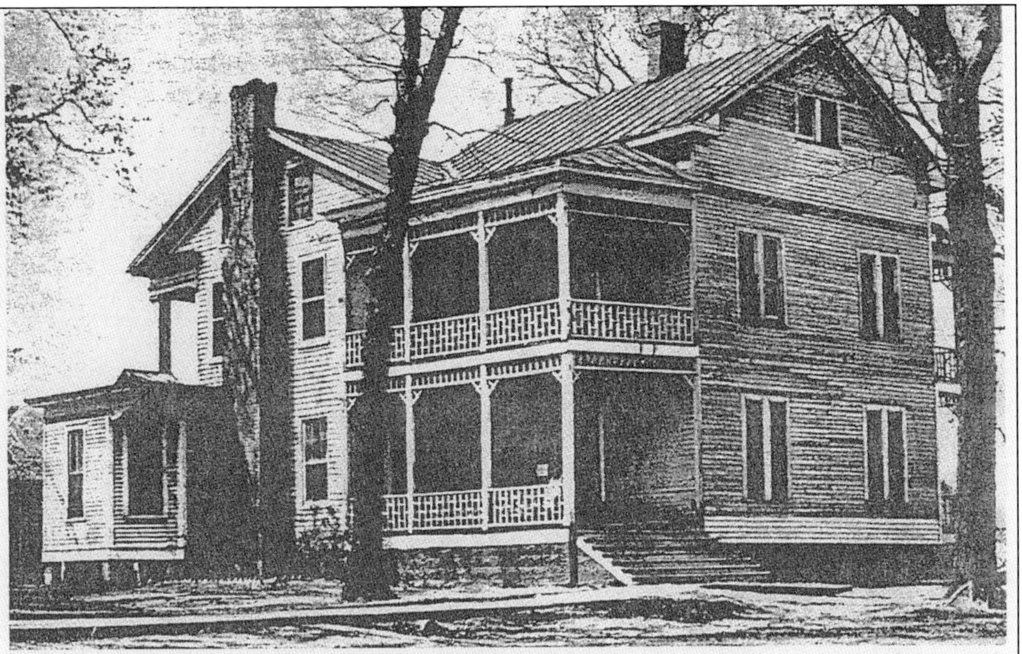

A group of doctors purchased the first hospital in 1909 on same location of the present hospital. It was named Marshall Hospital.

This is the first hospital in Marshall. Organized by a group of local doctors, it was located on the site of the present hospital. It was named Marshall Hospital. Later the name was changed to Kahn Hospital, then to Marshall Memorial Hospital, and it is now Good Shepherd Medical Center Marshall. (Courtesy of *Marshall News Messenger*.)

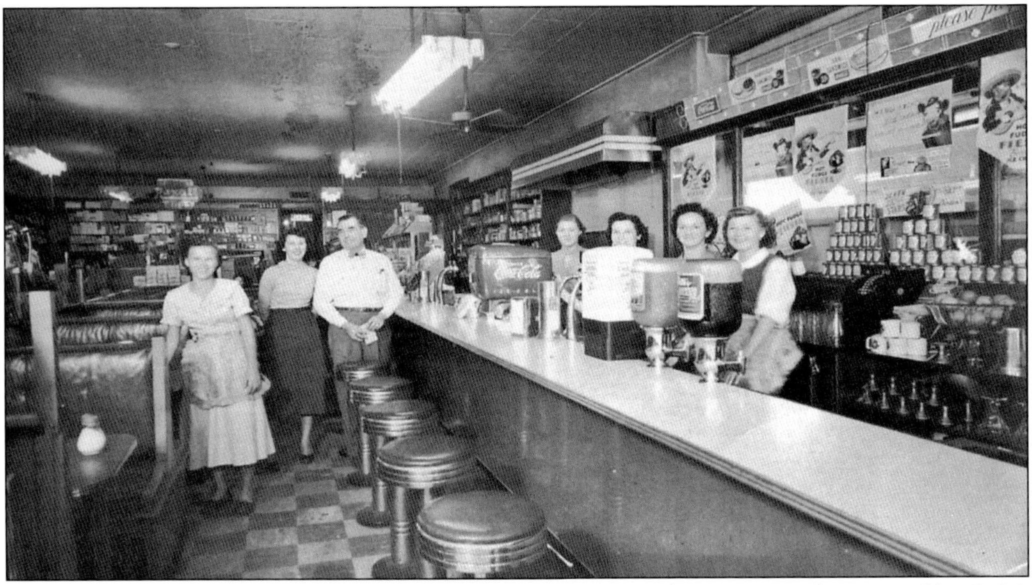

Established in Marshall in 1884, this is Fry-Hodge Drug around 1946. It was first owned by G. M. Phillips and called Phillips Drug. In 1884, it was sold to Maj. E. J. Fry and called E. J. Fry Drug. Fry operated it until 1900 at which time it was incorporated and became known as Fry-Hodge Drug. (Courtesy of *Marshall News Messenger*.)

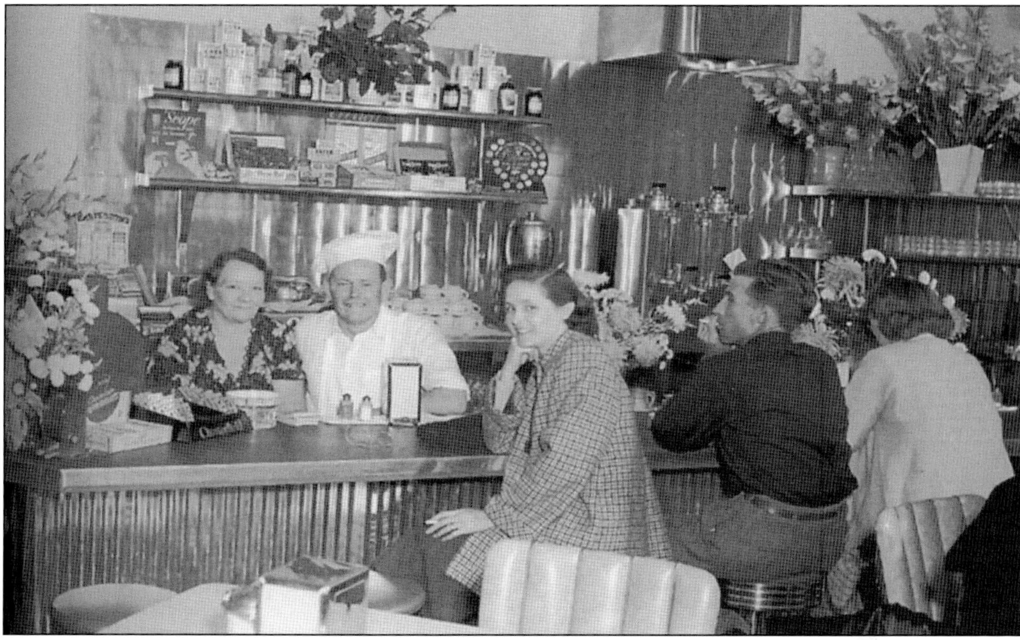

Marshall Waffle Shop was a popular gathering place for 50 years, from 1936 to 1986. (Courtesy of *Marshall News Messenger.*)

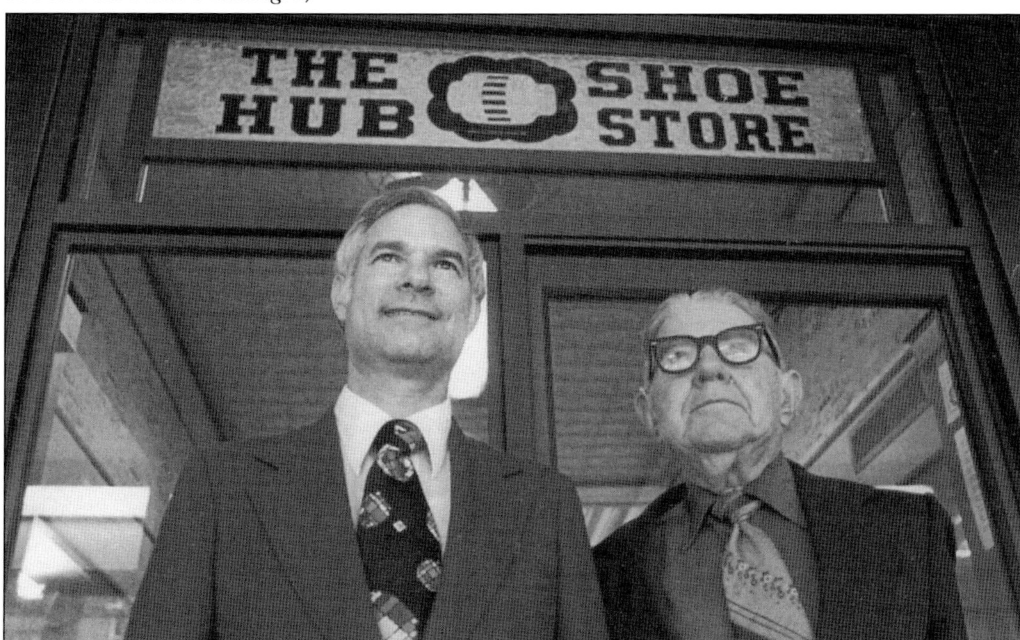

Louis Kariel Jr. (left) and Louis Kariel Sr. (right), in front of Hub Shoe Store in 1969.

In 1897, an exclusive shoe store was established in Marshall by M. L. Weisman. He operated it until 1924 when it was sold to L. W. Kariel and H. W. Pierpont. In January 1926, L. W. Kariel and his son Louis Kariel Jr. moved the store to 111A East Austin Street, where it was operated as the Hub Shoe Store. The store is now closed.

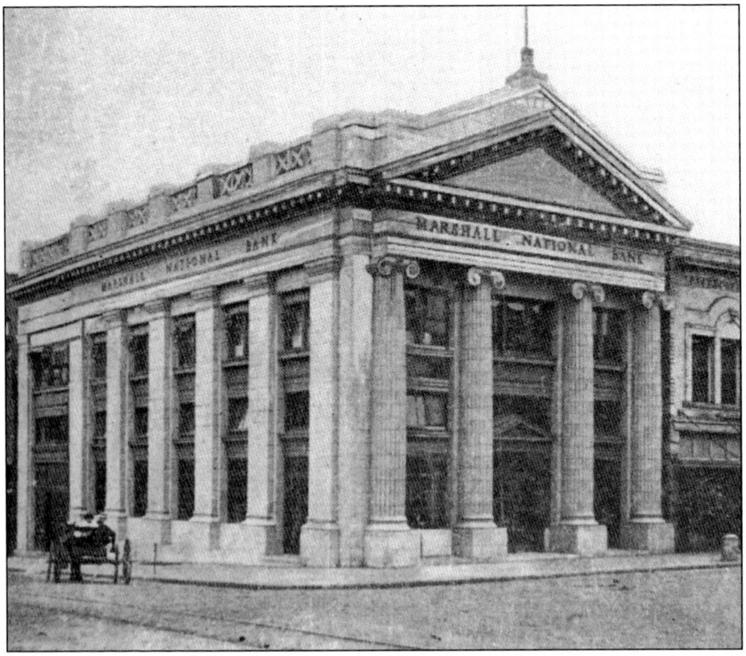

The Marshall National Bank was organized by several businessmen on July 25, 1889. A charter was granted in 1889 with the capital stock being $100,000. The first president was Will C. Pierce. One of the organizers, M. M. Rains, made the first deposit. The second president was W. L. Martin. He was succeeded by W. C. Pierce Jr., son of the first president. W. F. Young became president of the bank in 1947. This building is still standing and houses Chase Bank.

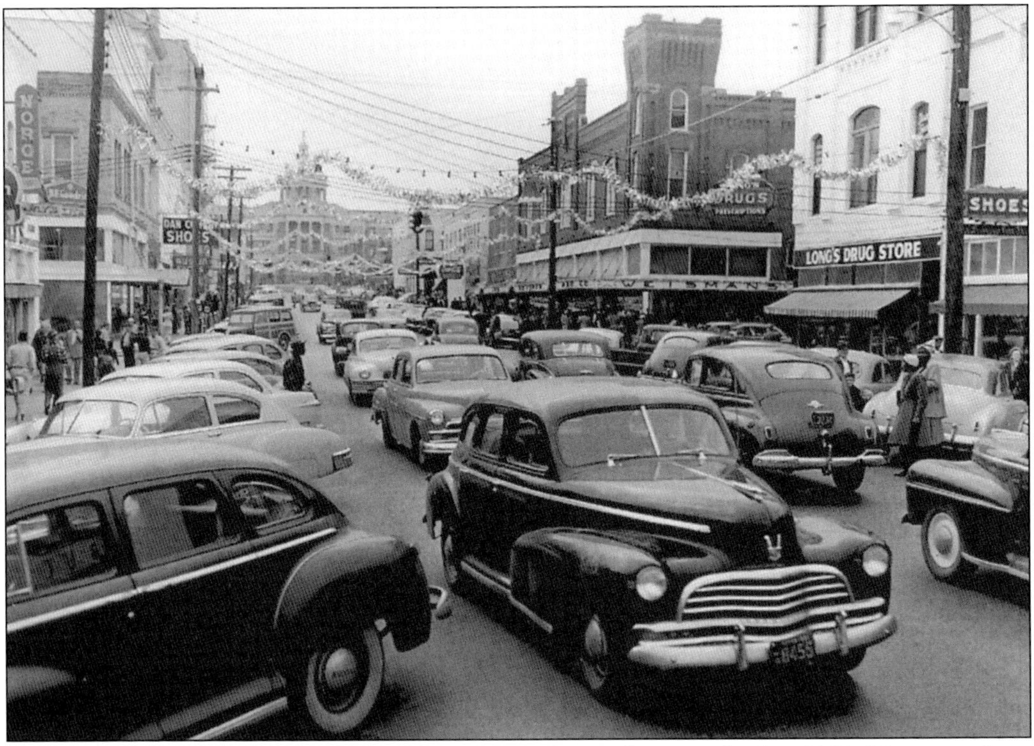

The Christmas traffic on North Washington Street was photographed in 1950. The scene here shows Weisman's Department Store and other stores that were in business at that time. (Courtesy of *Marshall News Messenger*.)

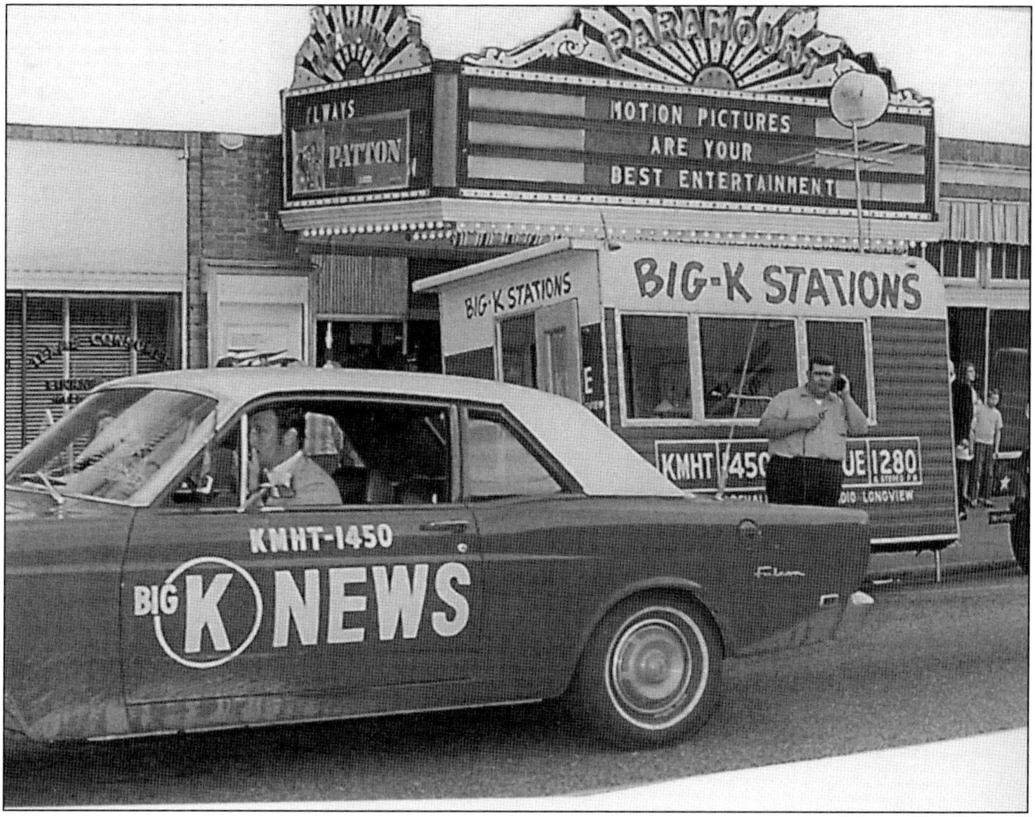

For many years, the Paramount Theater operated on North Washington Street in downtown Marshall. The building still stands today, but movies are no longer shown there. (Courtesy of *Marshall News Messenger.*)

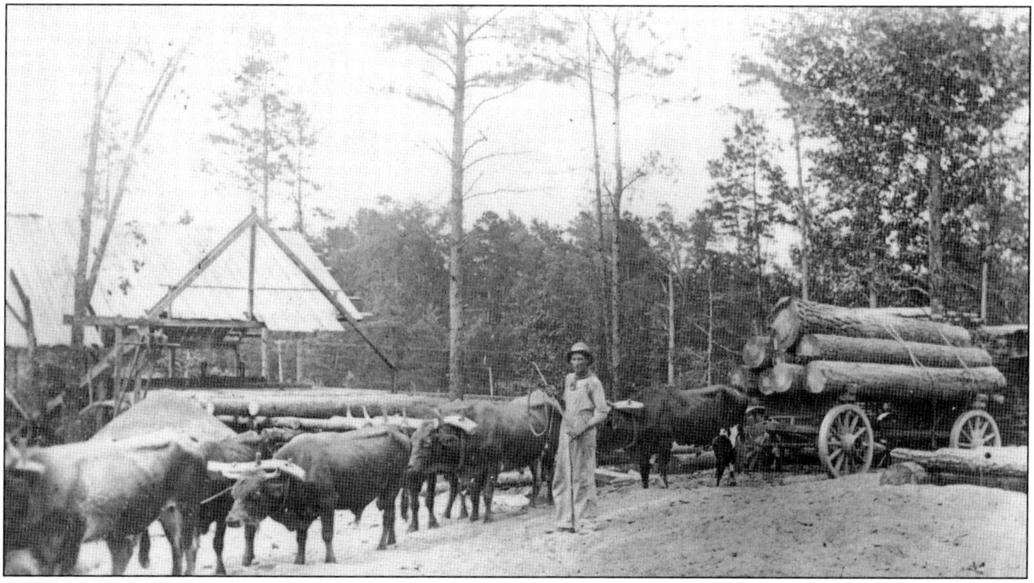

The lumber business was important in Marshall and all of Harrison County as communities began to grow and expand. Shown here is a horseless lumber wagon in use in 1908.

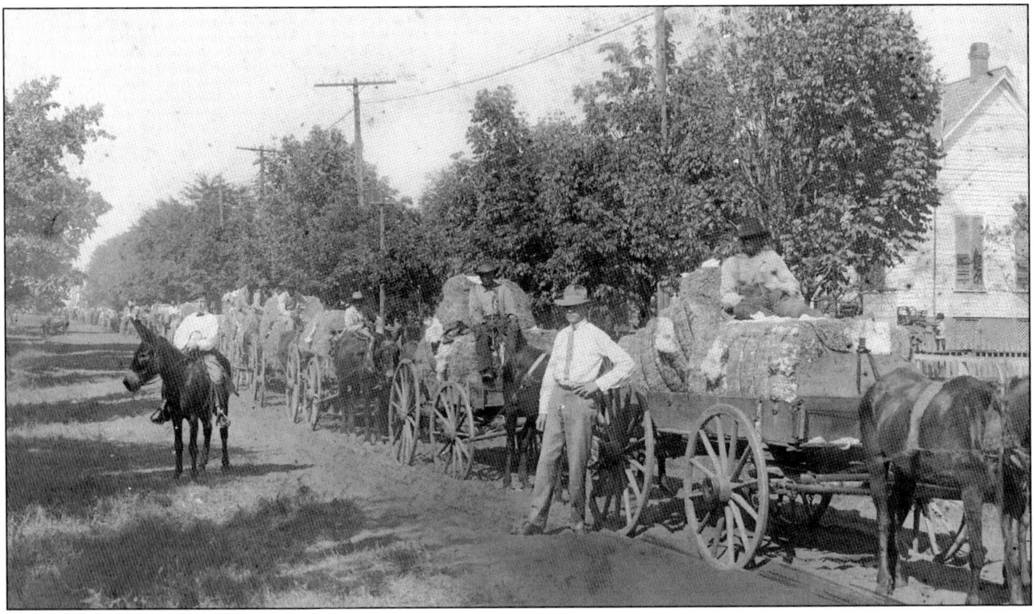

Wagons loaded with cotton bales line Bolivar Street. Most of the settlers of Harrison County were from the southern United States. They brought with them their cotton economy. In 1849, Harrison County produced about 4,600 bales of cotton. In less than 10 years, the number increased by almost 17,000 bales. Cotton was shipped to New Orleans markets.

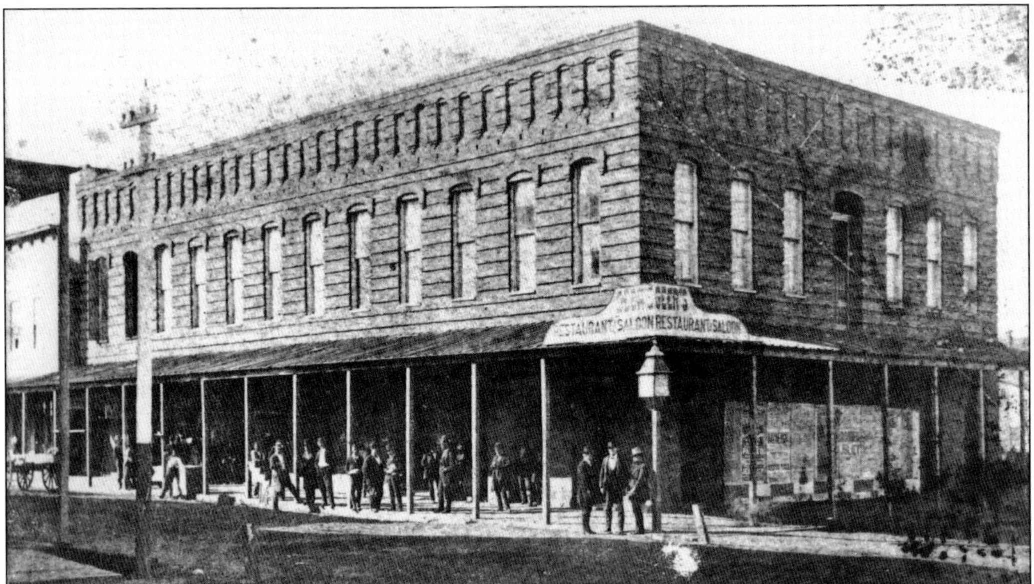

From 1877 to 1915, Marshall had five theaters; four of them were called "opera houses." The first theater was built before the Civil War by C. W. Rains, a prominent planter, and hosted local entertainers. Mahone's Opera House was built about 1875 by John R. Mahone. It was on the second floor of a building that still stands today at the corner of the intersection of Washington and Austin Streets in downtown Marshall. The theater had a seating capacity of about 600 and hosted many large companies. Occupying the ground floor was the Opera House Saloon. Mahone sold the opera house in 1883 for $5,000 to Katie and Mamie Knight of Dallas. It operated until 1887.

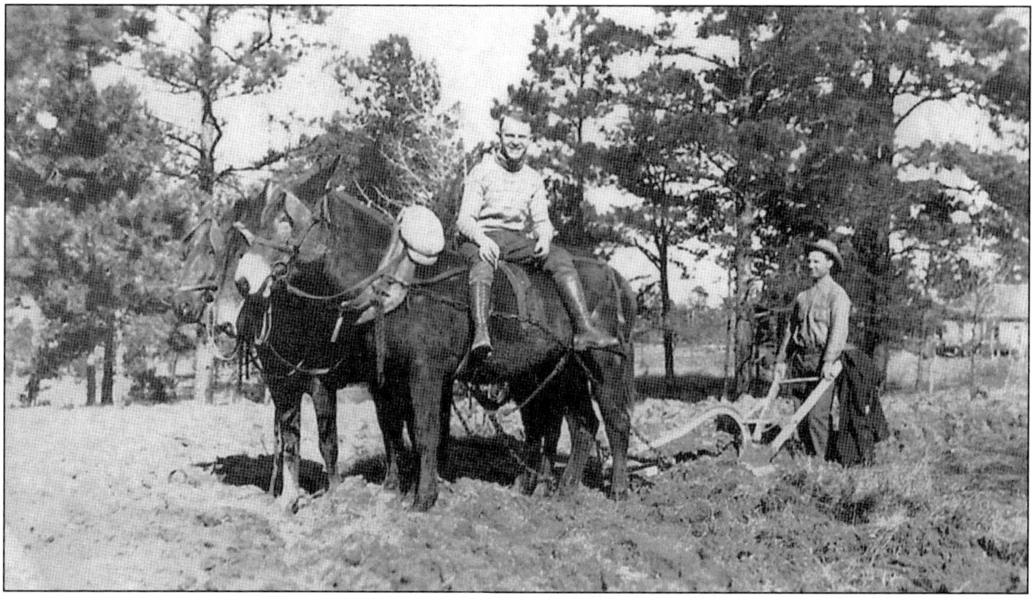

The importance of agriculture continued into the 20th century in Marshall and in Harrison County. Men are pictured plowing in 1927.

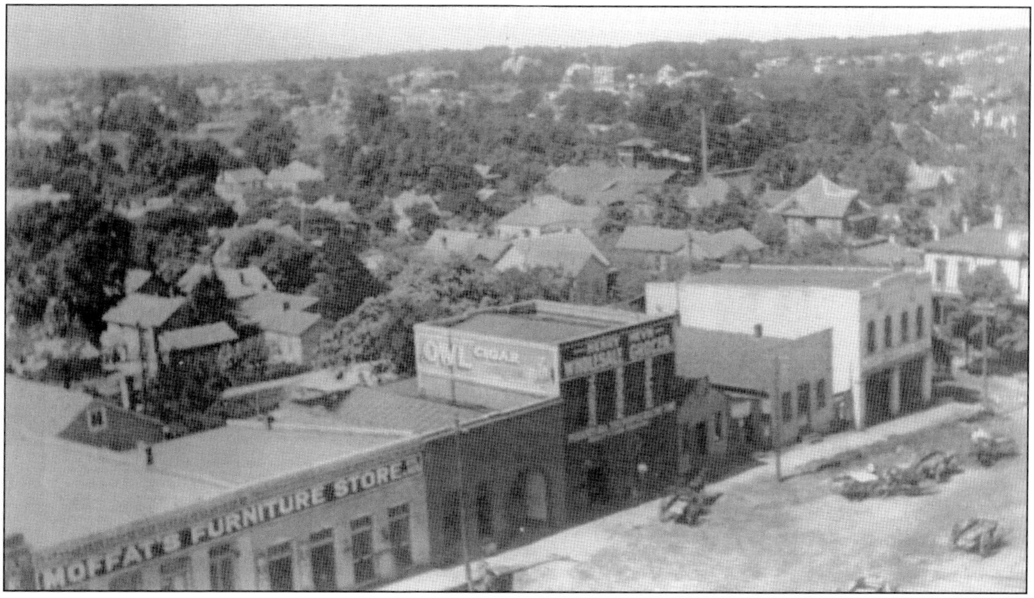

The first furniture company in Marshall was Moffat Furniture, built in 1899. It was located on the courthouse square and was partially burned when the courthouse caught fire. It was saved by volunteers who formed a bucket brigade.

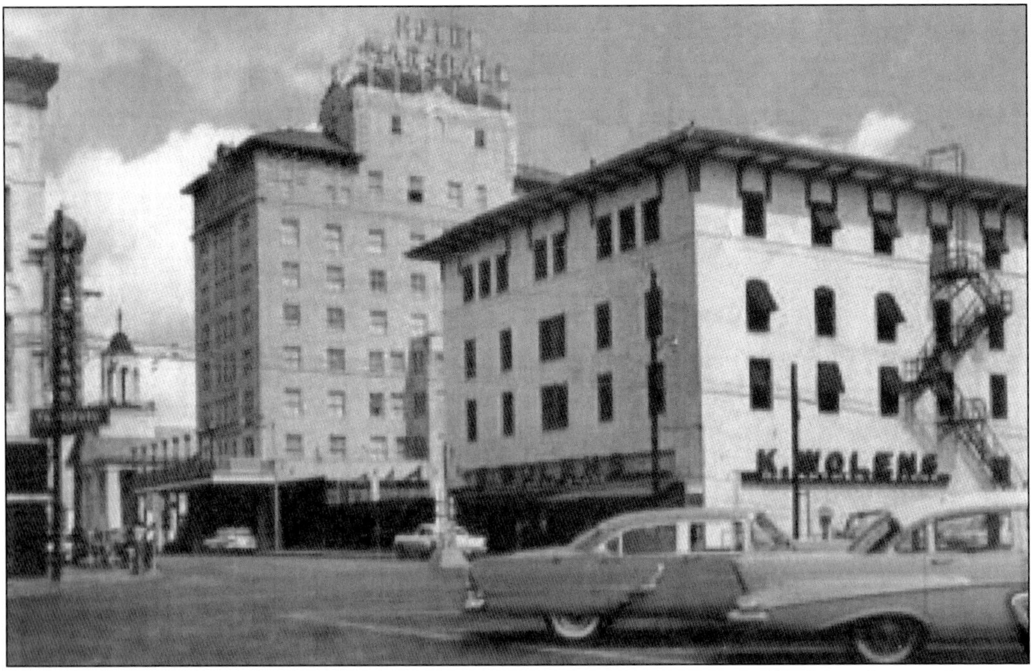

The Capitol Hotel was constructed on the corner of East Houston and Bolivar Streets by slave labor, with slaves both making and burning the bricks. Constructed in 1857 by Judge George B. Adkins, the hotel was reported by admirers to be the largest and best building in the Southwest. Adkins operated the hotel and entertained stagecoach passengers who stopped there. The building was purchased by Sam Perkins, who opened Perkins Department Store downstairs. Later this became K. Wolens Department Store. A walkway tied the two structures together. The Hotel Marshall, seen in the background, was constructed later and became one of the largest hotel complexes in the Southwest. It is still standing today.

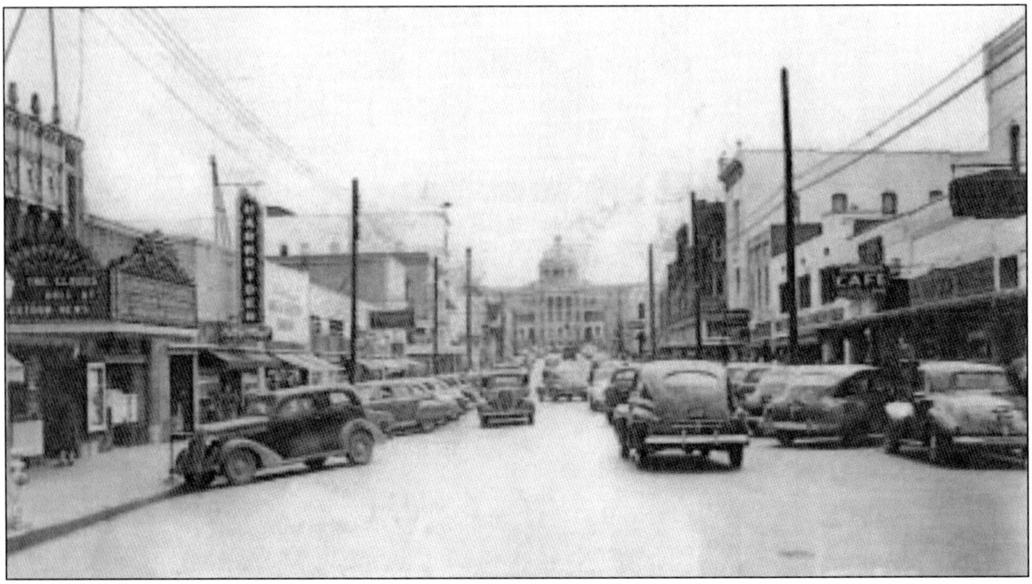

North Washington Street has been a busy street in Marshall since its beginning. This postcard scene shows how it might have looked on a busy day. (Courtesy of Henry Bradbury.)

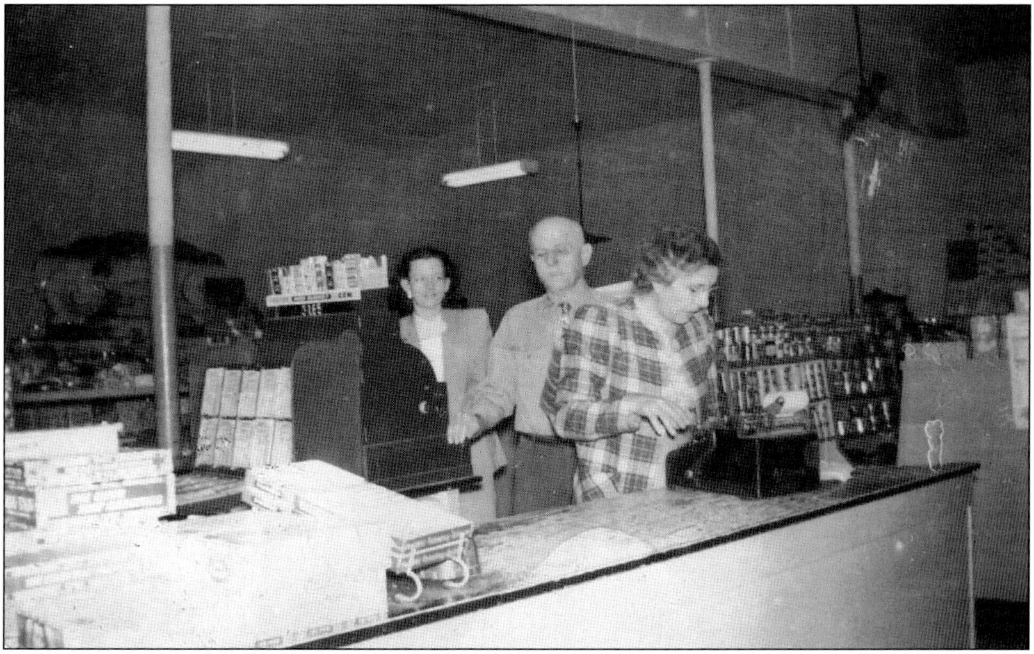

The first Lebanese came to Marshall in the early 1900s. The first generation of Lebanese in Marshall were peddlers. As they became successful and prosperous in this new land, they opened stores of their own. This store was Abraham Food Store, and Charlie and Helena Abraham are shown in this photograph. (Courtesy of the Barkett family.)

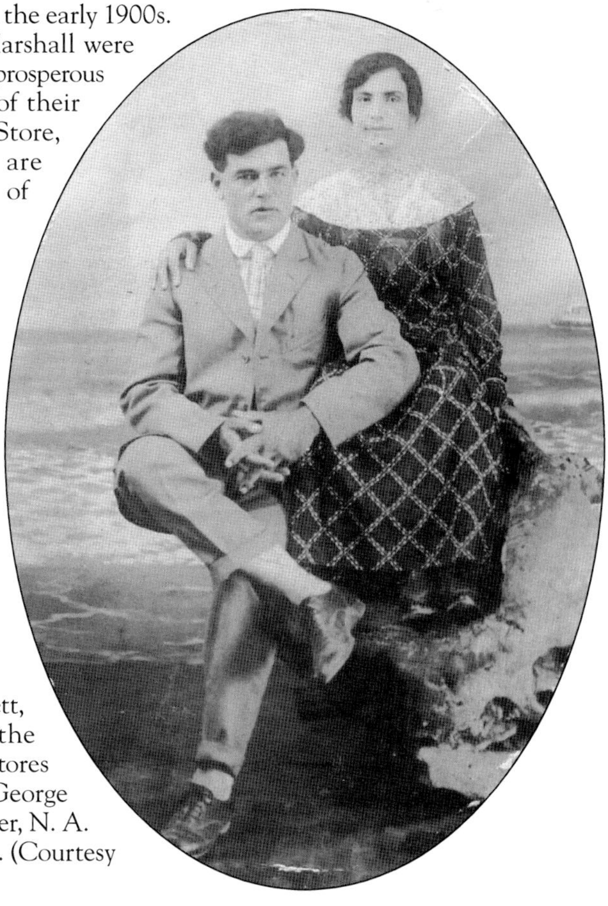

Shown here are Charlie and Asma Barkett, who operated a dry goods store in the McPhail block for a number of years. Stores on this block include Ameen Nader, George Asaff, E. T. Barkett, Sam Ellis, Lee Nader, N. A. Mack, Abraham Food Store, and others. (Courtesy of the Barkett family.)

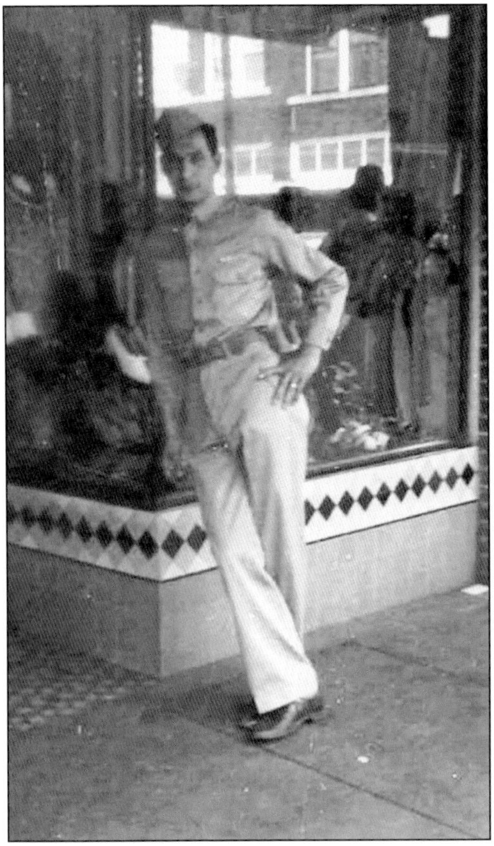

Sammy Barkett is shown here in uniform during World War II. He is in front of the store owned by his parents, Charlie and Asma Barkett. (Courtesy of the Barkett family.)

This photograph is of the McPhail Block. It was here that many Lebanese merchants opened stores. There were still peddlers in these early days, and it was not unusual for the women to join the men as peddlers. All of the peddlers had handmade goods, which were very popular. (Courtesy of the Barkett family.)

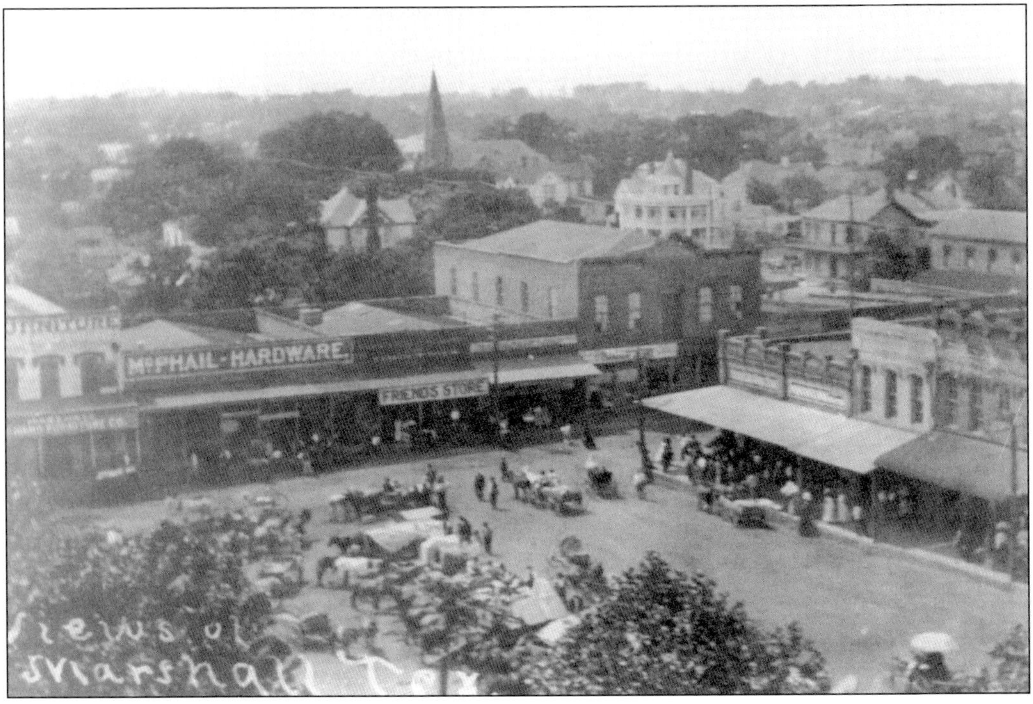

Five

Railroads in Marshall

Railroads have played an important role in the history of Marshall. The railroad exceeds all industries in bringing economic growth to Marshall. There were several attempts to charter and build railroads.

In 1850, a meeting was held to promote the idea that providing rail service to Caddo Lake ports would expand the agricultural interests in Harrison and other East Texas counties. An act incorporating the Vicksburg, Louisiana, and Texas Railroad was passed by the Texas Legislature in 1850. The railroad was granted 16 sections of land for each mile of track laid. The Marshall Railroad and Plank Company were chartered in 1850.

A Vicksburg, Shreveport, and Texas Railroad was chartered on February 14, 1852. It was to begin at the border of Harrison County and provide service to Austin and then on to El Paso. The Southern Pacific Railroad was chartered in 1852, and in 1853, the Marshall Railroad was chartered to run from Marshall to New Orleans. The Sabine and Sulphur Springs Railroad was chartered the next year.

The Southern Pacific Railroad was the only one of those chartered to actually lay track. Rails connected Marshall to Swanson's Landing on Caddo Lake in 1858.

The Civil War brought a halt to some railroad activities in Marshall. Confederate general John B. Magruder ordered some of the tracks removed and relaid to form a route between Marshall and Shreveport.

The Texas and Pacific Railway Company received a federal charter in 1871 to build a transcontinental railroad along the 32nd parallel from Marshall to San Diego. The Texas and Pacific built its shops in Marshall in 1873. Land was donated by the city. Harrison County issued $300,000 in bonds.

The Texas and Pacific (T&P) shops were situated on 66.5 acres of land in the northeastern part of Marshall. The shops operated until after World War II when industry advances rendered the Marshall shops obsolete. The Texas and Pacific Depot continued in use as a passenger station until 1974. Today it is one of Texas's restored historic depots, owned and operated by Marshall Depot, Inc., as a railway museum and Amtrak passenger station.

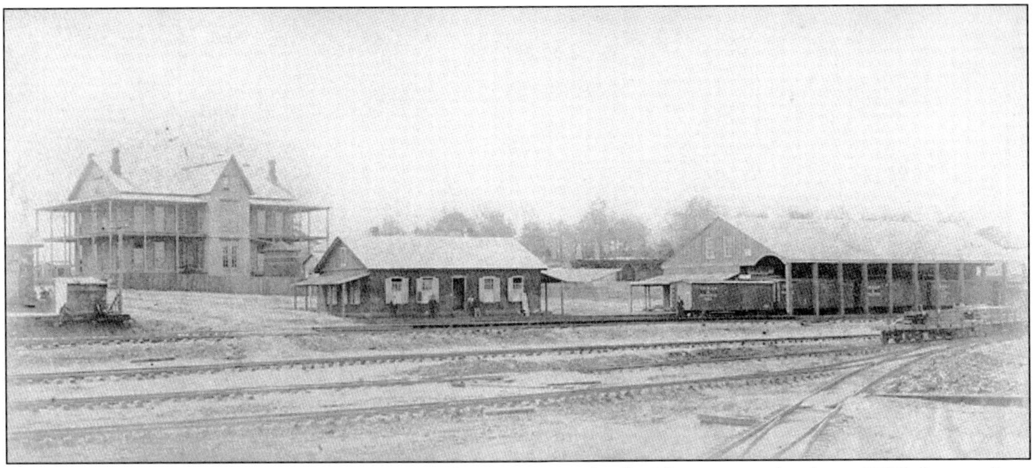

Pictured is the general office of the T&P shops in Marshall. These were built in 1873. Later they were used as a hospital. In the beginning, only four men were employed, and they worked in wooden buildings. A machine shop and roundhouse were built, and by 1900, a new roundhouse had been constructed, along with other improvements. Much of this was destroyed by fire in 1903. (Courtesy of *Marshall News Messenger.*)

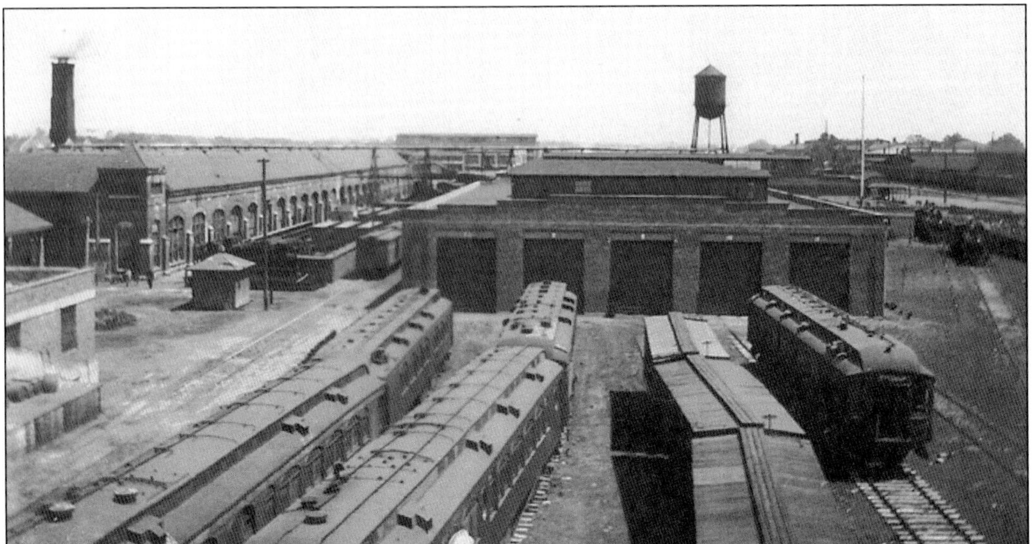

The T&P shops in Marshall continued to grow. In 1905, the first diesel engine was installed in the shop power plant at a cost of $15,000. It was a three-cylinder engine, generating 225 horsepower. Improvements continued to be made as long as the shops were in operation in Marshall. (Courtesy of *Marshall News Messenger.*)

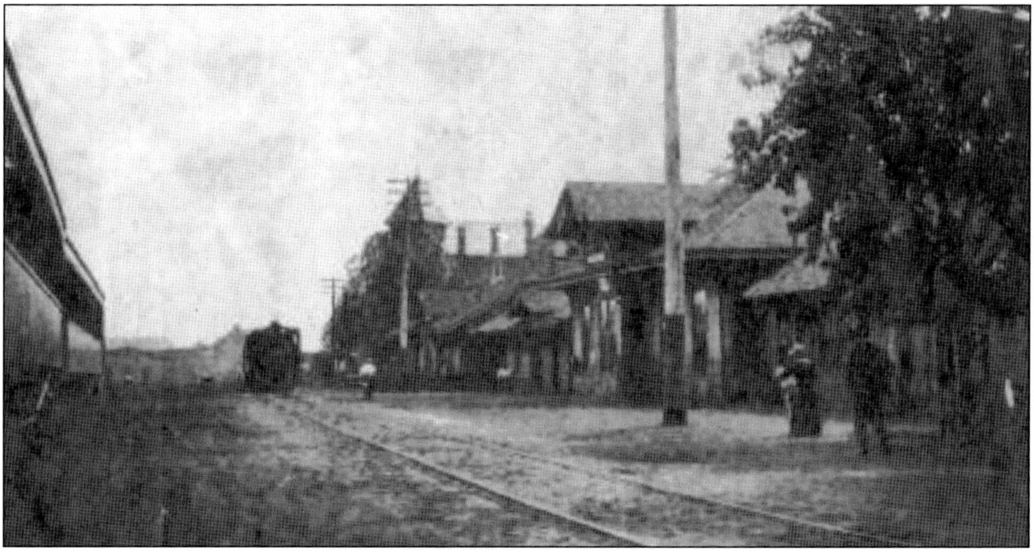

As did most railroad stations, the T&P in Marshall had hotels nearby for the convenience of travelers. This postcard advertising Marshall pictured the depot and the Elgin Hotel. (Courtesy of Henry Bradbury).

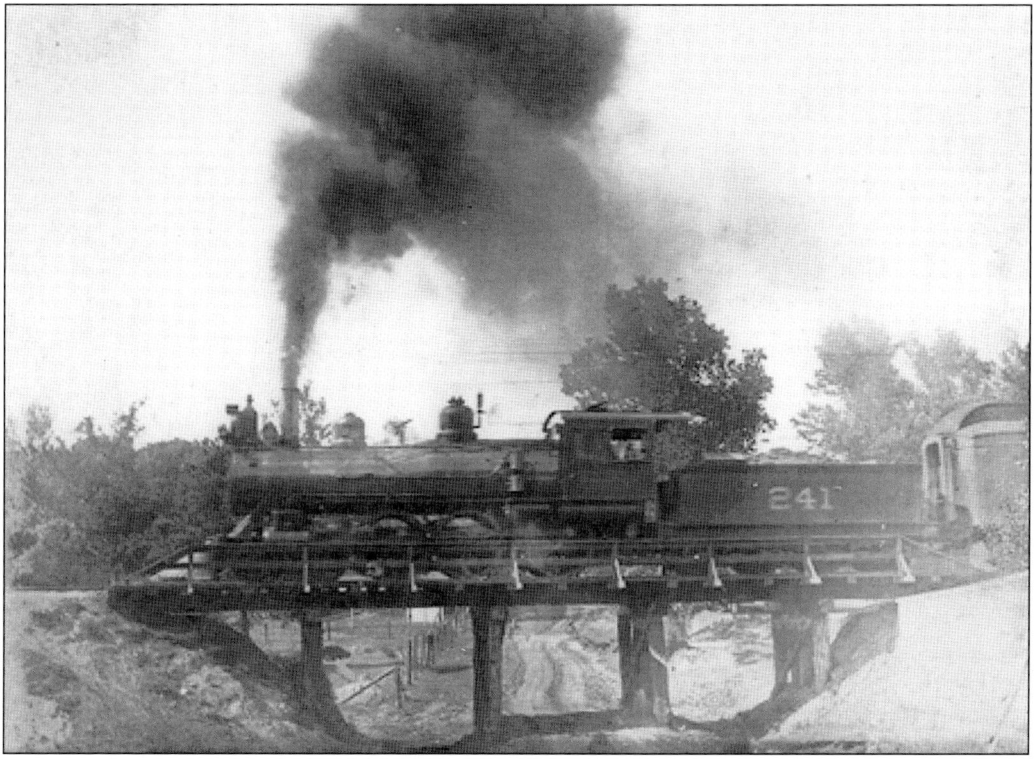

This is one of the many Texas and Pacific trains that operated near Marshall. The continual expansion of the railroad and the increasing number of trains operating in the area promoted economic growth, which was to last well into the 20th century. There were two well-known trains operating on the Vicksburg, Shreveport, and Texas Railroad: "Bull of the Woods" and "Ben Johnson."

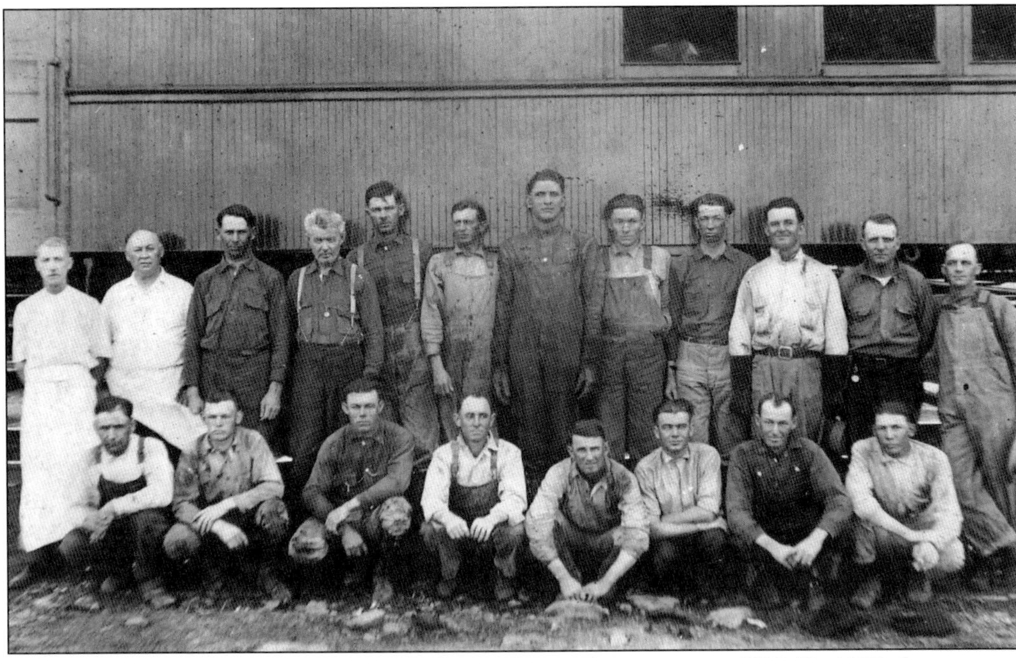

Employees of the railroad shops are standing in front of an engine in 1898. By 1918, the company employed about 1,600 men. Some worked in the blacksmith shop, repairing tools and working on different types of machinery. Some worked in the boiler shops where they created, cleaned, and repaired boilers, and some worked in the machine shop where designs and patterns were made for the new machinery. Repairs were also made in the coach shop.

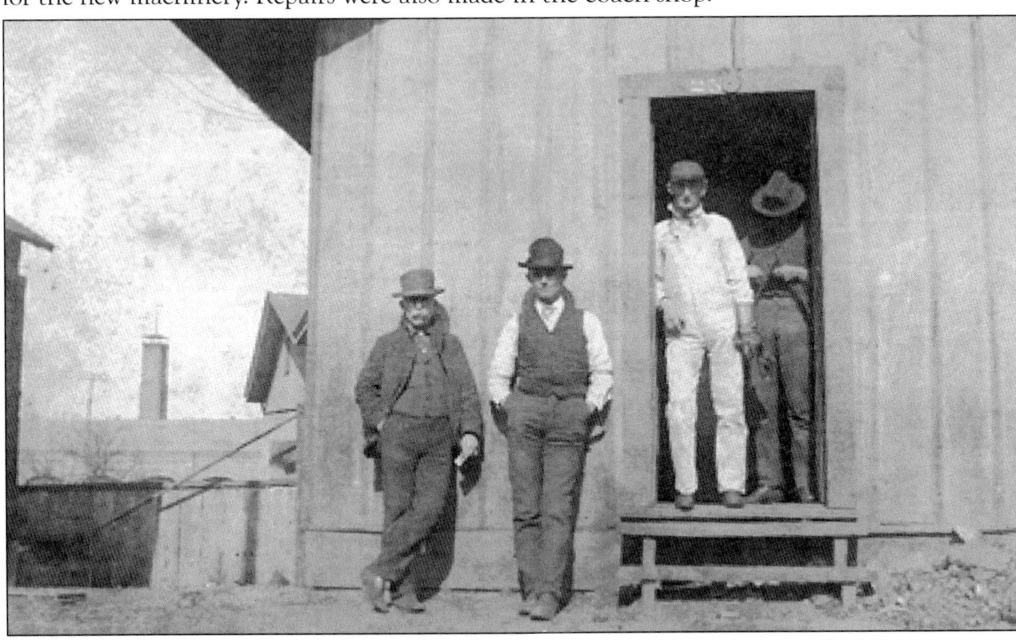

T&P workers are seen here in front of a switch shanty in 1898. Acquisition of the T&P operations was a boon to Marshall, as its geographic location was a benefit in obtaining the operation. Also, the fine water supply in Marshall was cited by railroad officials as one of the reasons for bringing the operation to Marshall.

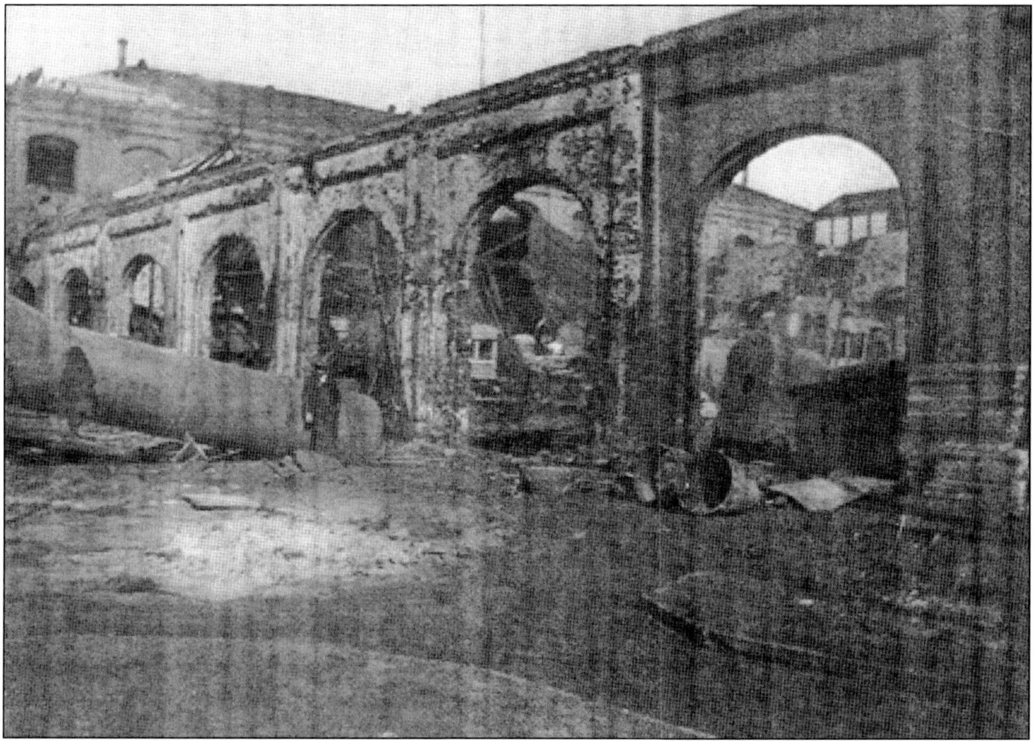

Railroad shops are shown here after the fire in 1898. Originally there were four buildings comprising the shop operation. Each of the buildings was wooden, and fire was an ever-present danger because of all the wood and the nature of their work. Only four men were employed.

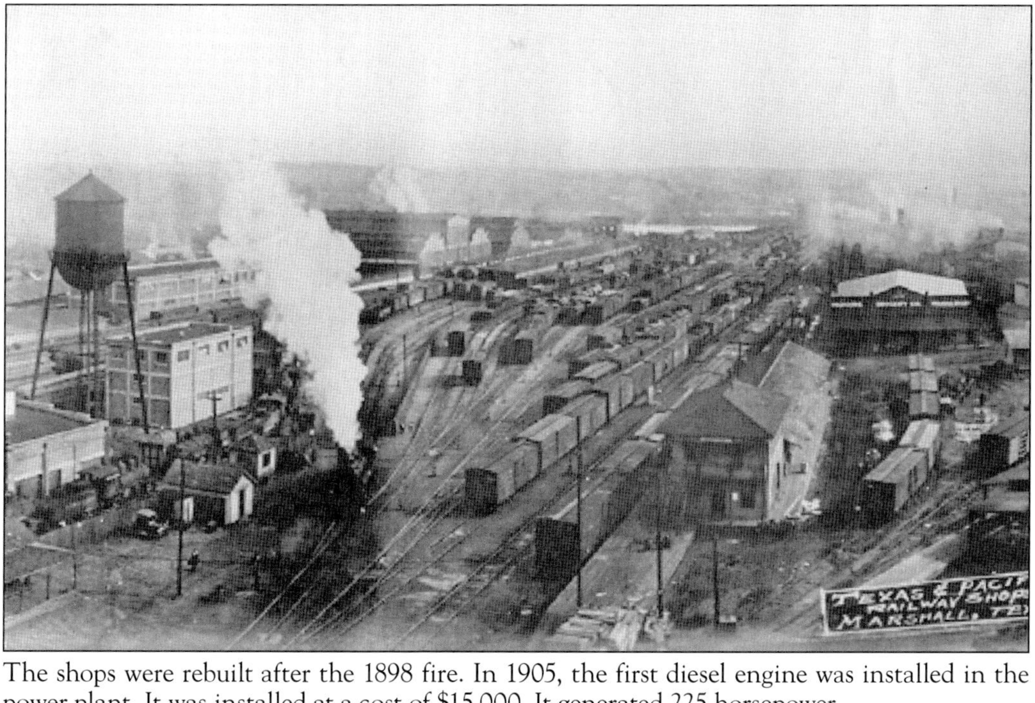

The shops were rebuilt after the 1898 fire. In 1905, the first diesel engine was installed in the power plant. It was installed at a cost of $15,000. It generated 225 horsepower.

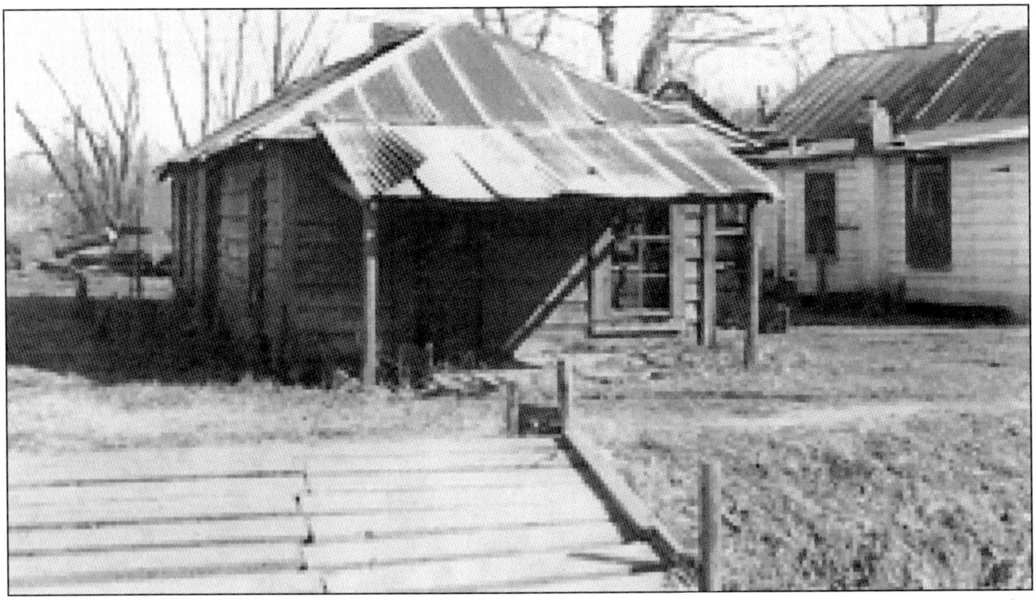

Shipping freight was an important source of income for the railroads. Shown here is the freight office, built in 1961 to serve Elysian Fields and other areas near Marshall.

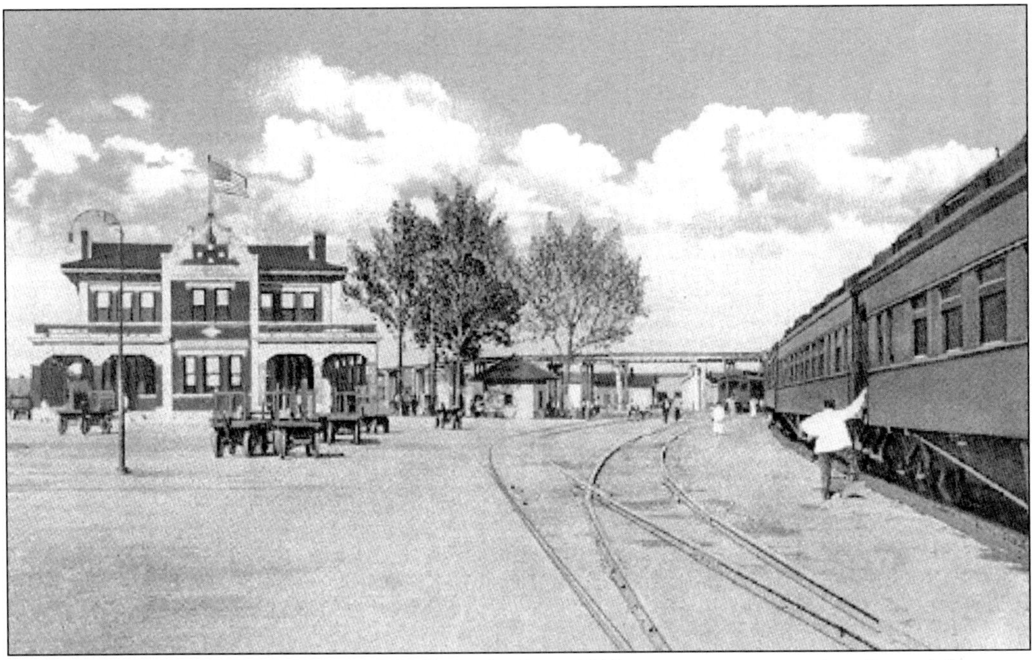

The Texas and Pacific Depot in Marshall was built in 1912 as a passenger station. Later it became an administrative center for the Texas and Pacific Railroad. It was the focal point for the entire operation of the T&P shops in Marshall. (Courtesy of Henry Bradbury.)

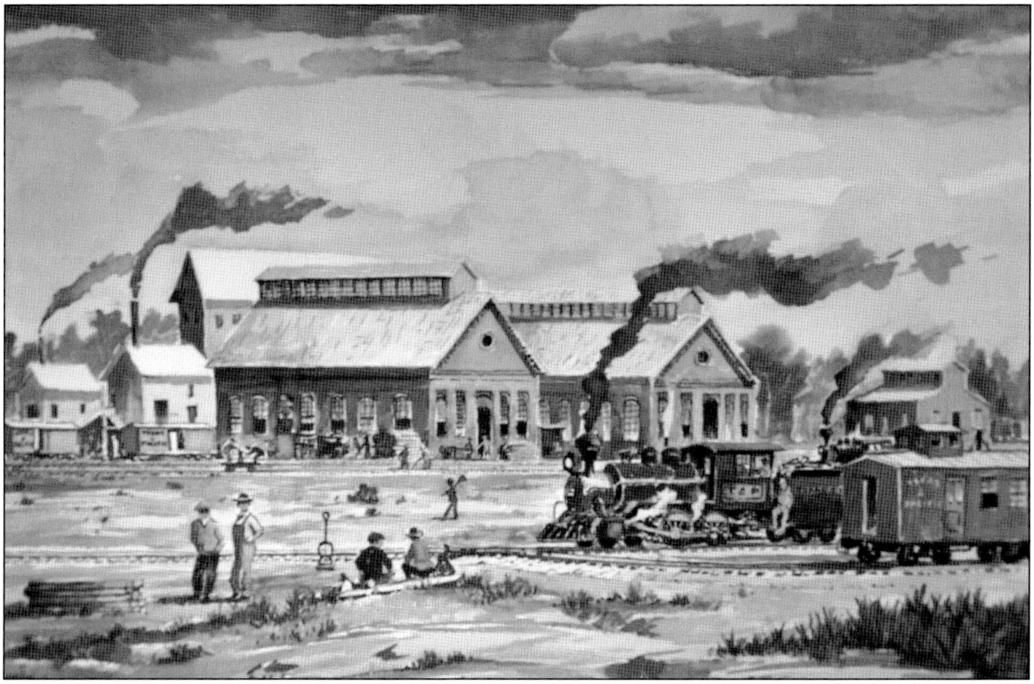

Marshall remained an important part of the Texas and Pacific operation until after World War II. The passenger depot closed in 1974, and Amtrak replaced the T&P trains the same year. Today it is a museum and also a ticket office for Amtrak, which still serves Marshall. (Courtesy of Henry Bradbury.)

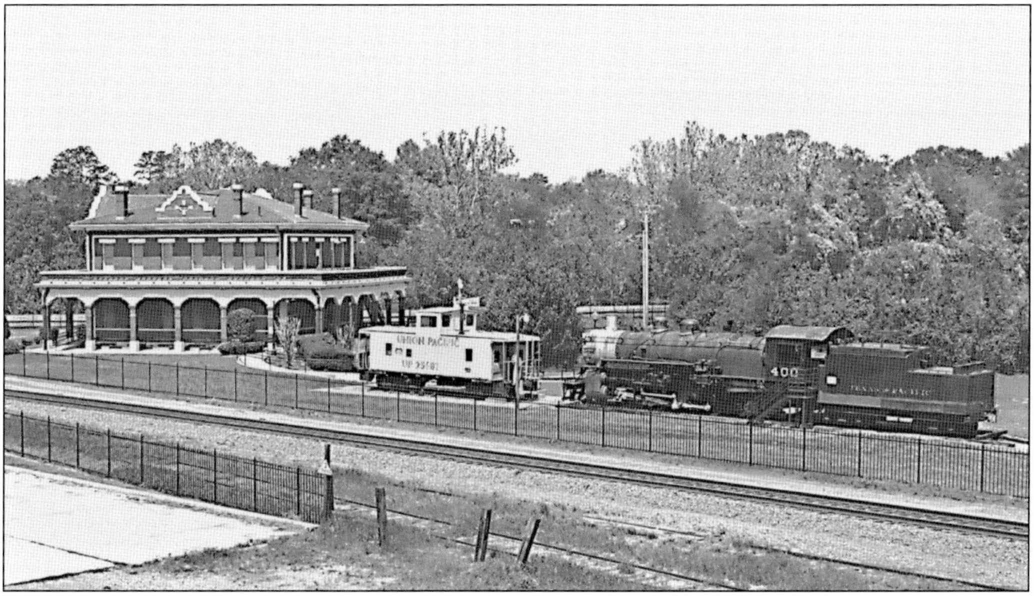

The depot closed in 1974, and Amtrak began service, which is still available. The exterior of the depot remained fairly consistent. Texas and Pacific merged with Missouri Pacific in 1976. The elegant T&P emblem was chiseled off the depot and the word "Marshall" was removed. This is a photograph of the depot in 2010. The depot today is operated by the Marshall Historical Society. (Courtesy of Ben Hughes.)

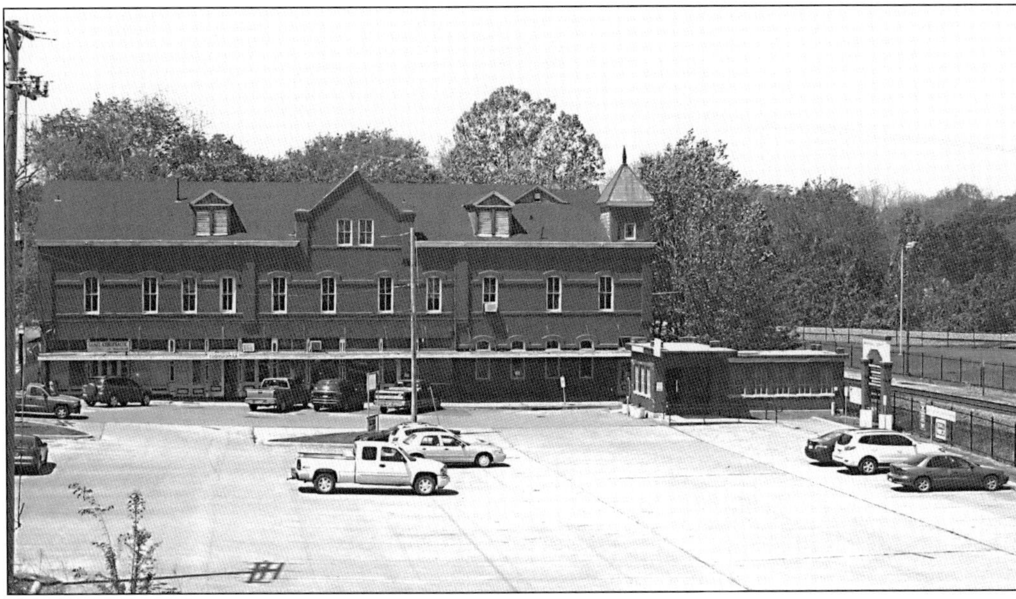

Missouri Pacific merged with Union Pacific in 1982. It appeared that the depot was doomed to be razed. However, citizens of Marshall stepped in, and the depot was saved. In 1990, a group incorporated as the Marshall Depot, Inc., and arranged for the lease of the building. The Texas Historical Commission awarded the Recorded Texas Historic Landmark to the depot in 1990 as well. Pictured is a current view of the Ginocchio Hotel, adjacent to the depot. (Courtesy of Ben Hughes.)

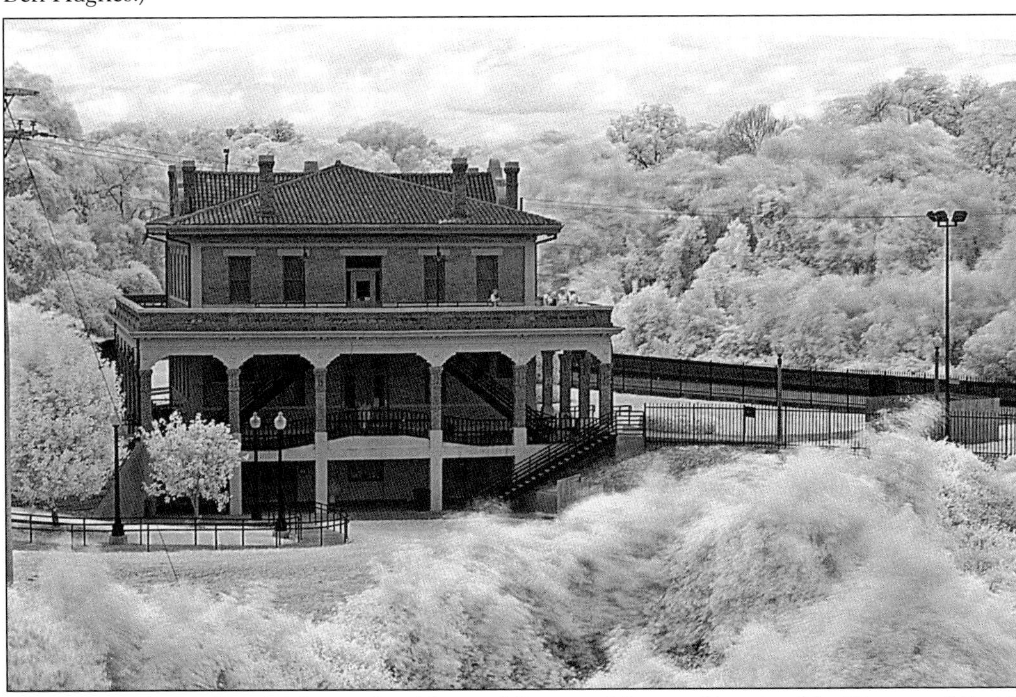

The depot is located in the Ginocchio National Register Historic District. The Texas and Pacific Railway Museum in the depot tells the story of railroading in Marshall. This is an infrared photograph of the depot as it exists today. (Courtesy of Ben Hughes.)

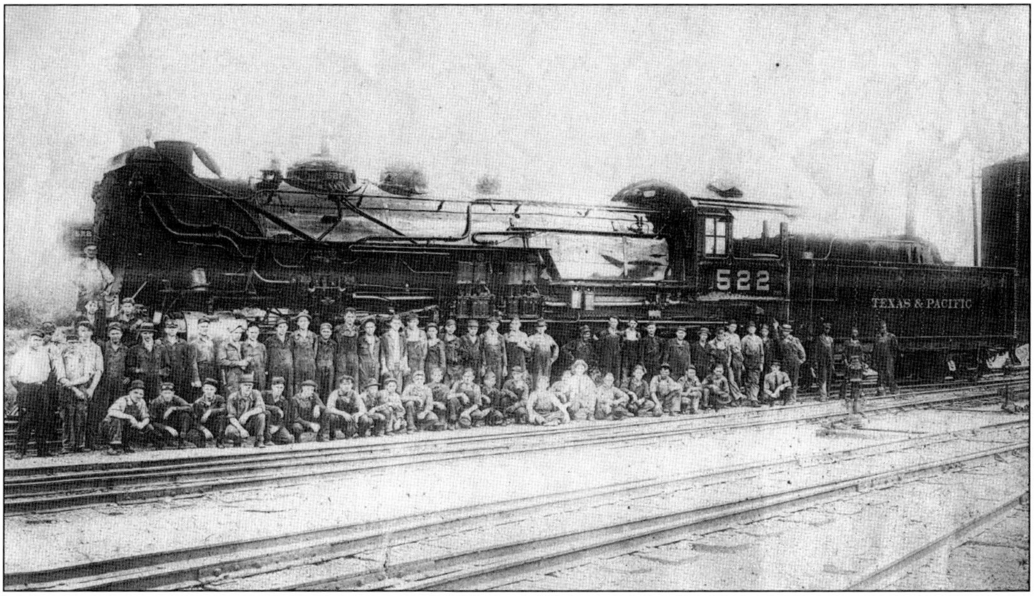

Seventy-five workers pose in front of Engine No. 522 near the Marshall depot. (Courtesy of Texas and Pacific Depot Museum, Marshall.)

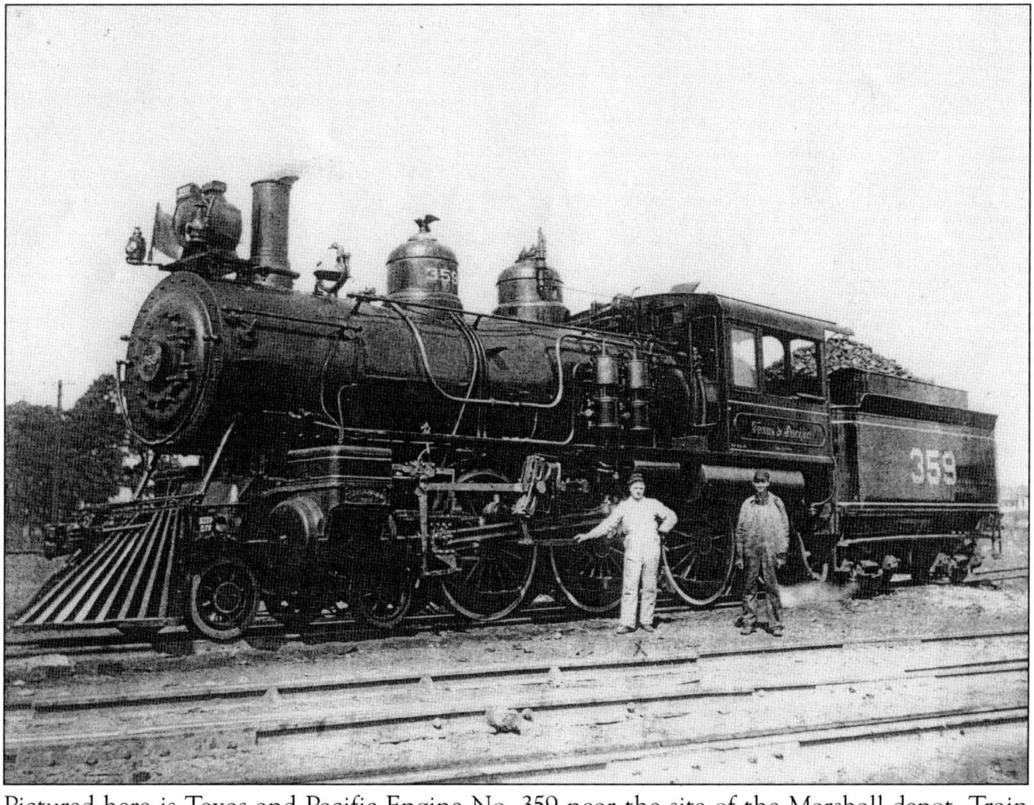

Pictured here is Texas and Pacific Engine No. 359 near the site of the Marshall depot. Train engines received much attention and were often immortalized in poetry and song.

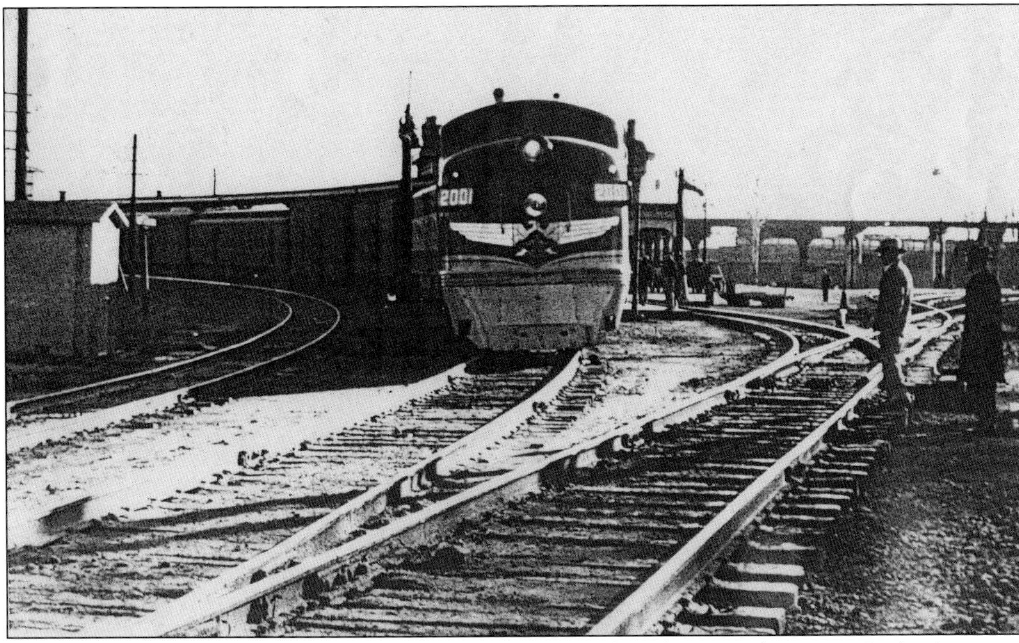

Pictured is the engine of the *Texas Eagle*. The depot and viaduct are shown in the background. (Courtesy of Texas and Pacific Depot Museum, Marshall.)

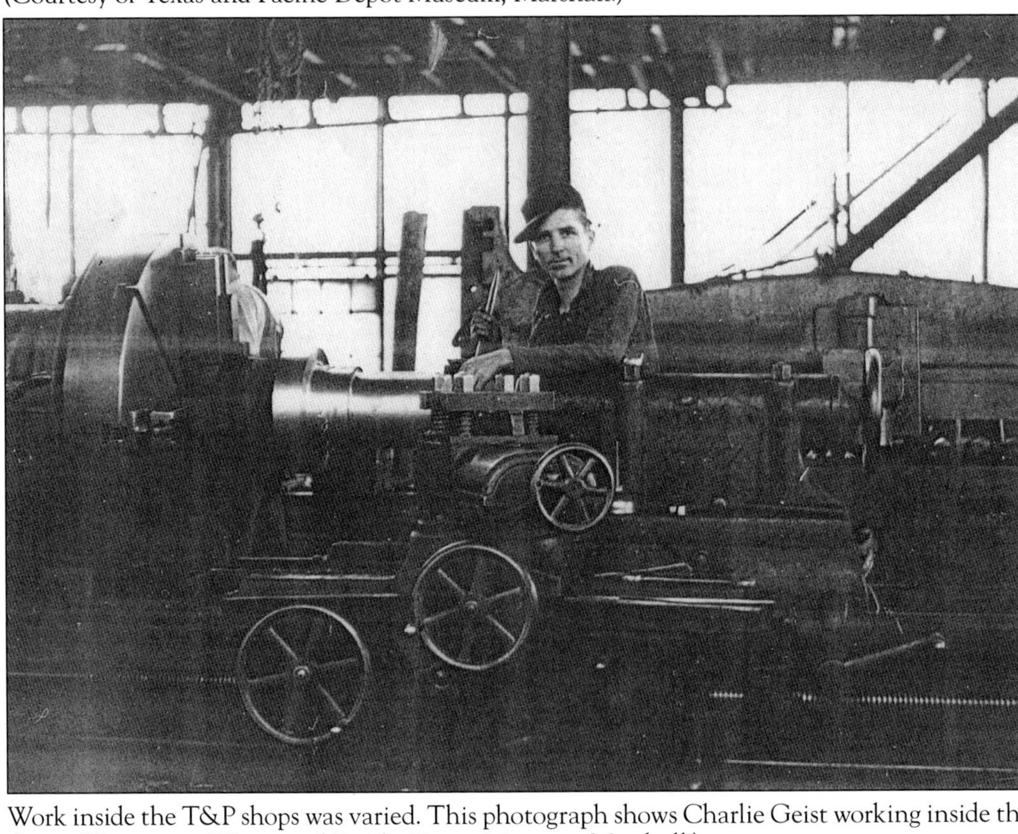

Work inside the T&P shops was varied. This photograph shows Charlie Geist working inside the shops. (Courtesy of Texas and Pacific Depot Museum, Marshall.)

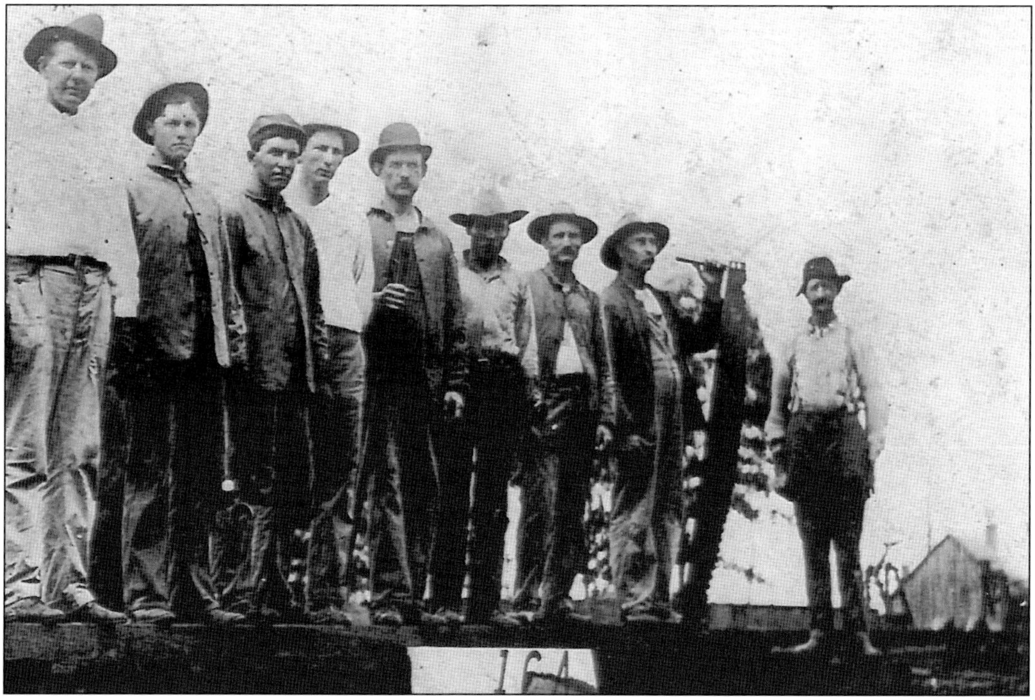

When the T&P was persuaded to open its office and shops in Marshall, the local economy and population boomed as the company's workers and maintenance shops moved into the city. Jobs brought to Marshall included crews that maintained the railroad lines. This crew worked on railroad bridges. John Staple Waller, far left, was the crew foreman. The date of the photograph is unknown.

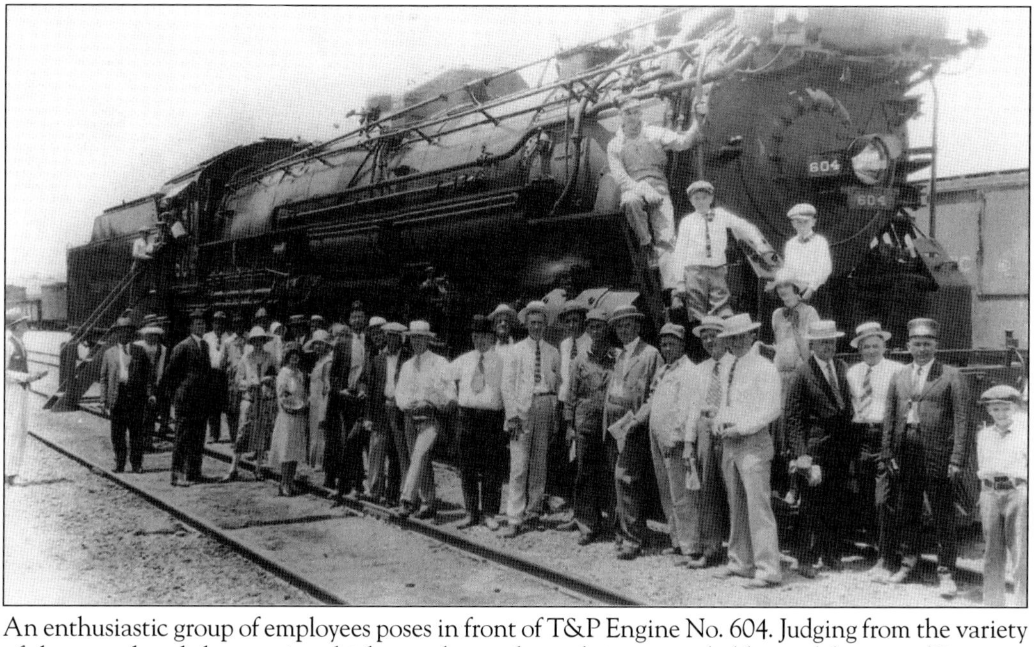

An enthusiastic group of employees poses in front of T&P Engine No. 604. Judging from the variety of the crowd and the way in which people are dressed, it was probably a celebration. (Courtesy of Texas and Pacific Depot Museum, Marshall.)

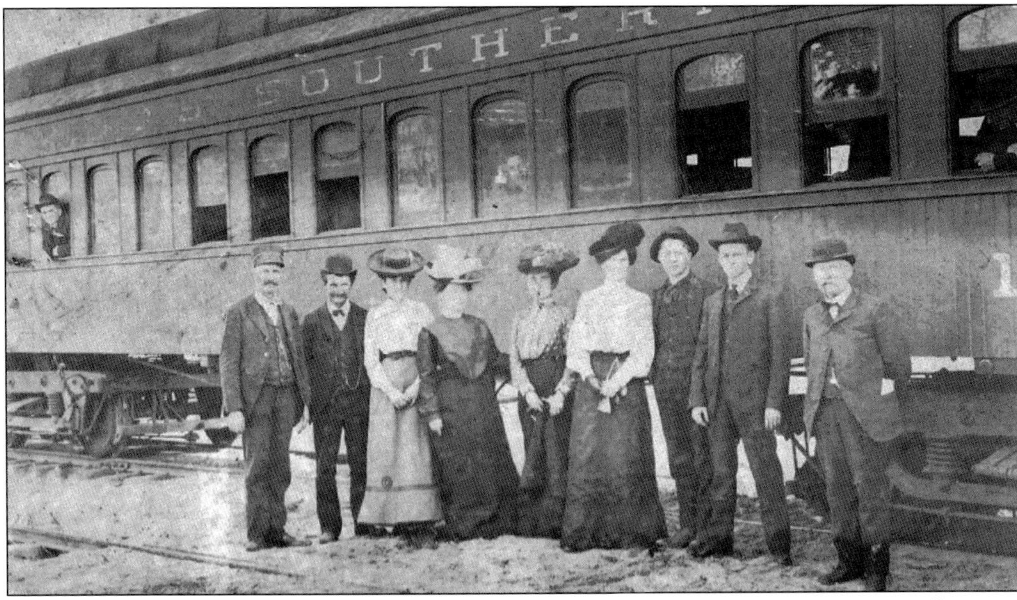

Trains, both in Marshall and elsewhere, were a popular means of traveling on small outings or vacations. This group appears to be ready to travel. (Courtesy of Texas and Pacific Depot Museum, Marshall.)

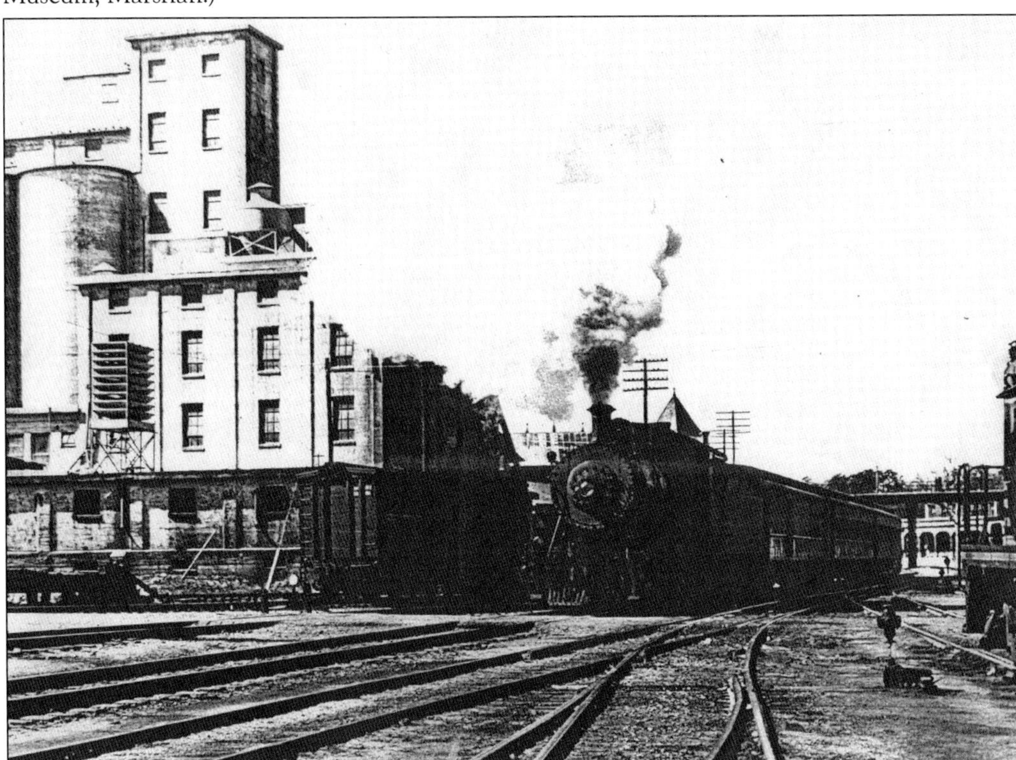

Marshall was an extremely busy station with trains entering the railroad yards both day and night. This shows an engine traveling through the underpass. Marshall Mill and Elevator are shown on the left. (Courtesy of Texas and Pacific Depot Museum, Marshall.)

Six

MARSHALL DURING THE CIVIL WAR

The geographic location of Marshall assured a significant role in the Civil War. Marshall had developed as a city by this time, and its location near inland steamboat ports at Jefferson and its connection by rail to Swanson's Landing on Caddo Lake made it a good location for manufacturing and shipping goods to the eastern areas of the Confederacy.

Citizens of Marshall were quick to respond in support of the secession. On April 19, 1861, the Walter P. Lane Rangers were organized with 103 men in the company. Other companies that formed included the Marshall Guards, the Texas Hunters, the Bass Grays, and the Texas Invincibles, the Clough Rangers, the Hendricks Company, the Harrison County Lanceers, the Marshall Mechanics, the Clough and Hill Avengers, the Cypress Tigers, McKay's Company, and Webb's Company. They fought in the Battles of Fort Donelson and Arkansas Post.

On November 25, 1863, Marshall became the government in exile for the state of Missouri. The house used as the capitol building was located at 108 East Crockett Street. The house that became the governor's mansion was located at 204 East Crockett Street. Neither structure is still standing.

Wyalucing Plantation was the Marshall home of Francis Wilkerson and Lucy Holcombe Pickens. By selling jewels given to her by the Czar of Russia, Lucy Holcome Pickens helped finance a Confederate army unit. Wyalucing Plantation was located at the west end of Silk Stocking Row (West Burleson Street) on what was later to become the campus of Bishop College.

Marshall was a major operations center of the Confederacy's Trans-Mississippi Department. A large powder mill operated in Marshall during the Civil War. It was located 1.5 miles from the city. It was used to manufacture and store gun powder for the Trans-Mississippi Department.

In 1865, the war was over. Federal troops arrived to occupy the city and brought news of emancipation of slaves. It was estimated that there were possibly 10,000 newly freed slaves in Harrison County. A Freedman's Bureau was set up in Marshall to help with the transition to freedom.

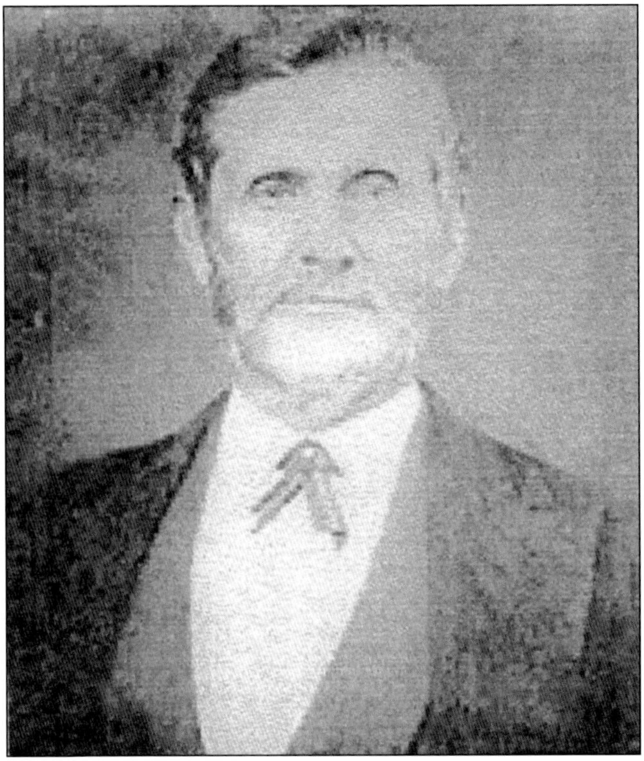

Walter P. Lane was born in County Cork, Ireland. The Lane family moved to Ohio in 1821, and Lane moved to Texas in 1836. He lived in several places in Texas before opening a mercantile store in Marshall in 1858. When the Civil War broke out, Lane joined the 3rd Texas Cavalry. The first volunteer company raised in Harrison County was named for him. Lane led the 3rd Cavalry at Franklin, Tennessee, where Confederate general Beauregard commended him for his bravery. He was severely wounded in the Battle of Mansfield in 1864. After the war, Lane returned to Marshall, where he helped to establish the Texas Veterans Association.

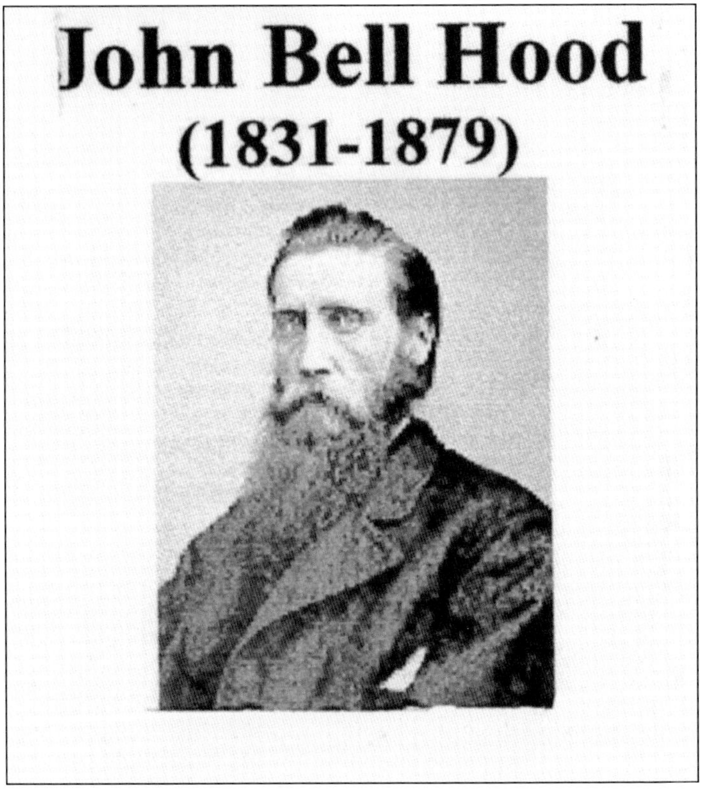

John Bell Hood resigned his commission in the U.S. Army in 1861 to join the Confederacy. He joined the 4th Texas Army in 1861 and took command of the Texas brigade on October 1, 1861. Following the second Battle of Manassas, Hood was removed from command for failure to follow an insignificant order. The Texans refused to move until he was restored to command. At one time, Hood's Brigade had 4,480 Texans. At the time of surrender, his brigade numbered 557. He had little contact with Marshall other than this leadership of Confederate forces, which included men from Marshall.

Lucy Holcomb Pickens had a legion in the Confederate army named for her; the Holcombe Legion was also partially financed by her. In order to do this, she sold jewels that had been given to her by the Czar Alexander II of Russia. Her portrait appeared on $1 and $100 Confederate bills. She is the only woman to have her portrait on Confederate money.

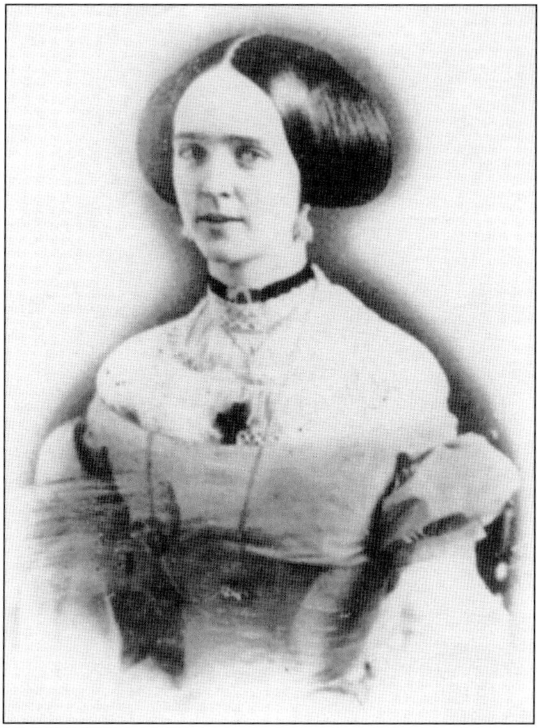

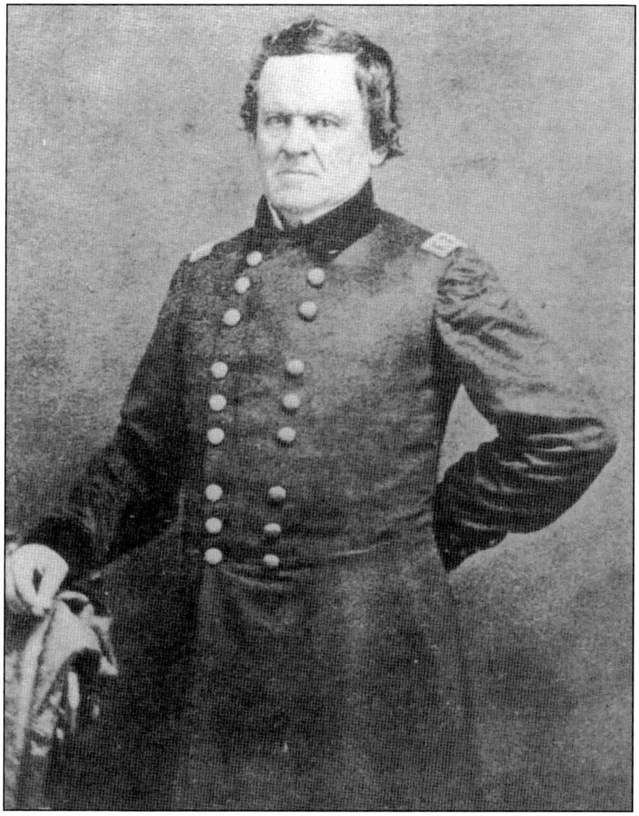

Col. Francis Wilkerson Pickens was ambassador to Russia prior to the Civil War. He returned home from Russia at the beginning of the Civil War and was elected governor of South Carolina in 1860. He died in 1867.

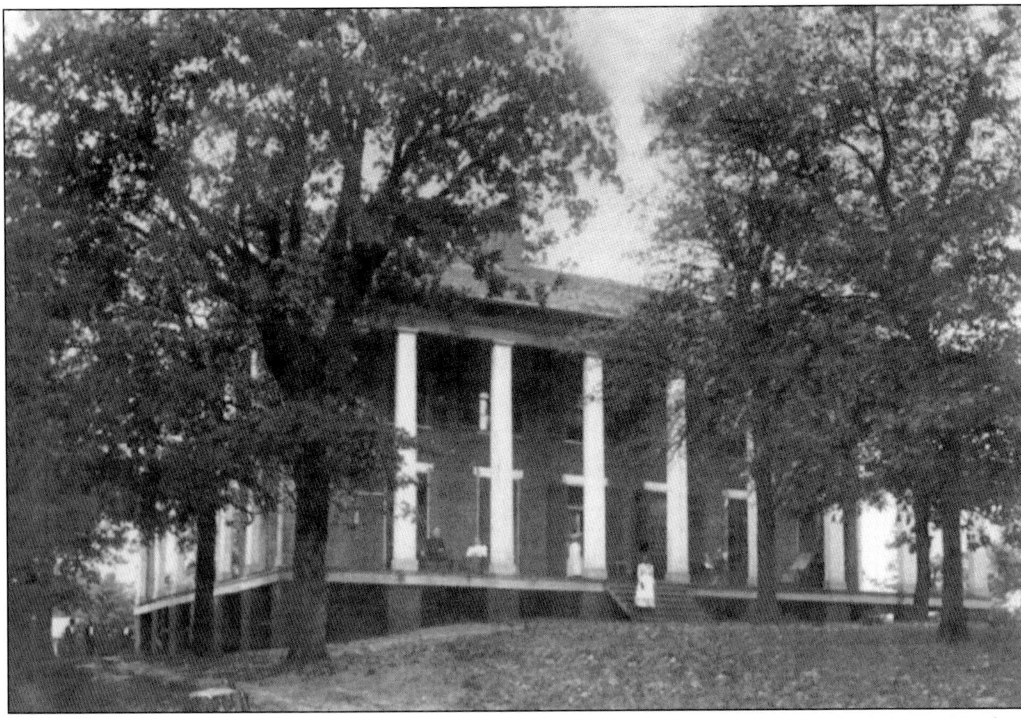

Wyalucing was located at the end of West Burleson Street on what was later the home of Bishop College. Wyalucing was built by Beverly Lafayette Holcombe, the father of Lucy Holcombe. It was begun in 1848 and completed in 1850. Brick for the house was fired on the site. The home was a gathering place for the entire family, but in 1880, the Holcombe heirs sold it to a real estate agency. Later it was sold to Bishop College.

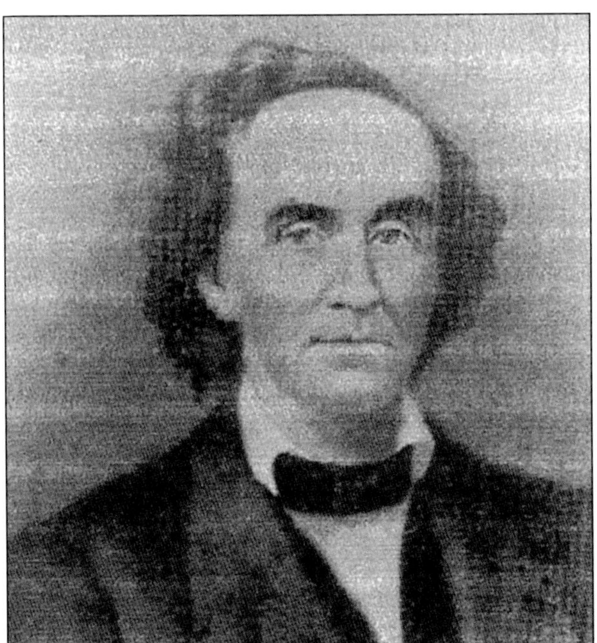

Gov. Claiborne Fox Jackson was the first governor of Missouri's government in exile in Marshall. The government of the Confederacy fully recognized this Marshall government as the government of Missouri. Jackson died in 1862.

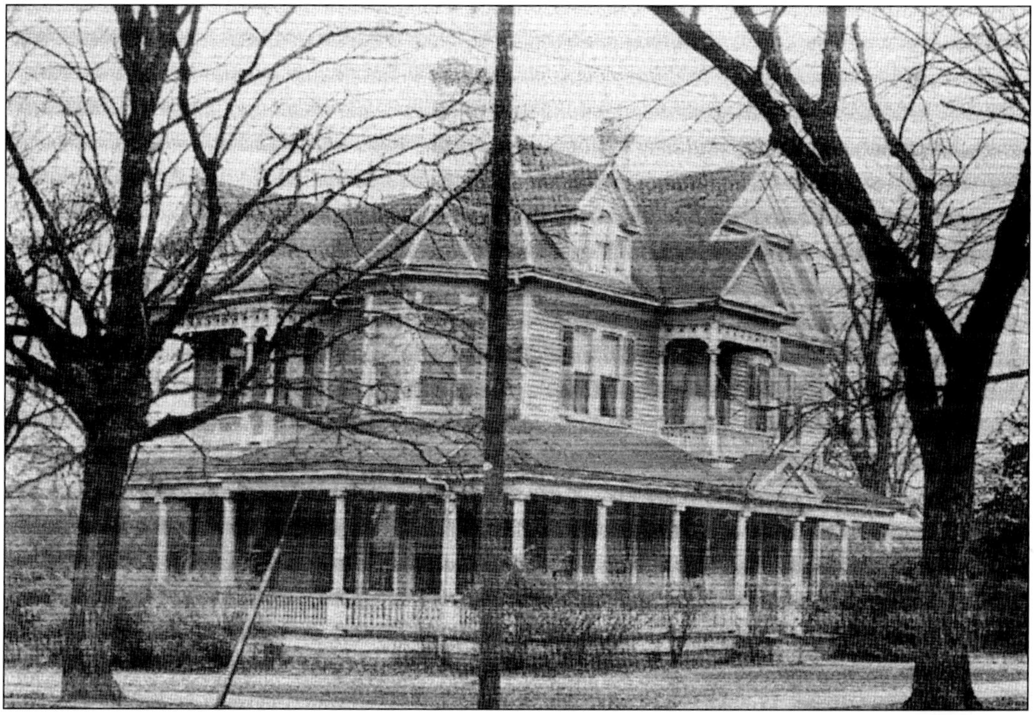

The capitol building for Missouri was located at 108 East Crockett Street in Marshall. The house was rented from Mary Key. Marshall was a town of about 8,000 at this time. The capitol remained in this house until the end of the Civil War.

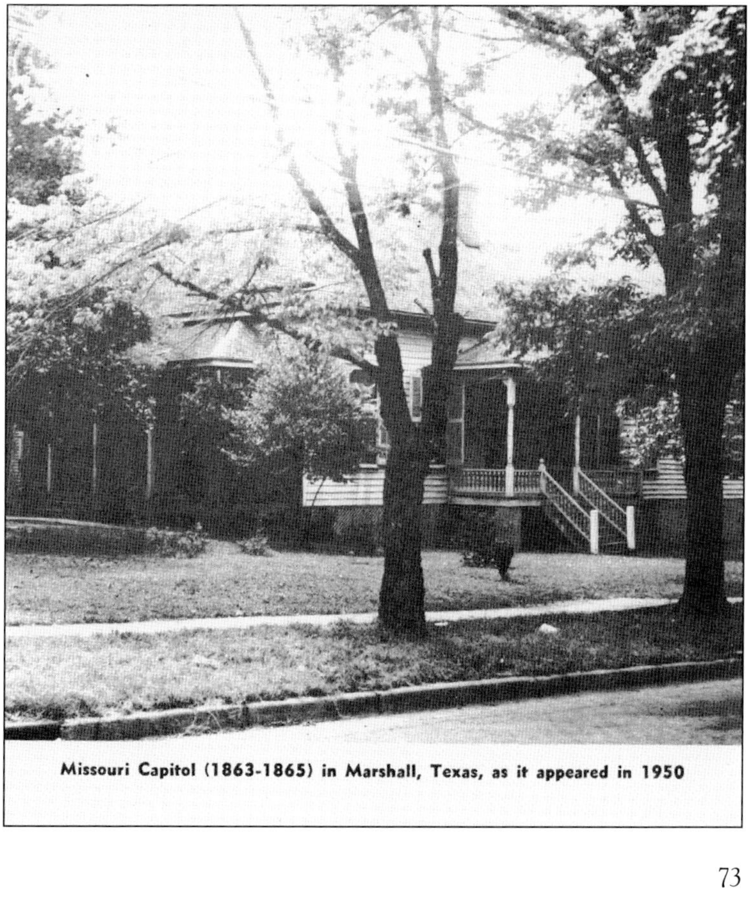

Missouri Capitol (1863-1865) in Marshall, Texas, as it appeared in 1950

The Missouri Governor's Mansion was located at 204 East Crockett Street. It was the home of Judge Asa Willie, who was serving on the Supreme Court in Austin. A letter in the files of the Harrison County Historical Museum from Hobart Key, grandson of Mary Key, verifies the location of the governor's mansion.

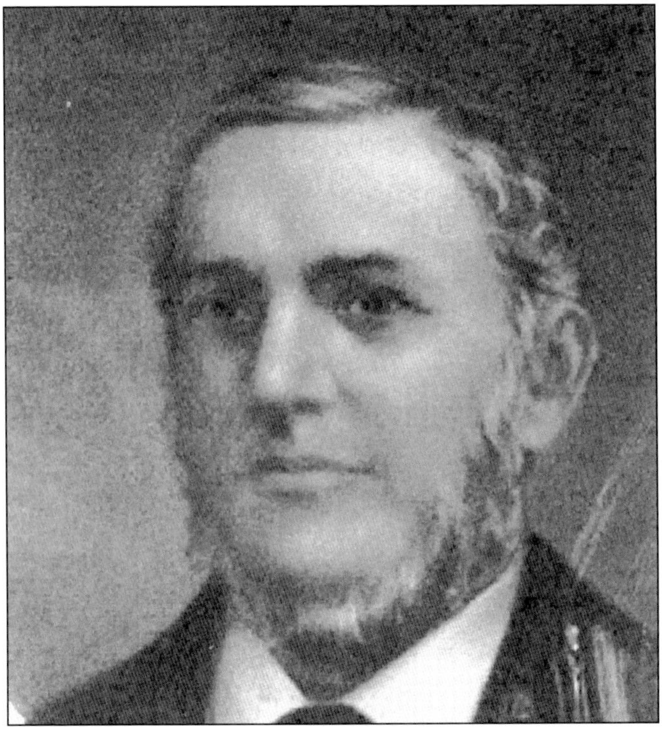

Lieutenant Governor Reynolds came to Marshall with Governor Jackson and became governor of Missouri when Jackson died in 1862. He served in that capacity until the end of the war.

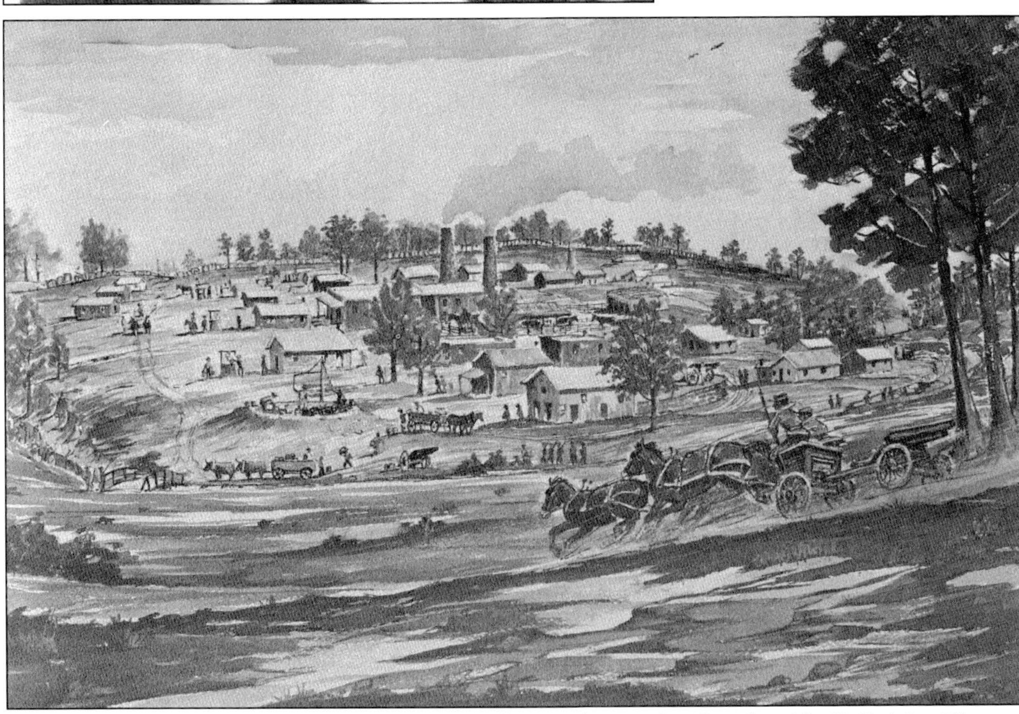

A powder mill operated near Marshall during the Civil War. On October 25, 1863, Maj. Thomas C. Rhett, chief of ordnance and artillery for the Trans-Mississippi Region, reported that he was building this facility. Eventually there were about 40 buildings used to manufacture gunpowder, make and repair weapons, and make ammunition.

Edward Clark was elected lieutenant governor of Texas in 1859. Sam Houston was serving as governor at the time. In 1861, when Houston refused to give allegiance to the Confederacy, he was removed from office and Edward Clark was sworn in as governor. On June 8, 1861, Clark called for volunteers for the Confederate army and eventually there were 15,000 recruits from Texas in the Confederate army.

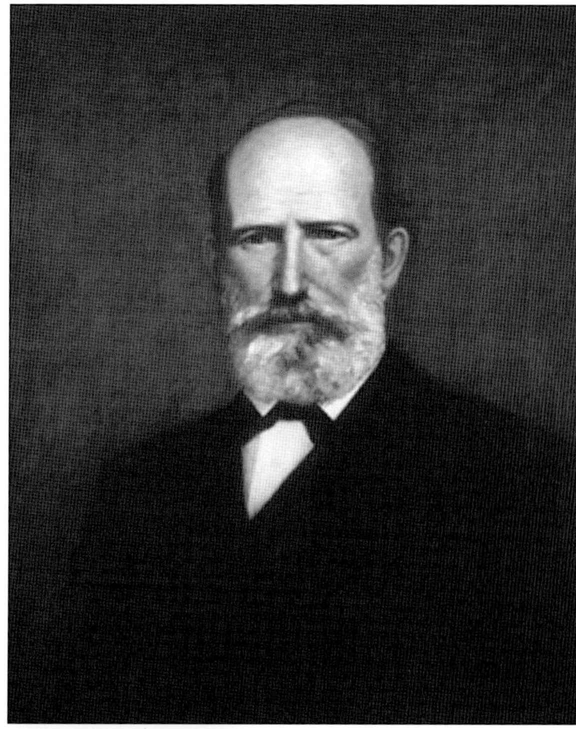

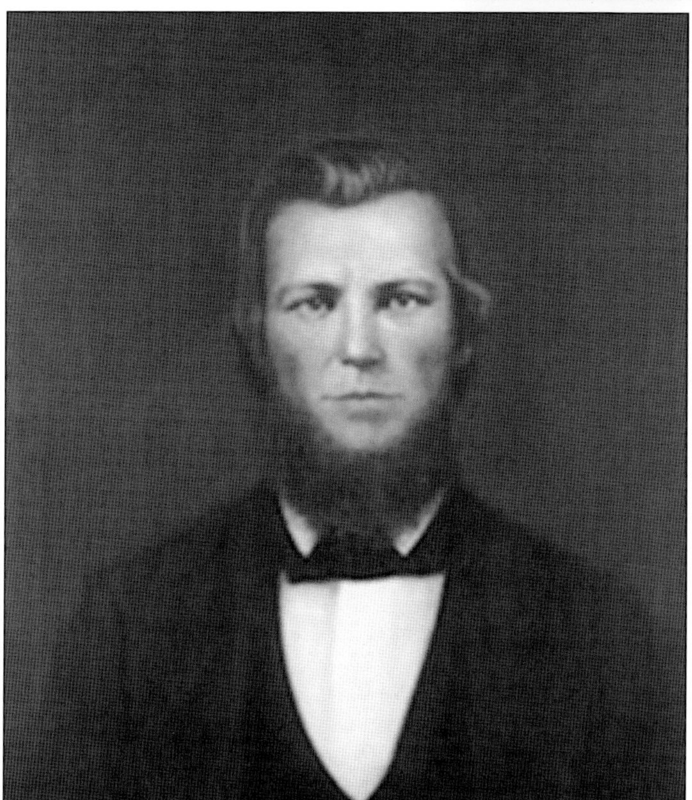

Marshall was home to the last Texas Confederate governor, Pendleton Murrah. Murrah served as governor from 1863 to 1865. Prior to being elected governor, he was a successful lawyer and businessman in Marshall. Sixteen months of his term were while Texas was in the Confederacy.

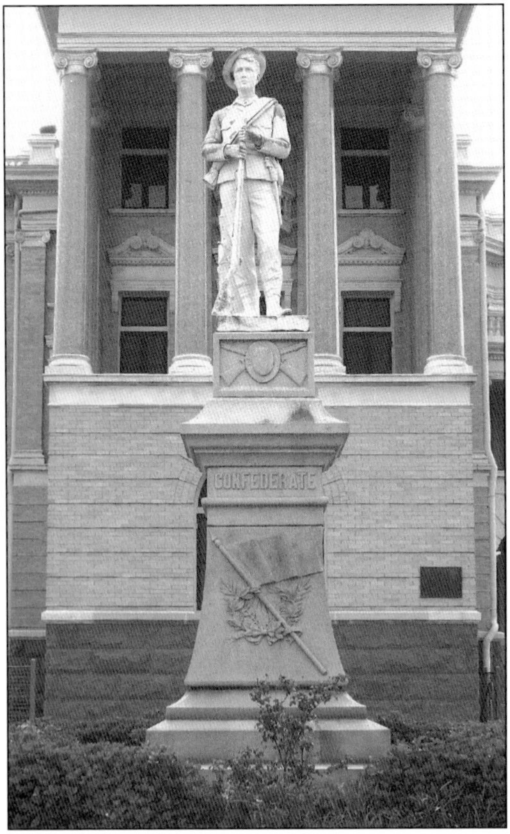

A monument honoring the Confederate soldier is on the east side of the courthouse. Citizens of Marshall erected the monument after the war ended.

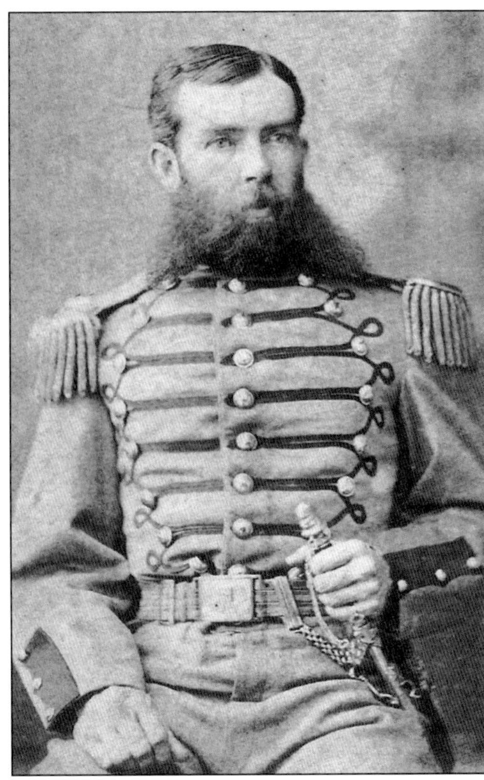

Rev. C. G. Rivers is shown here in a Confederate uniform. Many men from Marshall joined the Confederate army and served during this conflict.

Seven

Education in Marshall

Education has always been in the forefront in Marshall, as evidenced by the operation of two early institutions in Marshall: Marshall University (1842) and the Marshall Masonic Female Institute (1844). They operated for 50 and 65 years respectively.

White children in Marshall were taught in the Old Marvin Chapel School, organized in 1878. In the 1890s, Marshall High School was organized to teach white children. In 1900, the first class graduated from Marshall High School.

Central School was the first public school in Marshall. H. B. Pemberton organized it in 1894 for Marshall's African American elementary children. Pemberton arranged a loan to build the school at the intersection of Travis Street and Alamo Boulevard. The African American community repaid the loan. In 1970, Marshall's separate public schools for whites and African Americans were combined, eliminating school segregation.

In 1873, Wiley College was founded by the Freedmen's Aid Society of the Methodist church as an institution for the education of African American men and women freed by the Civil War. In 1893, Isaiah S. Scott, a former slave preacher, became the first African American to preside over the college. Beginning in 1896, under the 46-year administration of Dr. Matthew W. Dogan, the school experienced significant growth.

The College of Marshall was organized in Marshall in 1912. It first opened its doors to the public in 1917 with Dr. T. C. Gardner as the president. He was succeeded by Dr. H. E. Watters, who selected the first faculty. In 1944, the name was changed to East Texas Baptist College, and then East Texas Baptist University in 1984.

Bishop College was founded by the Baptist Home Mission Society in 1881. It was chartered in 1885. In 1929, Joseph J. Rhoads was elected the first black president. The college moved to Dallas in 1961 and closed in 1988.

Texas State Technical College (TSTC) began operation in Marshall in 1991 as a campus of the Texas State Technical College System, the only state-operated system of two-year colleges in Texas. In 1999, the TSTC-Marshall campus became a separate college.

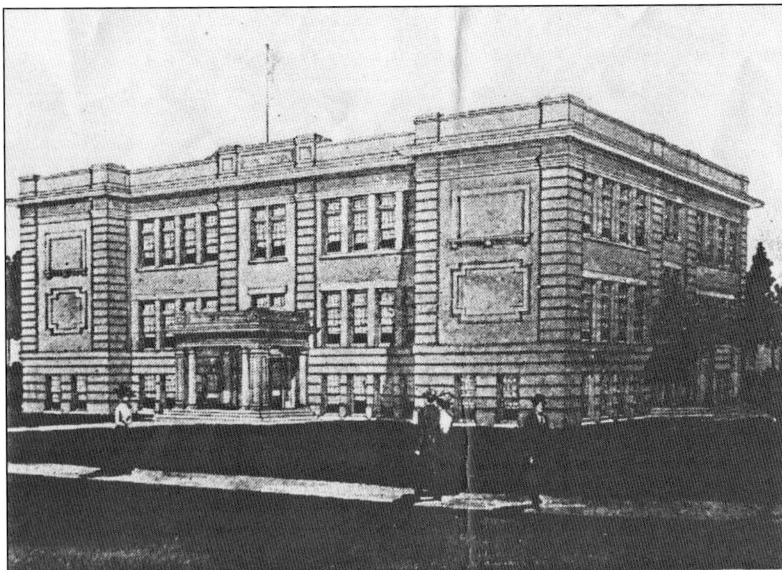
Marshall High School—C. G. Lancaster, Architect

Marshall High School was organized in the 1890s to educate white children in the community. It was preceded by Marshall University and the Marshall Masonic Female Institute. Shown here is a picture of Marshall High School. The date is not known. (Courtesy of Henry Bradbury.)

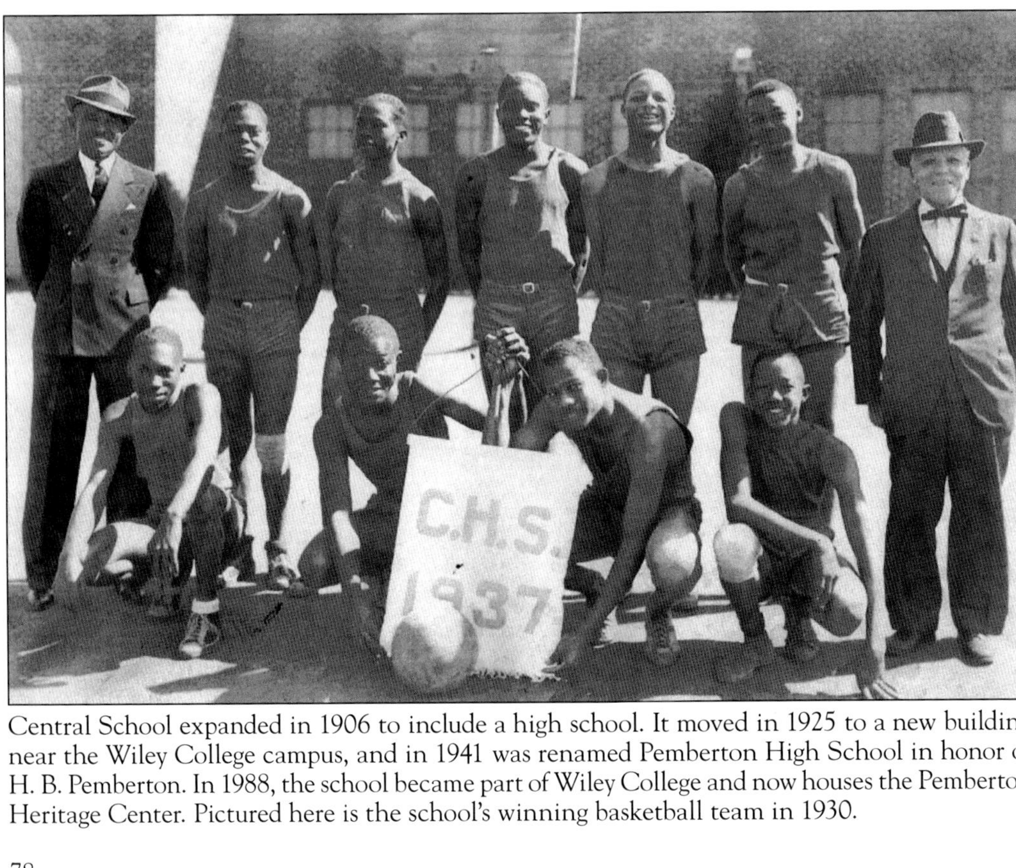

Central School expanded in 1906 to include a high school. It moved in 1925 to a new building near the Wiley College campus, and in 1941 was renamed Pemberton High School in honor of H. B. Pemberton. In 1988, the school became part of Wiley College and now houses the Pemberton Heritage Center. Pictured here is the school's winning basketball team in 1930.

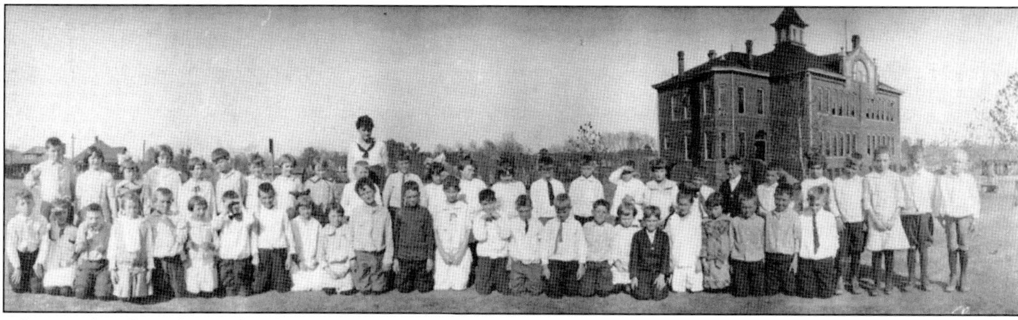

This is the fourth grade class at Sam Houston School in 1914. The school building has not been used for many years and was recently destroyed by fire.

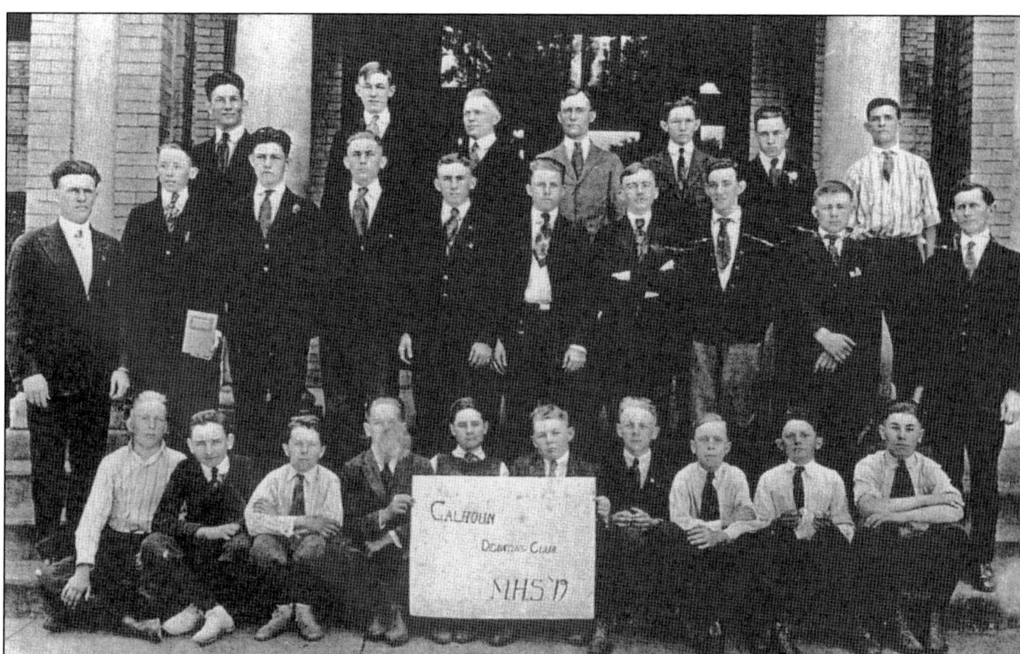

Pictured here in 1914 are members of the Marshall High School Calhoun Debating Club. No additional information was available about this team.

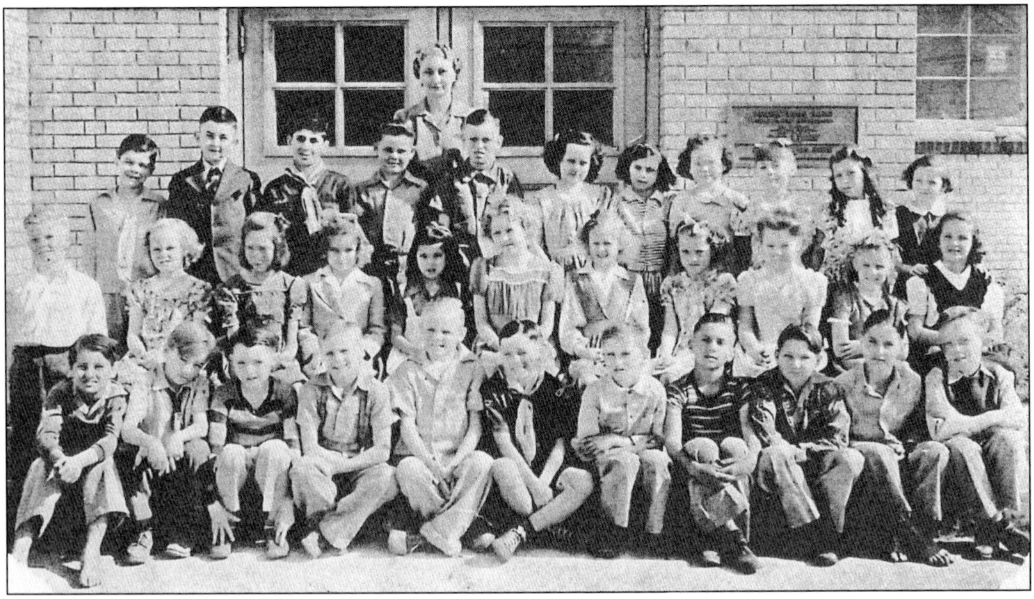

This is the 1943–1944 third grade class at Stephen F. Austin School. At one time, this school was known as West End School. However, as the number of schools increased in Marshall, the board of the Marshall Independent School District began the practice of naming schools for Texas heroes rather than designating them by the part of town in which they were located.

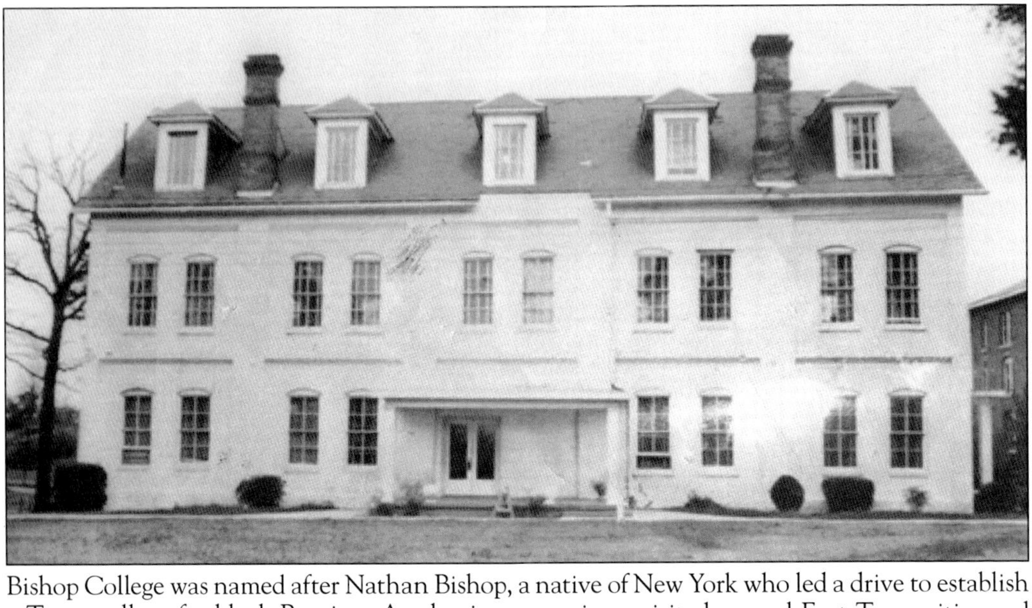

Bishop College was named after Nathan Bishop, a native of New York who led a drive to establish a Texas college for black Baptists. A selection committee visited several East Texas cities and selected Marshall. Local Baptist ministers raised the money to purchase the former Wyalucing Plantation for the school.

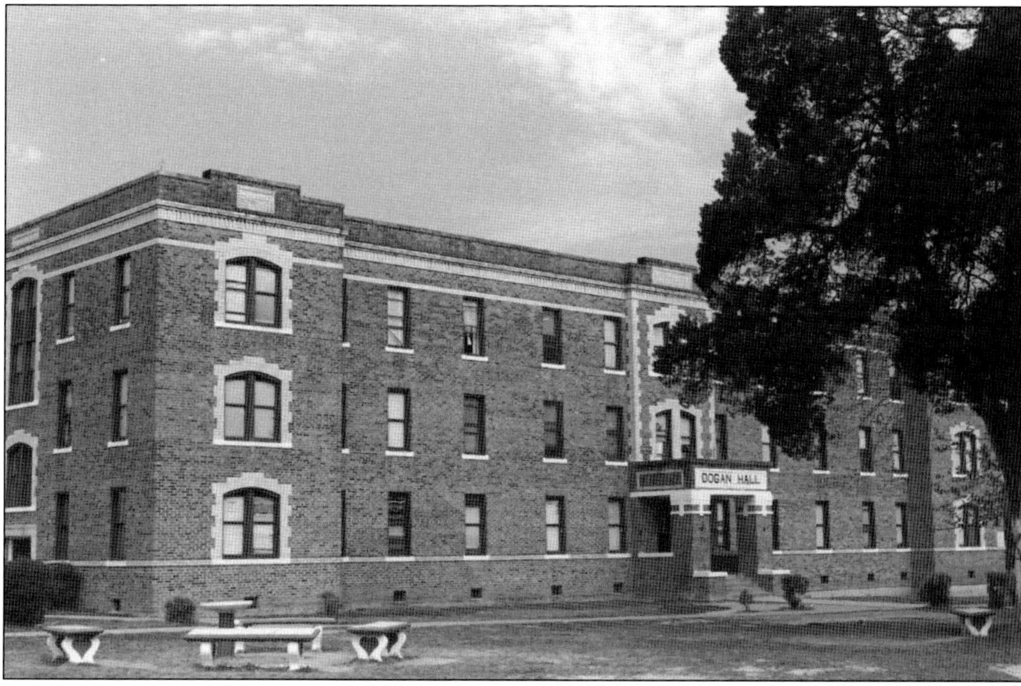

M. W. Dogan was president of Wiley College in the 1940s. Dr. Dogan initiated a program that offered students scholastic studies and practical training. The program, known as the "Wiley Method," was widely used by black colleges. Pictured here is a building named in his honor. Wiley College was awarded a Carnegie Library. The building still stands today.

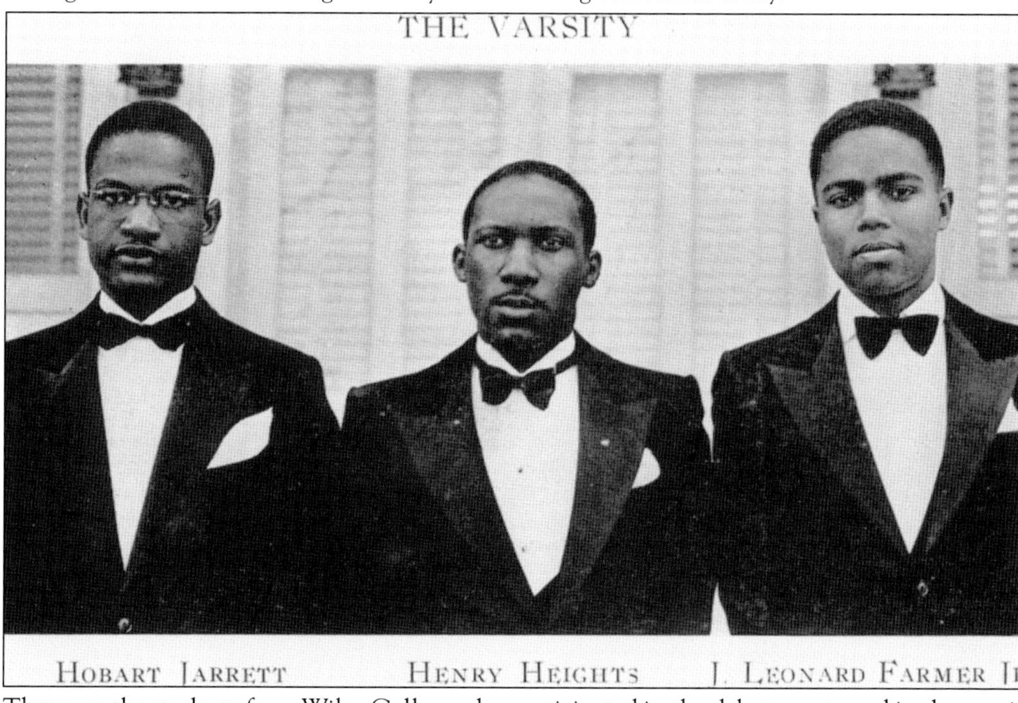

These are the students from Wiley College who participated in the debate portrayed in the movie *The Great Debaters*. The movie adds a woman on the team, but this was not the case.

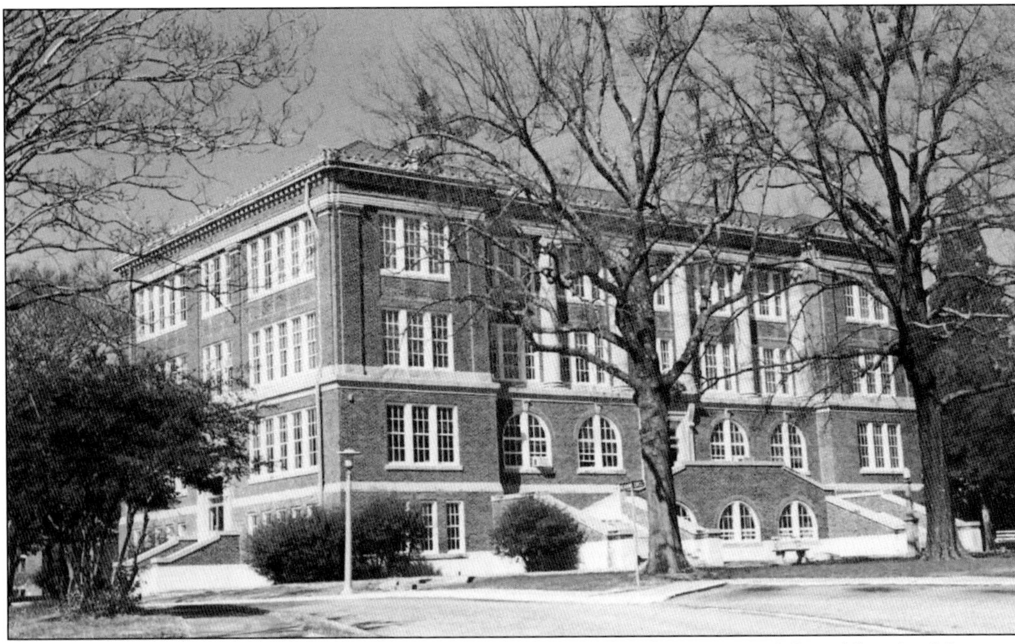

Marshall Hall on the grounds of East Texas Baptist University is one of the oldest buildings on the campus. There have been several presidents, including Dr. H. D. Bruce, Dr. George Bennett, Dr. Jerry Dawson, Dr. Robert Craig, and Dr. Bob Riley.

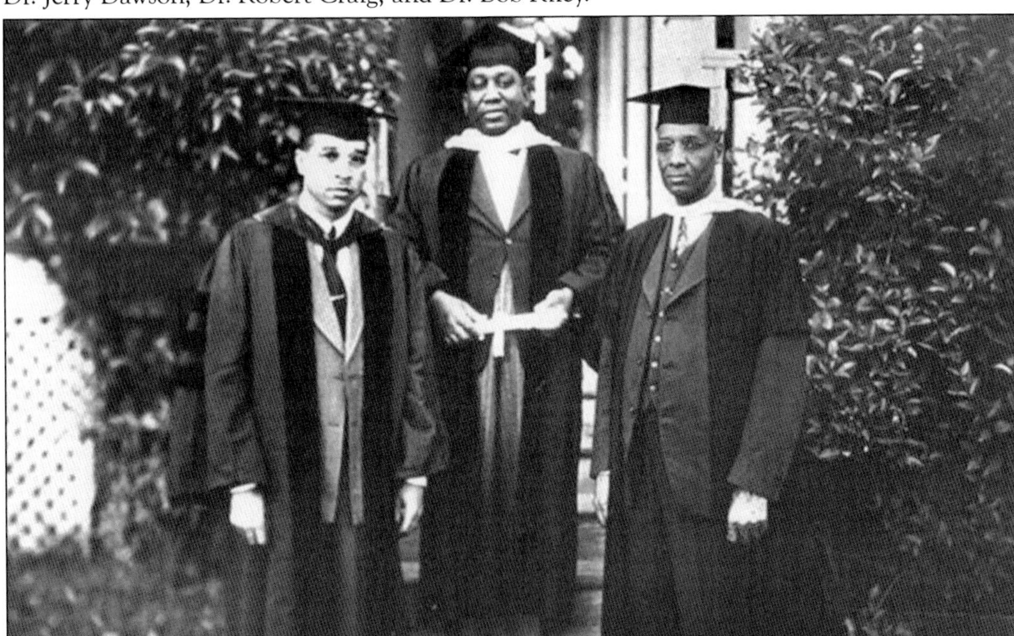

Bishop College first opened its doors to students in 1881. It was chartered in 1885 and named for Nathan Bishop, a New York lawyer. Pictured here at the 1941 graduation exercises at Bishop College are, from left to right, Dr. Boone, Jules Bledsoe, and Joseph J. Rhoads, president of Bishop College.

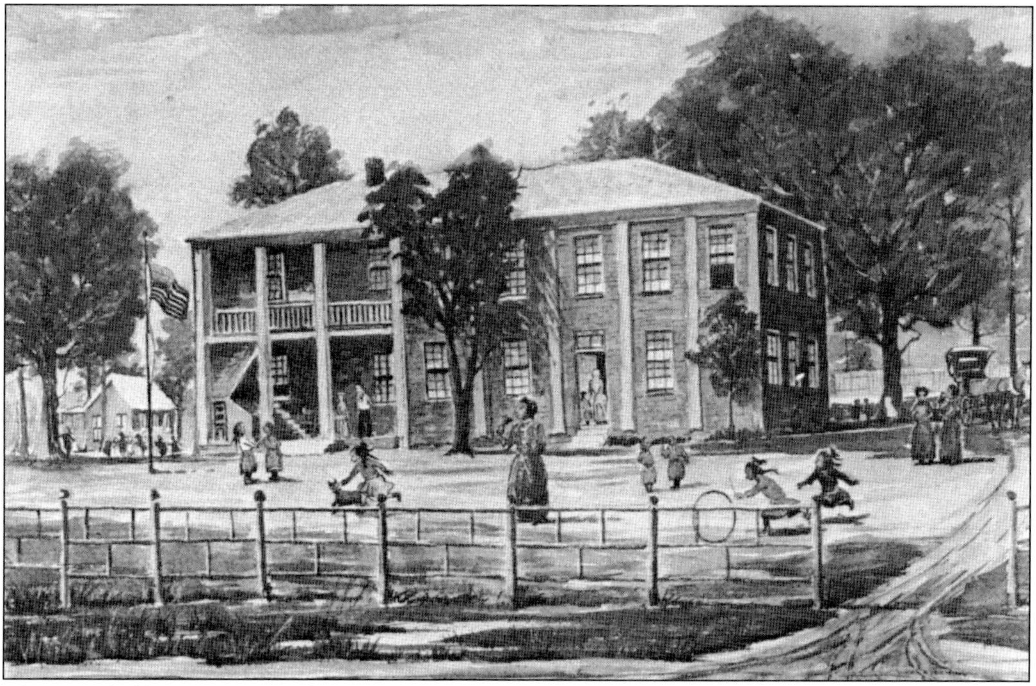

The Marshall Masonic Female Institute began operation in 1842 as a part of Marshall University. It operated until 1882, at which time it was closed for lack of enrollment. The buildings were leased to the public schools for many years.

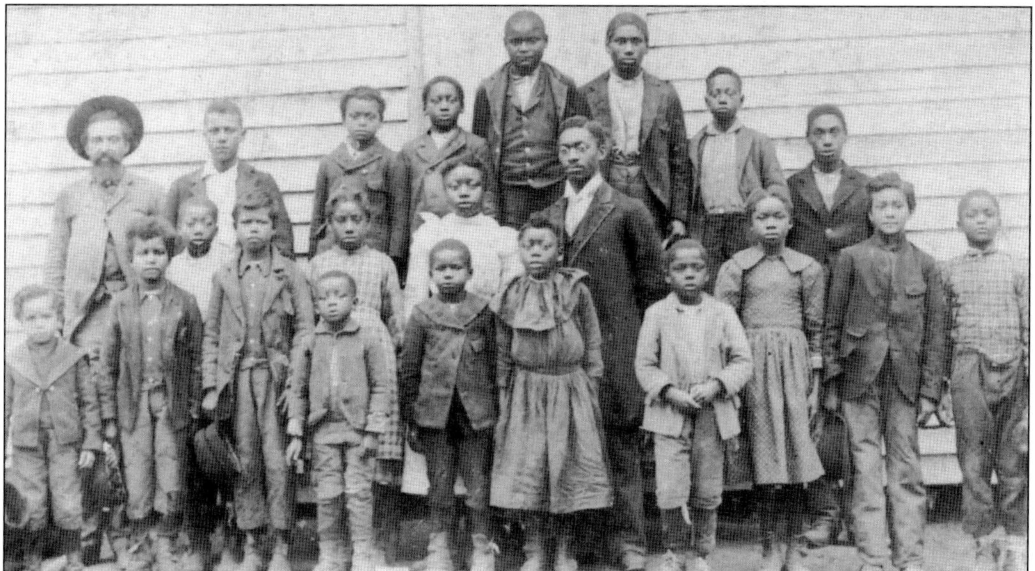

Rosenwald Schools played an important role in education in Harrison County. Twenty-one schools were built by the Rosenwald Foundation to improve educational opportunities for African Americans. None of these schools are left standing in Harrison County today. Pictured here are students from Long Ridge School, which was a Harrison County Rosenwald School that was funded during the 1926–1927 Rosenwald budget year. It was built at a cost of $3,500, with $1,250 raised by African Americans, $1,550 by the public, and a $700 grant from the Rosenwald Foundation.

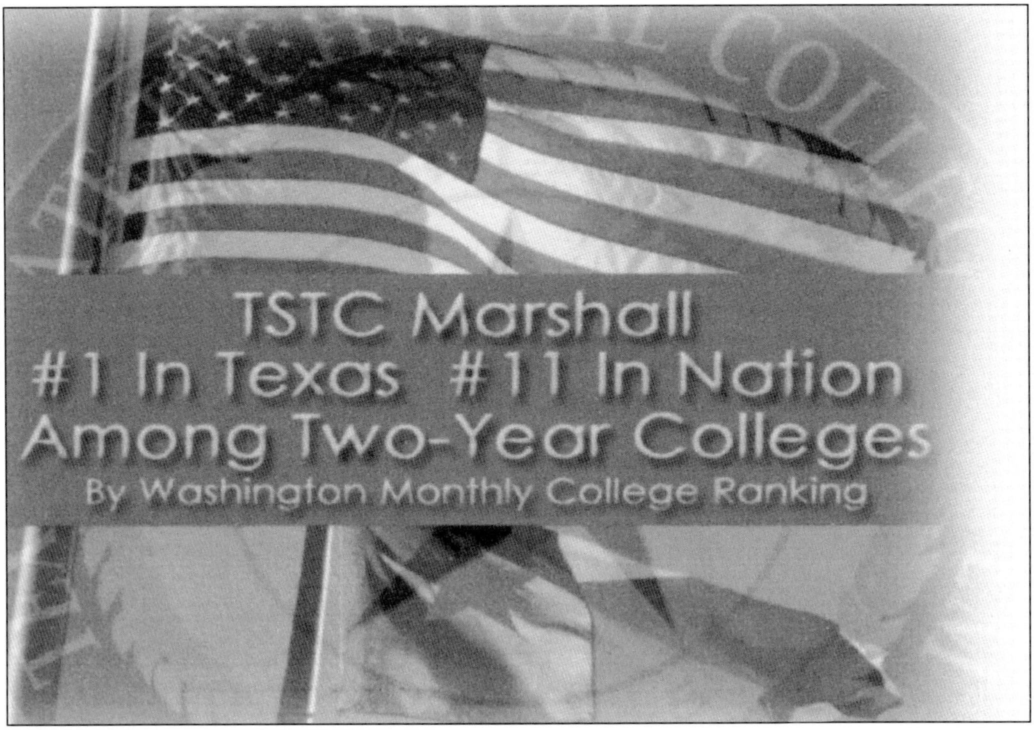

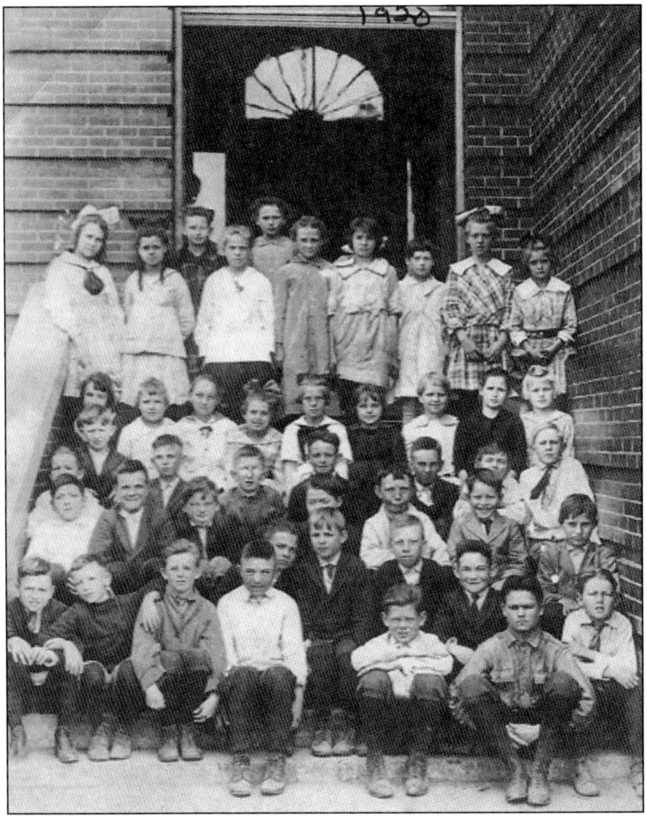

The land for TSTC was purchased by Marshall's economic development organization and offered free to the college as an incentive for it to locate in Marshall. The community wanted to develop a highly skilled workforce as a part of its economic development effort.

Pictured here are students from East End School. The photograph was taken about 1920.

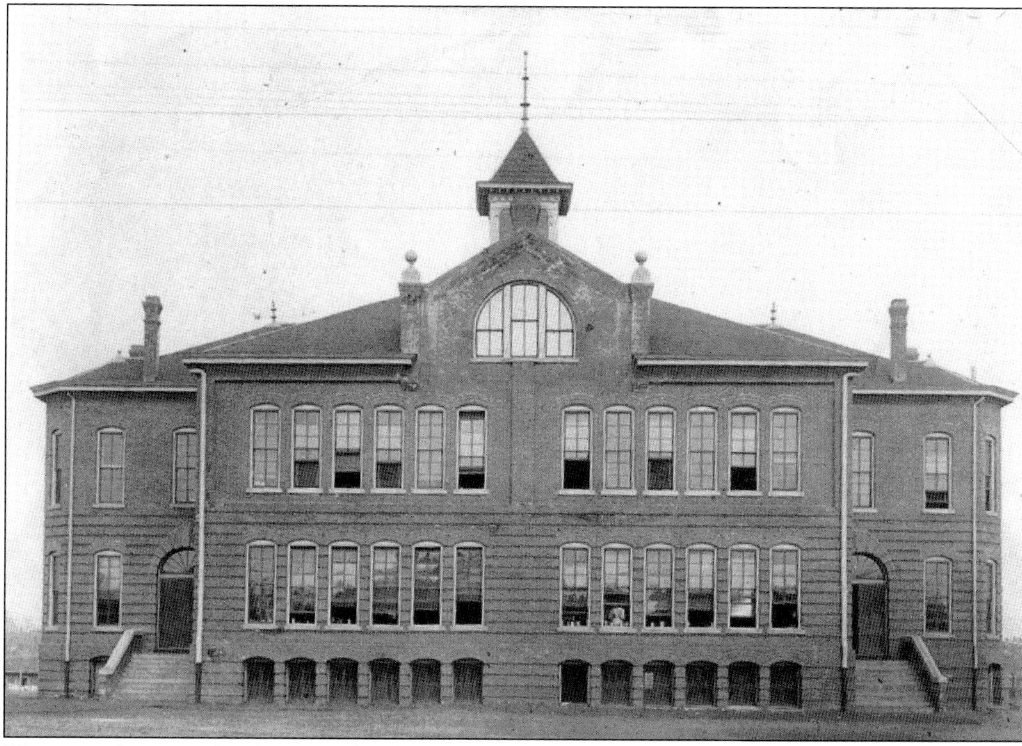

This is a photograph of East End School in 1906. The school was used for many years and was eventually named Sam Houston School. It was left standing vacant for several years after it closed but was recently destroyed by fire.

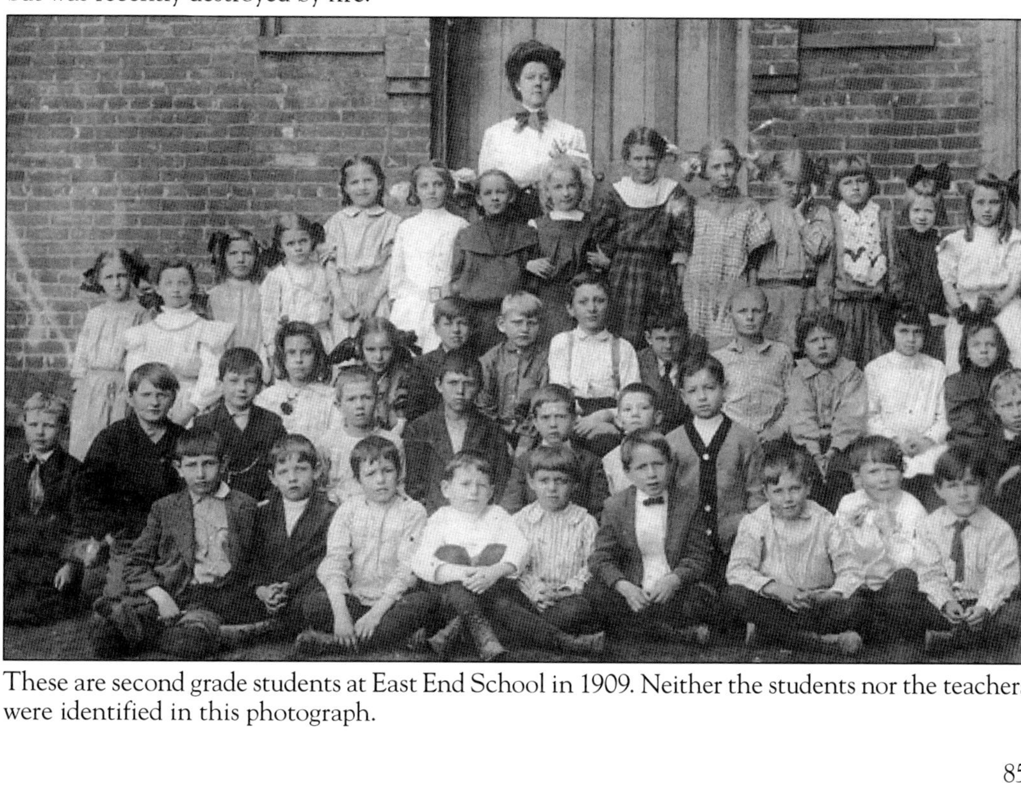

These are second grade students at East End School in 1909. Neither the students nor the teachers were identified in this photograph.

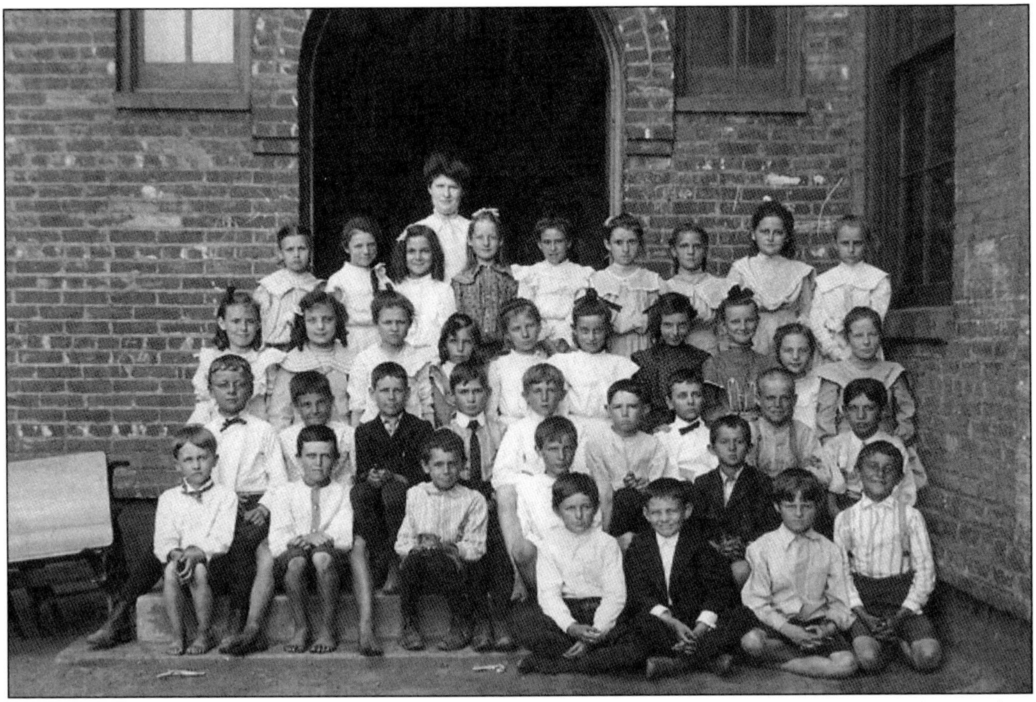

Pictured here are students at West End (Stephen F. Austin) School in 1902. Neither the teacher nor the grade level was identified on the program.

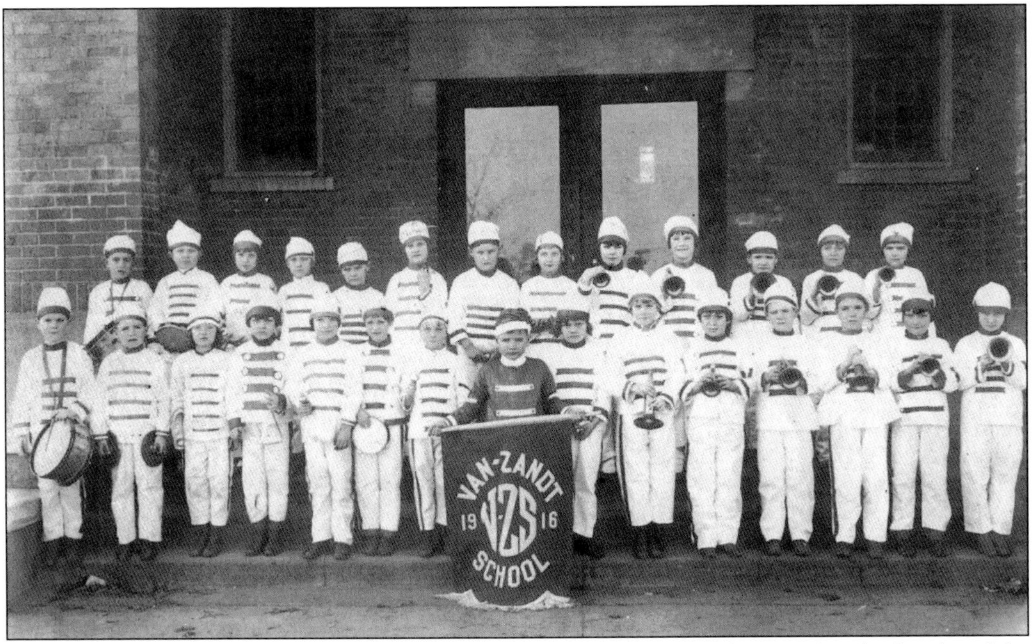

Many schools had rhythm bands in the 1920s and 1930s. Pictured here is the rhythm band for Van Zandt School. The year was 1923.

Eight

Churches in Marshall Prior to 1900

Religion rivals education in the importance it has played in the history of Marshall. Circuit riders from the Methodist Episcopal church came into Harrison County in 1839. A church was organized in 1845, and in 1861, a building was completed.

The First Baptist Church of Marshall was established May 6, 1845. A building was completed for the church in 1893. The Cumberland Presbyterian Church was founded April 11, 1848, with Rev. T. B. Wilson as the first pastor.

The First Presbyterian Church of Marshall was organized May 30, 1850, with 14 charter members. The church dissolved and was reorganized 39 years later (1888). Trinity Episcopal Church was established on Christmas Day in 1850. Twenty-two people were present, including the Rev. Henry Sansom and "The Southern Firebrand" Wigfall and his wife, Charlotte. The Ebenezer United Methodist Church was founded December 11, 1867. The first pastor of the church was Rev. Elijah Blair. Also in 1867, William Massey founded Bethesda Baptist Church. The church was destroyed by fire in 1953, after which the present building was erected.

Three black churches operated in Marshall early in its history. Miles Memorial CME Church was organized in 1872 and is the oldest CME church in Texas. In 1874, the Jerusalem Missionary Baptist Church was founded. A third church was organized as the Prince Monroe and Jacob Martin Church.

The St. Joseph's Catholic Church in Marshall was established on May 3, 1874, when the first baptism was performed. The Northside Methodist Church was organized in 1885 or 1886, preceded by Marvin Mission. The name changed to Summit Street Methodist Church in 1947.

The Temple Moses Montefiore was organized in 1887. The first president of the congregation was Adath Israel Daniel Dopplemeyer. The First Christian Church came into existence in 1888 in a meeting at Cumberland Presbyterian Church.

Marshall's First Church of Christ Scientist began in 1888 on the second floor of the Capitol Hotel. It operated in several locations until a new building was dedicated on April 4, 1943.

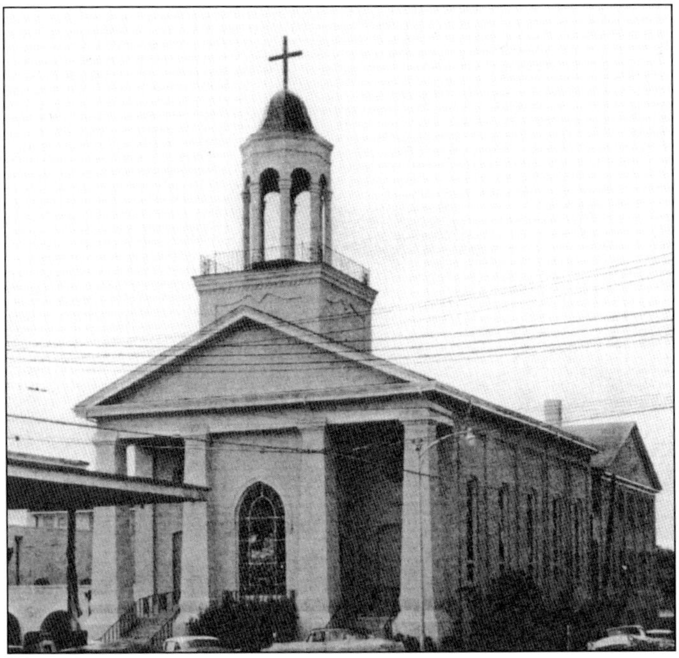

Land for the First Methodist Church was donated by Peter Whetstone. However, it was determined that the lot he donated was not suitable. This lot was sold and land was purchased from Thomas and Mary Bennett. Construction on the original building began prior to the outbreak of the Civil War. Today's church complex has expanded greatly, but the original building, the sanctuary, is still in use. This church, as did other churches in Marshall, donated its bell to be used for cannon. Their bell was not used and was recovered after the war by Marshall natives W. W. Heartsill and W. M. Johnson.

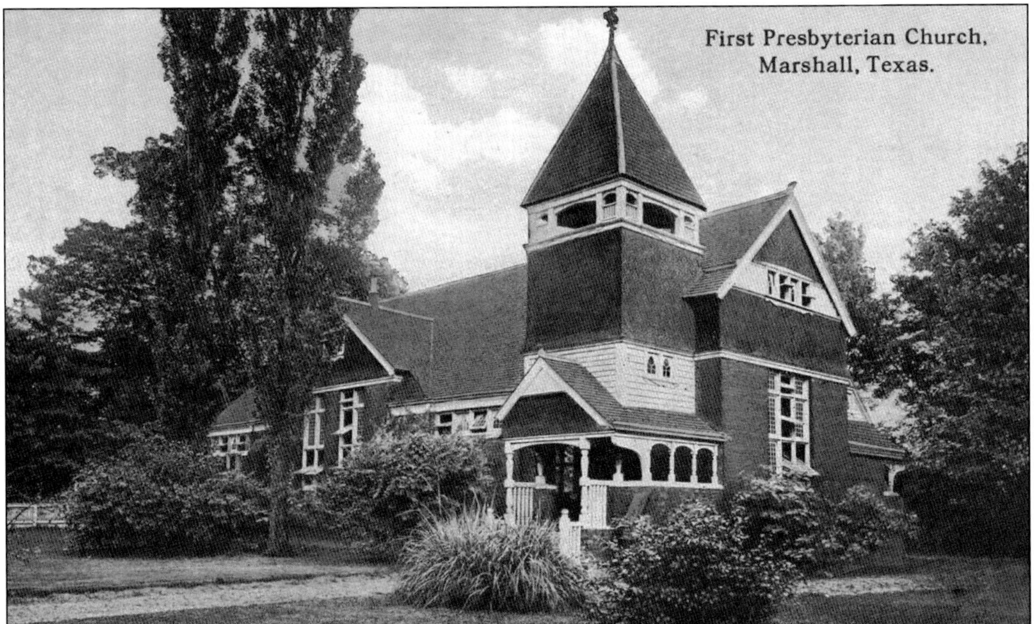

The First Presbyterian Church of Marshall is located at the corner of West Burleson and North Fulton Streets. W. M. Staples came to Marshall to organize the church only to find that there was one family of Presbyterians in Marshall. As the number grew, they met in the courthouse until their own building was completed. In 1851, Dr. W. C. Dunlap came to serve the church as pastor. When the Texas and Pacific Railroad came into prominence, the church grew, and in 1884, a new building was completed.

The First Baptist Church of Marshall was organized with 12 charter members. Dr. John Bryce came from Georgia to be a missionary in Texas, Arkansas, and Louisiana. He came to Marshall and organized the First Baptist Church in 1845. At first they met on a lot which is now in the 200 block of West Burleson Street. After they built their first church on land donated by James McCown, they often shared the building with other congregations who did not have a church structure.

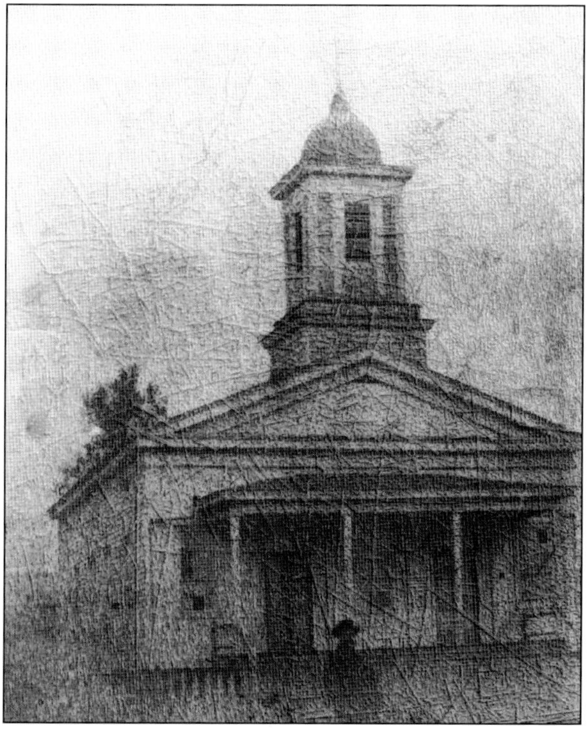

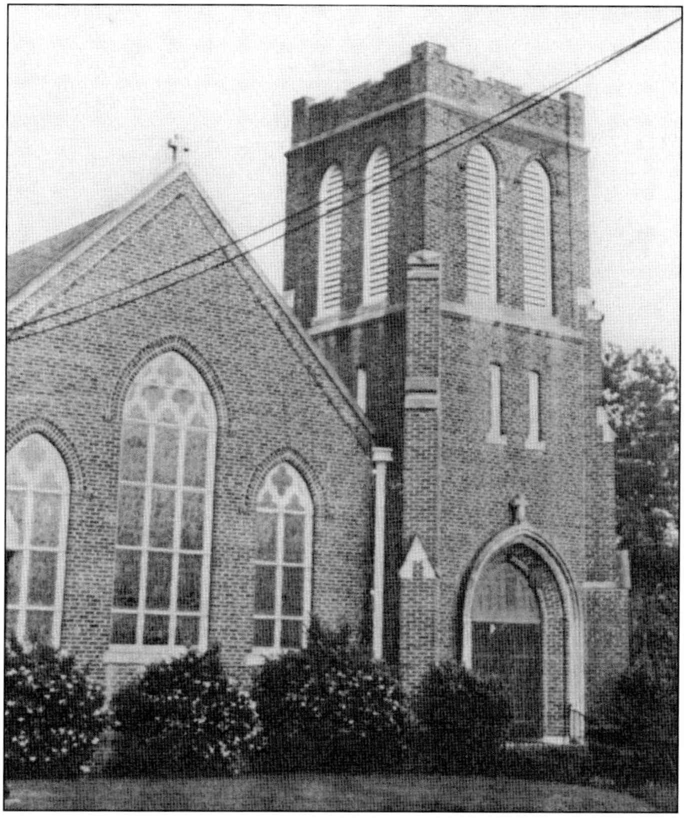

Trinity Episcopal Church was the 13th Episcopal church organized in the state. In June 1851, Bishop Freeman, a missionary of Arkansas and Texas, held the first confirmation meeting in Marshall. Mrs. J. P. Henderson, wife of the governor of Texas at that time, organized a mission for the purpose of building Episcopal churches in East Texas. Her work was interrupted by the Civil War, but eventually the building was completed. Dr. James Starr and his family were instrumental in the completion of the first building.

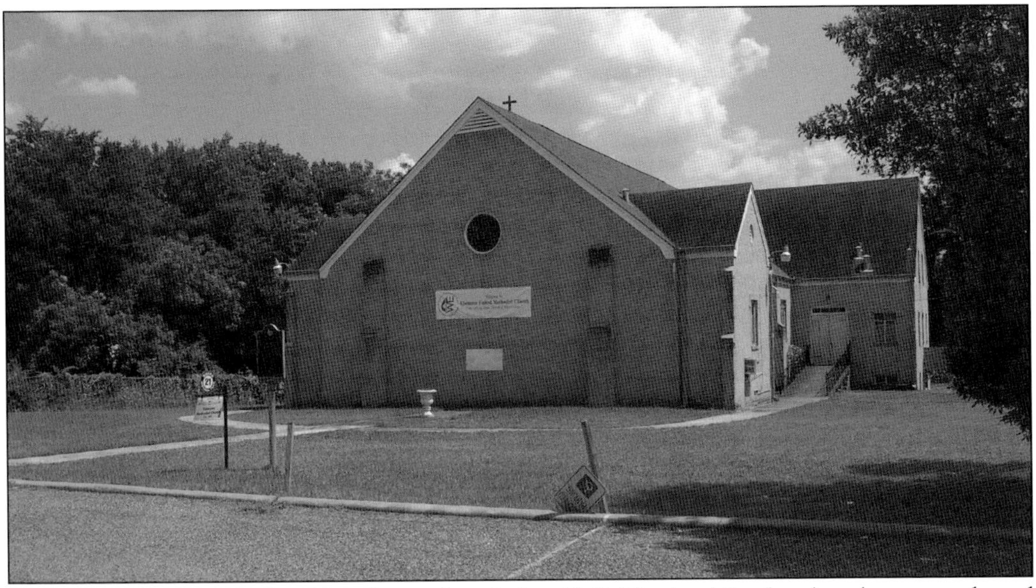

Ebenezer United Methodist Church was founded in 1867. The land for the church was purchased from R. P. Brown on December 11, 1867, at a cost of $100. The church operated a school for African American children.

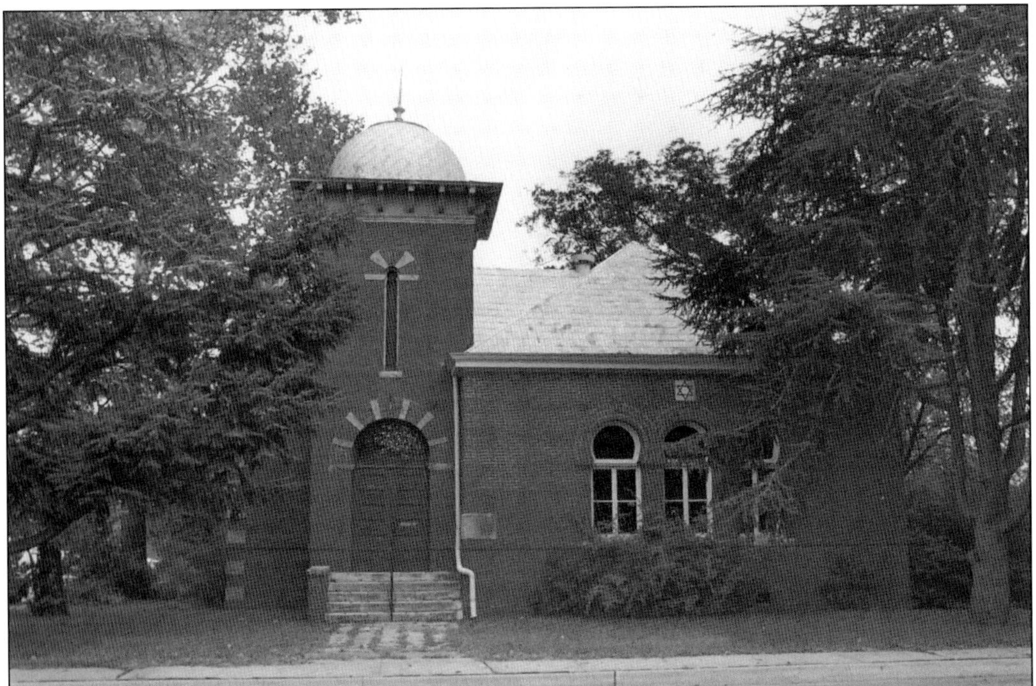

Temple Moses Montefiore was named for a noted British financier and philanthropist from England. It was organized on June 12, 1887. The Jewish people had a presence in Marshall since early in its history. The Marshall Hebrew Benevolent Society was organized in 1868 and is still in operation. The Temple Moses Montefiore was built in 1900. It was located on the corner of North Fulton and West Burleson Streets. On May 4, 1973, the Temple Moses Montefiore was demolished. The congregation merged with Temple Emanuel in Longview.

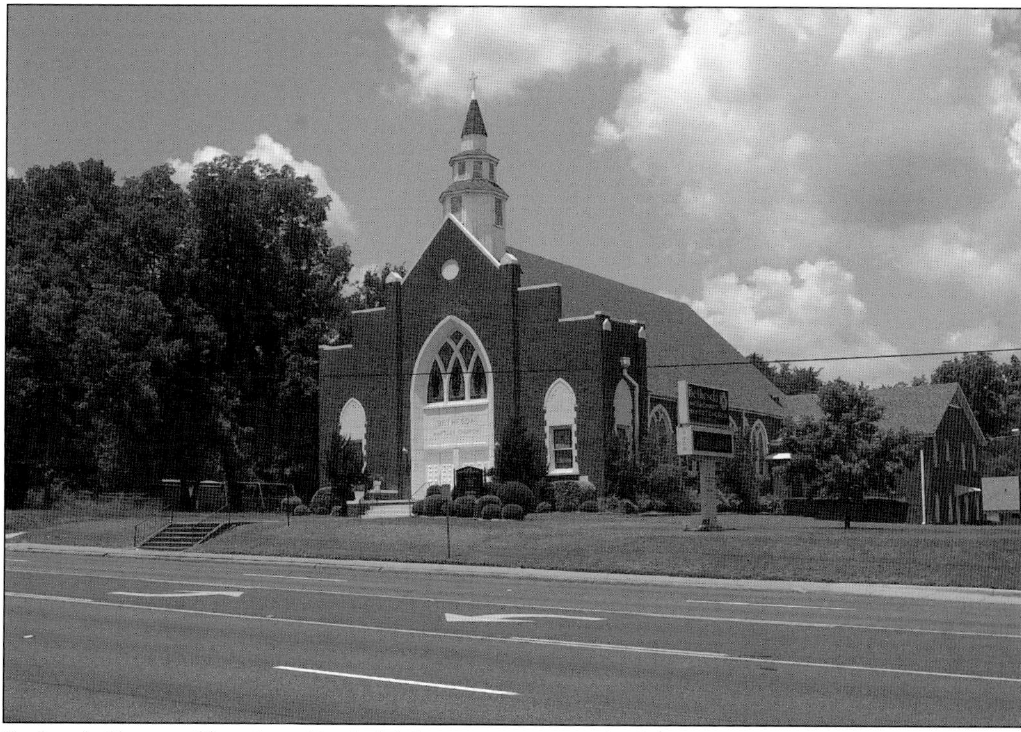

Bethesda Baptist Church at first held their meetings in the home of their minister, Rev. William Massey. It stands today as a historic church in Marshall. It has a historical marker to designate its significance to the community. (Courtesy of Lucile Estell.)

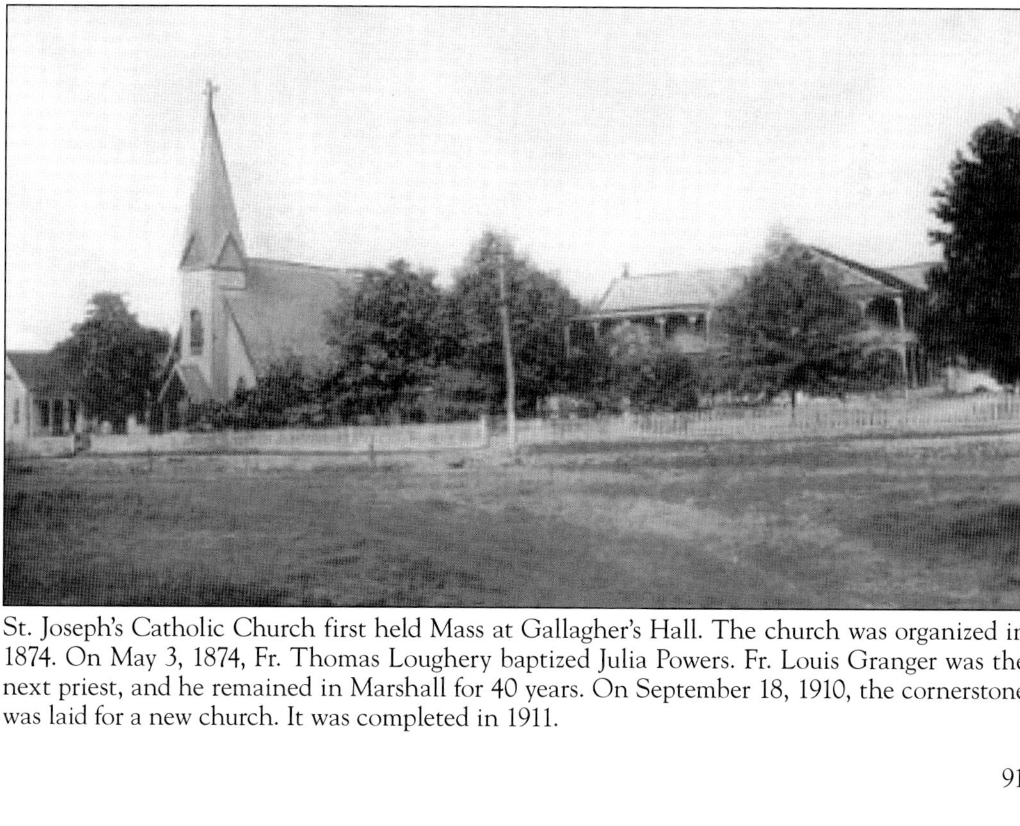

St. Joseph's Catholic Church first held Mass at Gallagher's Hall. The church was organized in 1874. On May 3, 1874, Fr. Thomas Loughery baptized Julia Powers. Fr. Louis Granger was the next priest, and he remained in Marshall for 40 years. On September 18, 1910, the cornerstone was laid for a new church. It was completed in 1911.

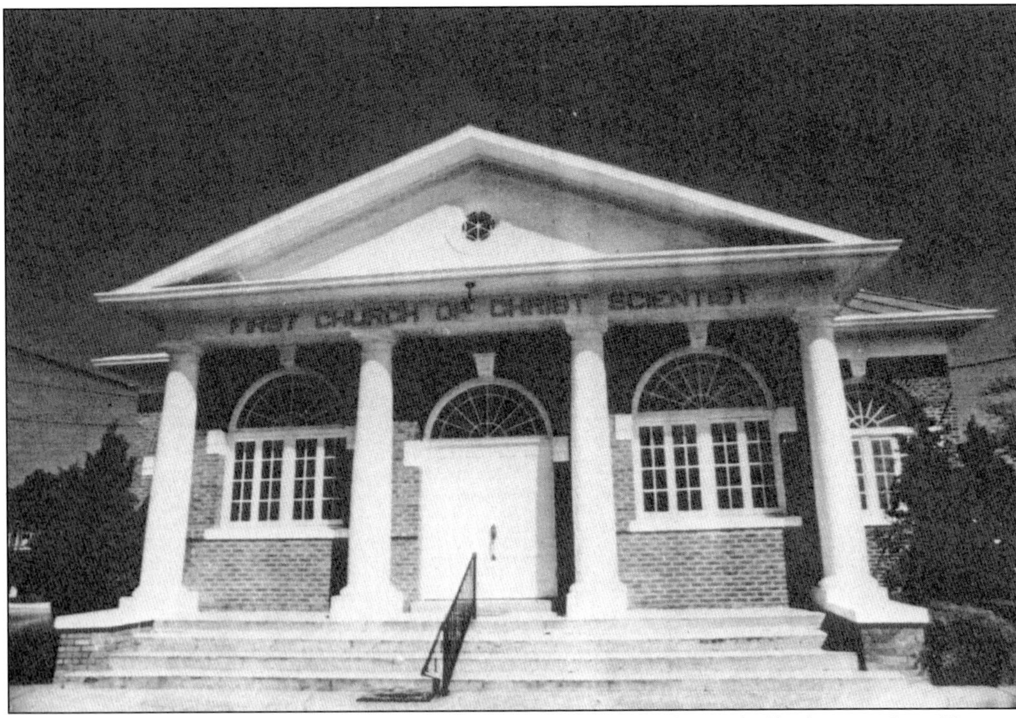

The First Church of Christ Scientist is located near the site of Marshall's famous Sam Houston Oak. In 1889, the church was granted a charter by the State of Texas. The present church building was erected in 1904. Prior to that time, the congregation met in the Capitol Hotel, the Marshall National Bank, and the Starr National Bank.

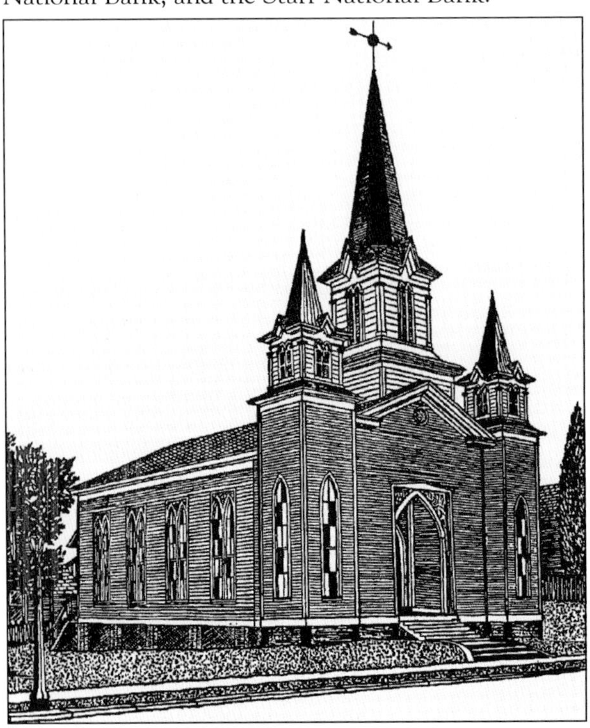

By 1842, the Cumberland Presbyterian Church was one of three churches well established in Marshall. The other two churches were the Baptist and Methodist. Rev. T. B. Wilson was the first pastor. He served from 1850 until his death in 1878. The Sunday school was organized in 1851, and the Ladies Aid Society was organized in 1869. In 1898, the Women's Missionary Society was organized. This was their first building, located at the corner of North Washington and East Grand Streets. (Drawing by Richard Magrill.)

Nine

More about Marshall

In the eight chapters preceding this one, the story of one community and its growth over the past century and a half have been chronicled. Told in these first eight chapters is much of the story, and it is told in segments generally related to periods of time. Yet there are people and events that do not fall naturally into this framework. These are the places and events that give Marshall a sense of place and are uniquely Marshall. They fall well into the scheme of things when one considers that in the study of history and in the marking of history for perusal by local citizens, tourists, and young people, one must consider two distinct bodies of knowledge: the land and the people. The first eight chapters of this book consider both. This ninth chapter makes the story come full circle by focusing on things that should always be a part of Marshall's history.

First, consider important places that should be recognized. This is a partial listing of places that make Marshall unique and are a special part of its history: Hynson Springs, the Old Stagecoach Road, Ginocchio Hotel, the Old Powder Mill Cemetery, Scratch Eye Cemetery, Marshall Cemetery, Greenwood Cemetery, and New Town.

Next, there are people with strong Marshall ties, who lived and worked in Marshall and who went far from Marshall to exert influence, which was felt worldwide. These are not the only ones, but there are those who did not fall into any category in the initial chapters because most of their lives were spent outside of Marshall. Included in this list are Y. A. Tittle, Sam Hall Jr., Lady Bird Johnson, Bill Moyers, Franklin Jones Jr., Quinton and Mildred Carlile, and Peter Whetstone.

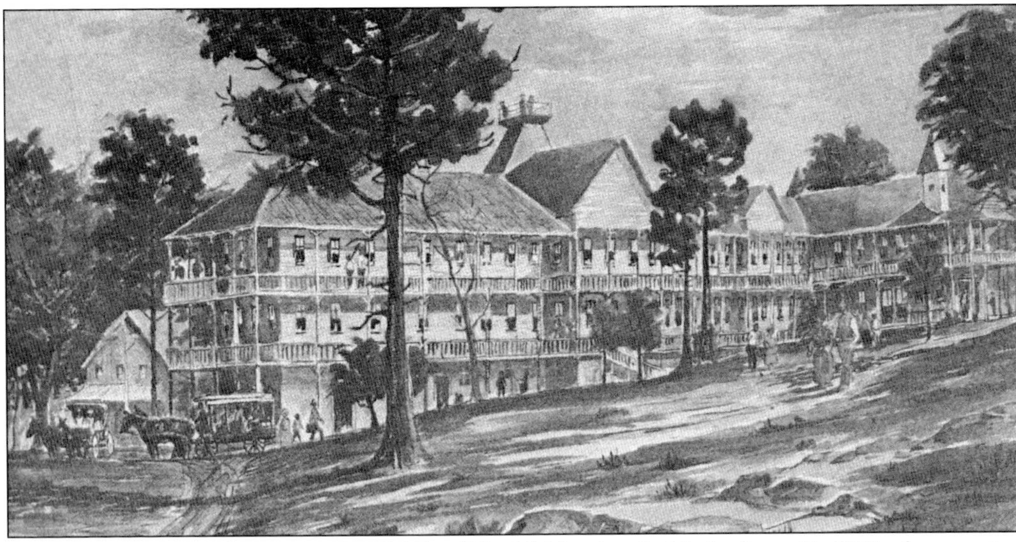

Hynson Springs was known as the "Hills of Health" by the Caddo Indians. By 1861, these springs had achieved national significance. During these early days, they were known as Marshall Springs or Iron Springs. A man named Colonel Hynson became interested in the springs, and by 1860, he had built a home overlooking the springs. During the Civil War, Hynson became involved in a tanning business in Shreveport. The springs were sold, and the Interstate Investment Company of Shreveport erected a huge hotel. The hotel operated there until 1905.

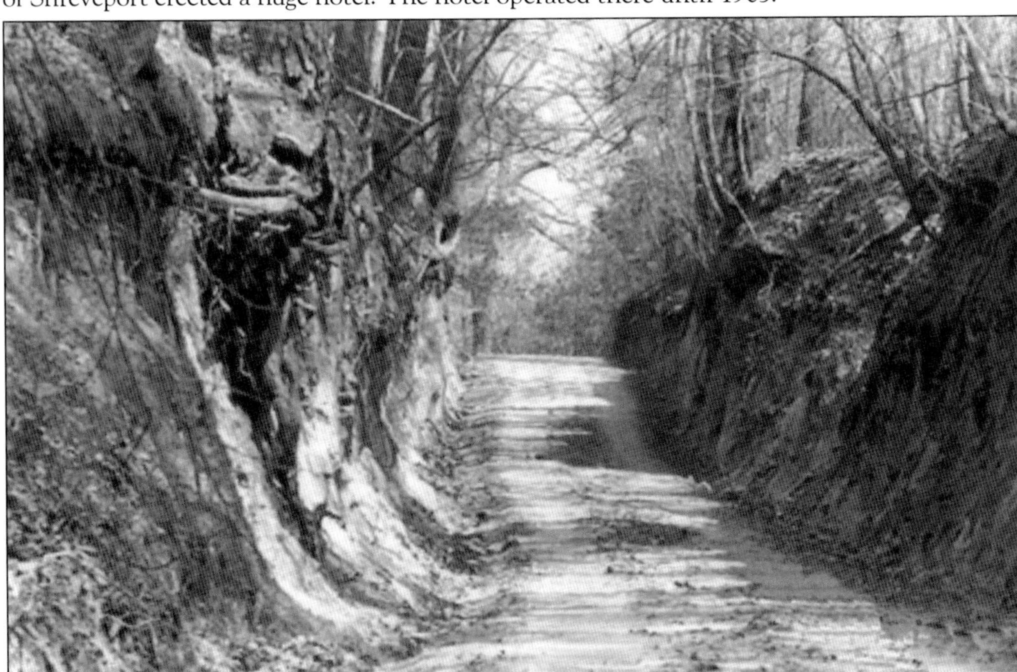

Before the Civil War, the major thoroughfare between Marshall and Shreveport was the Old Stagecoach Road. One of the advantages of this was the fact that it opened the door to trade with New Orleans. The heavy traffic dug as deeply as 12 feet into the dirt as the use of this road progressed. It is still visible today. Access to the road is on Highway 43 to Karnack. The road declined in use after the Southern Pacific completed a rail line to Shreveport.

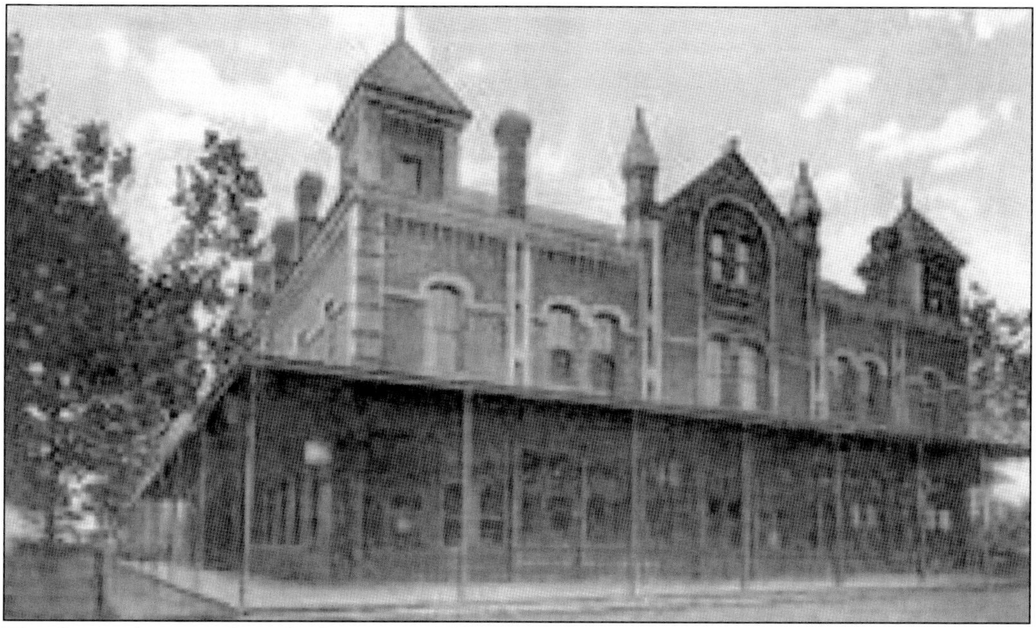

The Ginocchio Hotel was built in 1896. The bricks used in the building were made on-site. It was constructed just a few yards from the ticket office for the railroad and is one of the most imposing structures, architecturally and historically, ever built in Marshall. There is a sealed tunnel that runs from the hotel to the Ginocchio home located directly across the street. It is also rumored that the hotel has a "friendly" ghost.

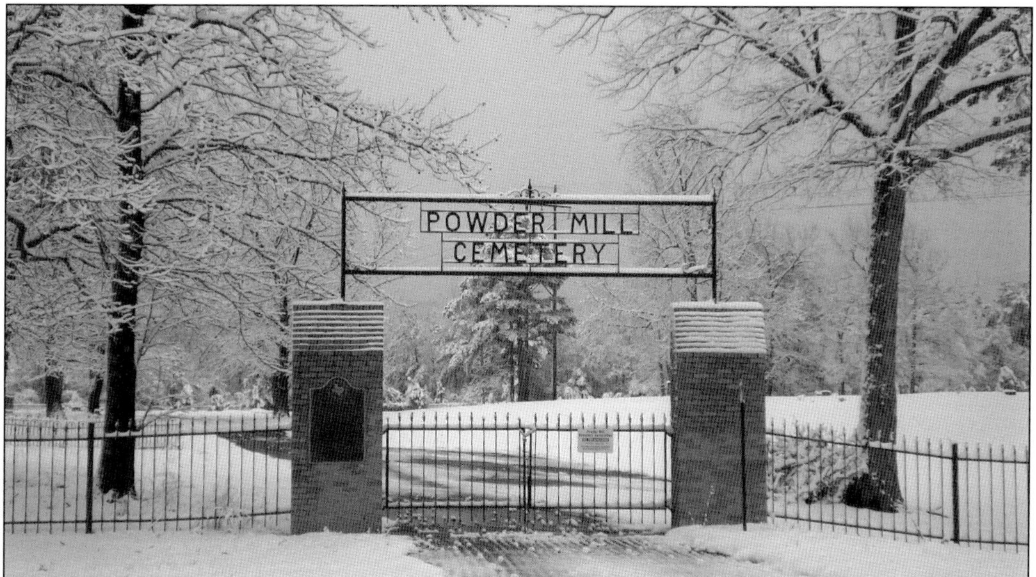

Powder Mill Cemetery is located at the site where the powder mill operated during the Civil War. A cemetery had been located there. After the Powder Mill was destroyed, the acreage fell into private ownership. One of landowners, M. M. Rains, began recording the graves in 1880. David Abner, a previous member of the Texas Legislature and former Harrison County treasurer, is buried here with his wife, Millie. Many of the early black leaders of the community are buried here, including H. B. Pemberton, J. R. E. Lee, and William Gross. (Courtesy of Elaine Sutton.)

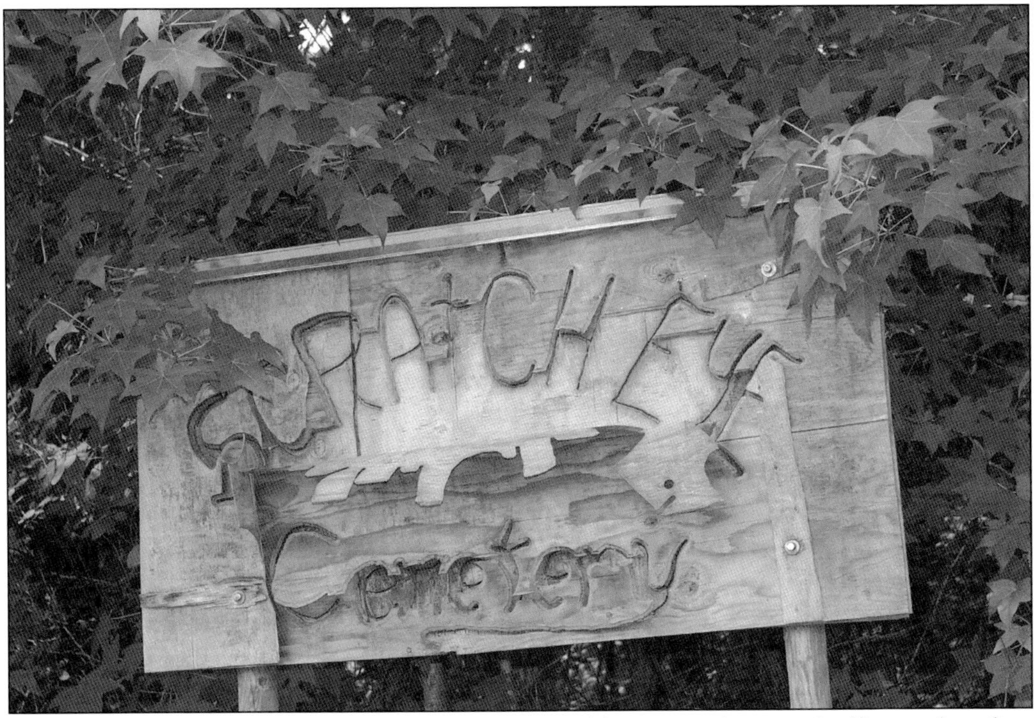

According to legend, Scratch Eye Cemetery was named for a man who scratched his eye by riding under a low hanging tree. His eye became infected, causing his death. He was buried under the tree. The first white child born in Harrison County, Amaryllis Beaty Cole, is buried here. The first grave in this cemetery is that of William Burns, who was buried in 1876. (Courtesy of Lucile Estell.)

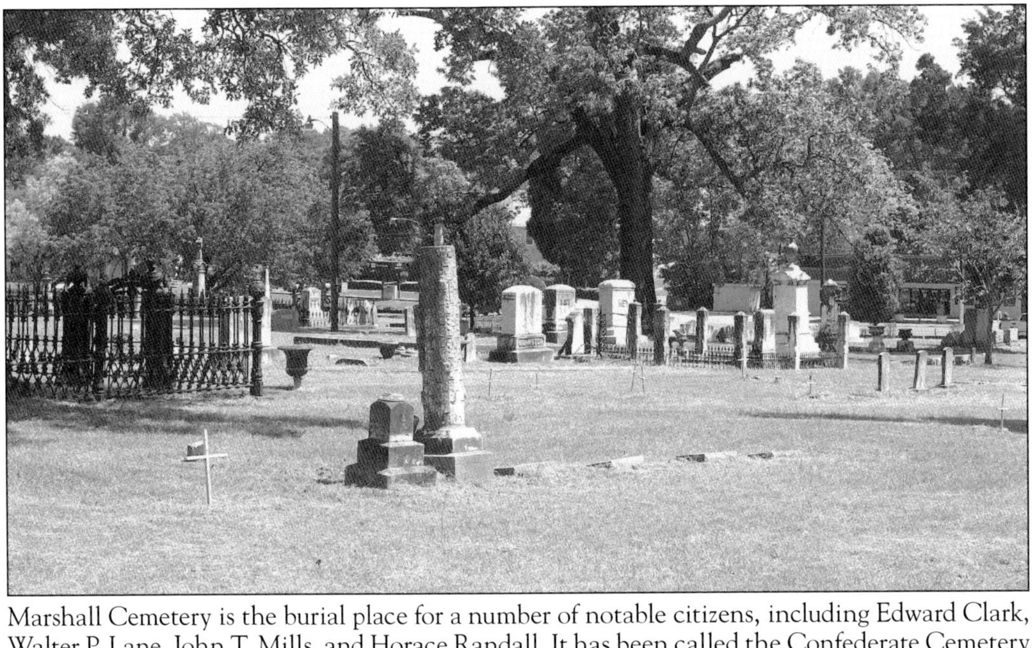

Marshall Cemetery is the burial place for a number of notable citizens, including Edward Clark, Walter P. Lane, John T. Mills, and Horace Randall. It has been called the Confederate Cemetery because of the large number of Confederate soldiers buried here. (Courtesy of Ben Hughes.)

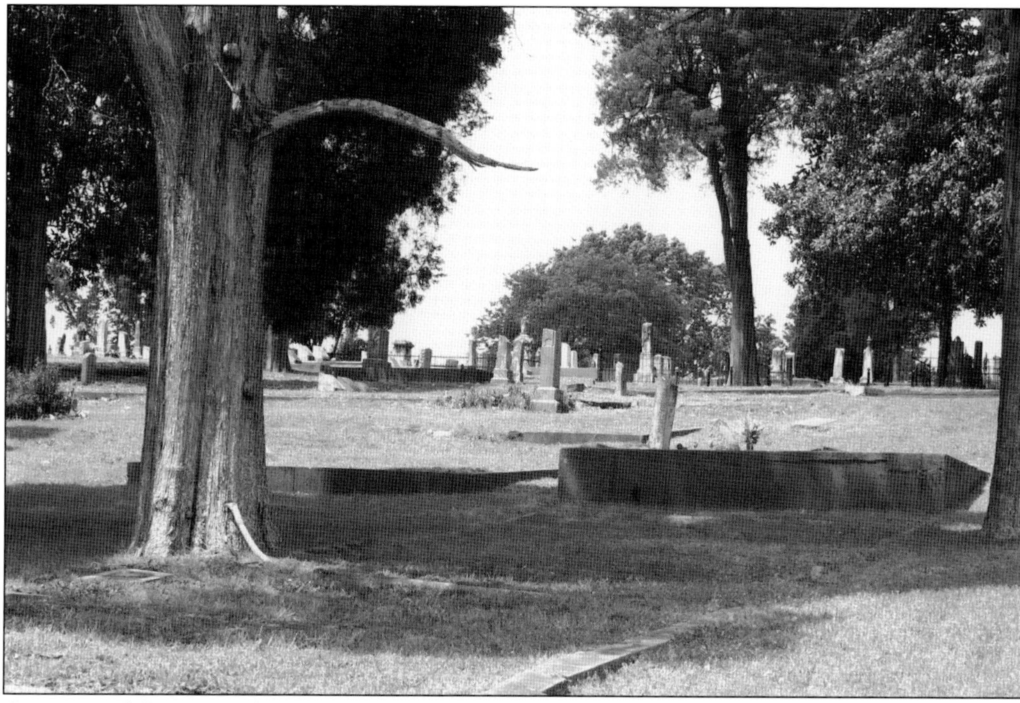

Greenwood Cemetery began in 1840 as a private burial ground. Notables buried here include Isaac Van Zandt, James Harper Starr, Matthew Duncan Ector, Alexander Travis Hawthorne, and Charles Raguet Bring-Ups (grandson of Sam Houston.) (Courtesy of Ben Hughes.)

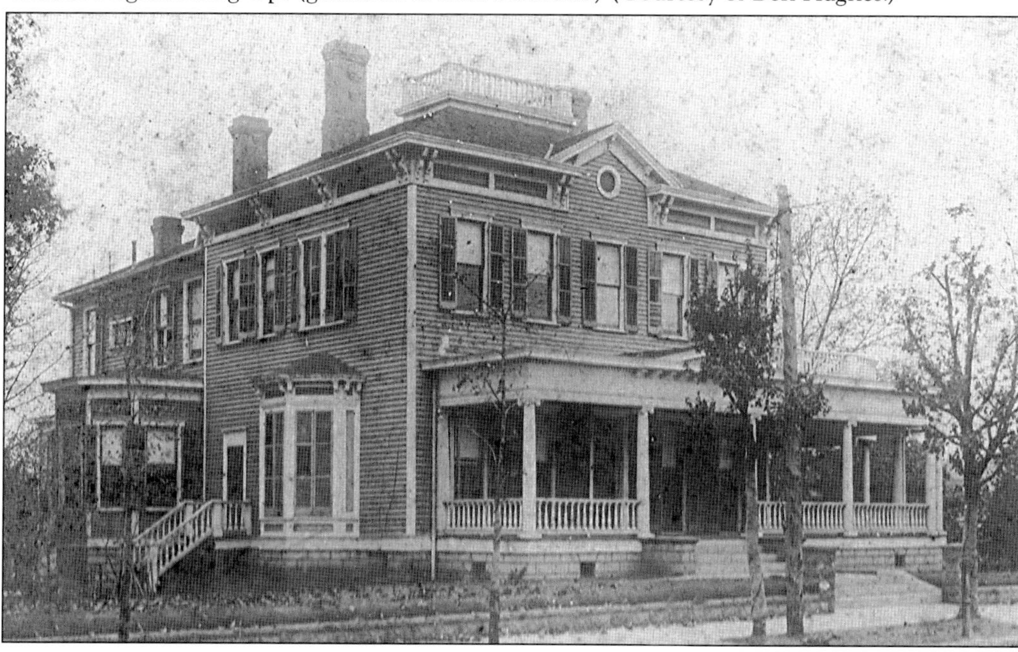

The Confederate Hat Factory was located at 109 West Grand Avenue. The factory operated in the basement of the house at this location. They made military hats for Texas and other troops. The house burned in 1862, and the Edmund Key family donated the site to the Harrison County Conservation Society to be used as a park.

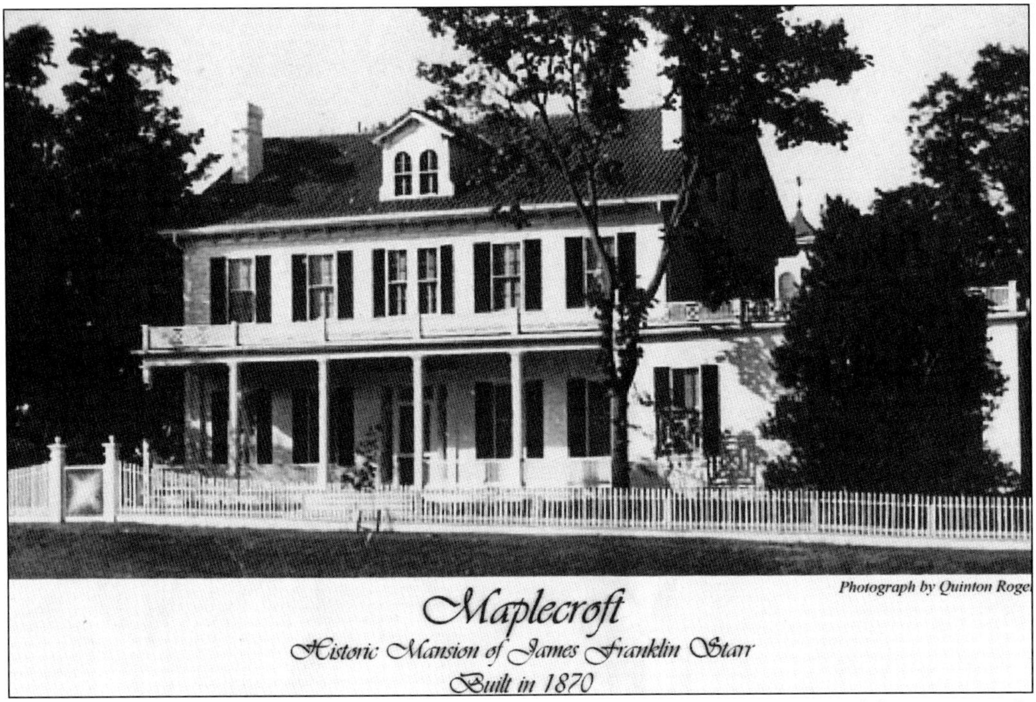

Maplecroft, the Starr Family Historical Site, is now owned by the Texas Historical Commission. It was built for James Frank Starr in 1870–1871. It was built with joints mortised on property owned by Dr. James Harper Starr, secretary of the treasury in the Republic of Texas. Later he served as postmaster general of the Trans-Mississippi Department. The home is located at 407 West Travis Street. (Photograph by Quinton Rogers.)

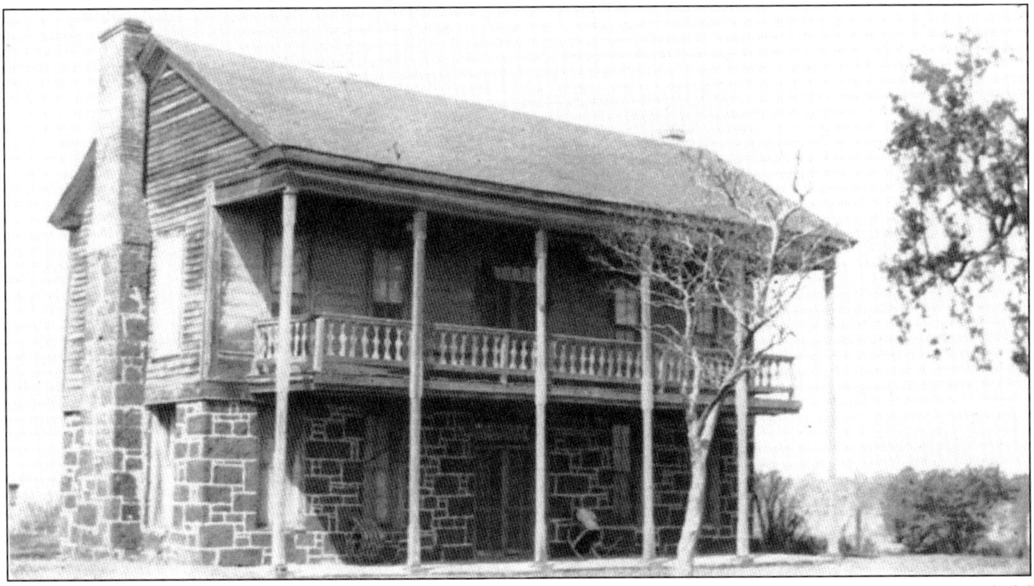

Old Stagecoach House (John Barry Henderson home) was located on the Shreveport to Daingerfield Stage. The main part of the house was built between 1868 and 1871. The ground floor walls were constructed of local iron ore rock. The second floor has a narrow, cantilevered porch with ornamental railing.

Citizens of Marshall have always been quick to answer the call of their country. Pictured here is Sgt. S. E. Short in 1918. He was one of many young men to leave home in defense of his country.

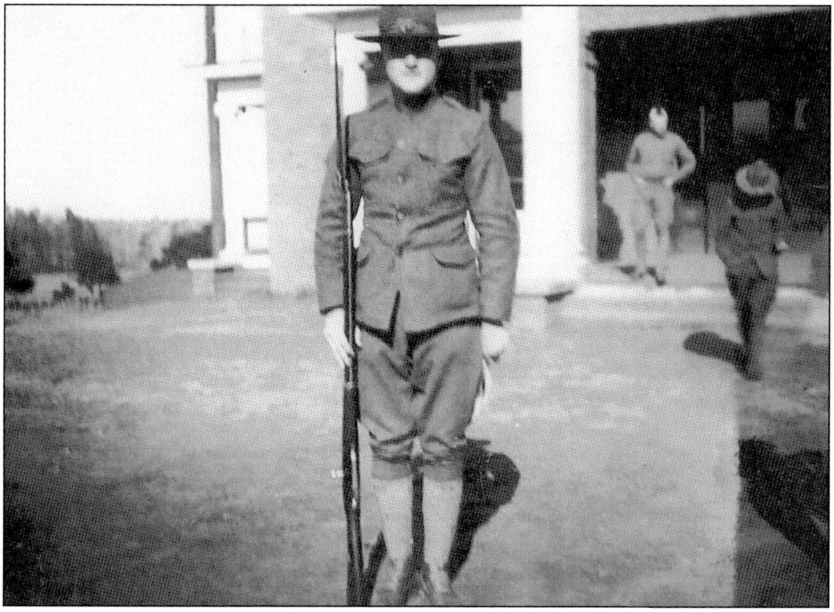

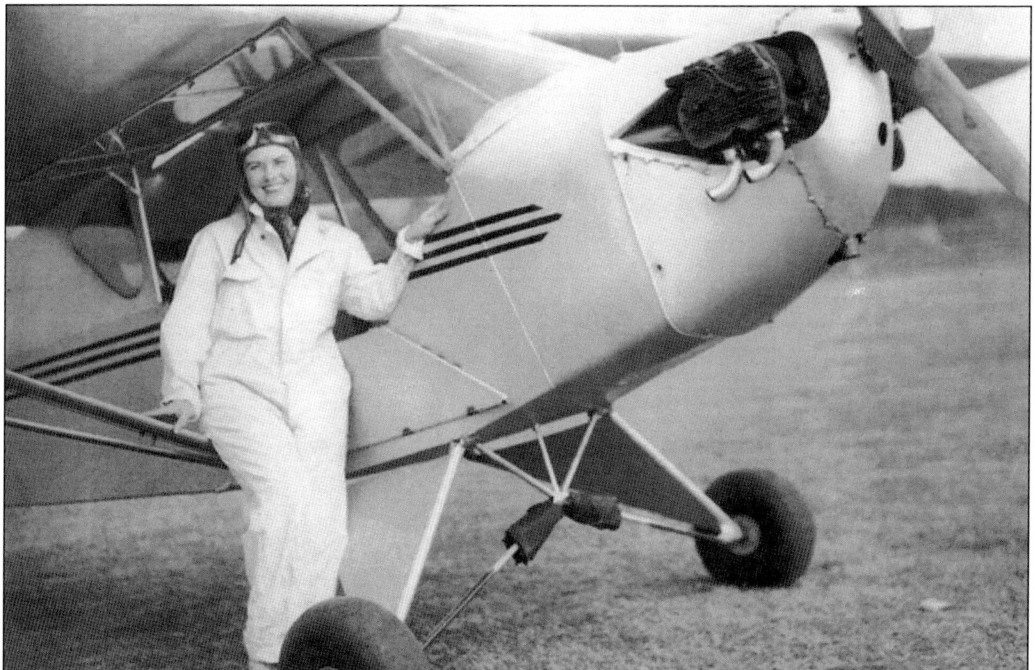

Pilot Katherine Van Hook Carroll is pictured here with an airplane in 1932. Pilots were scarce at this time, especially female ones. The museum did not reveal anything about her career.

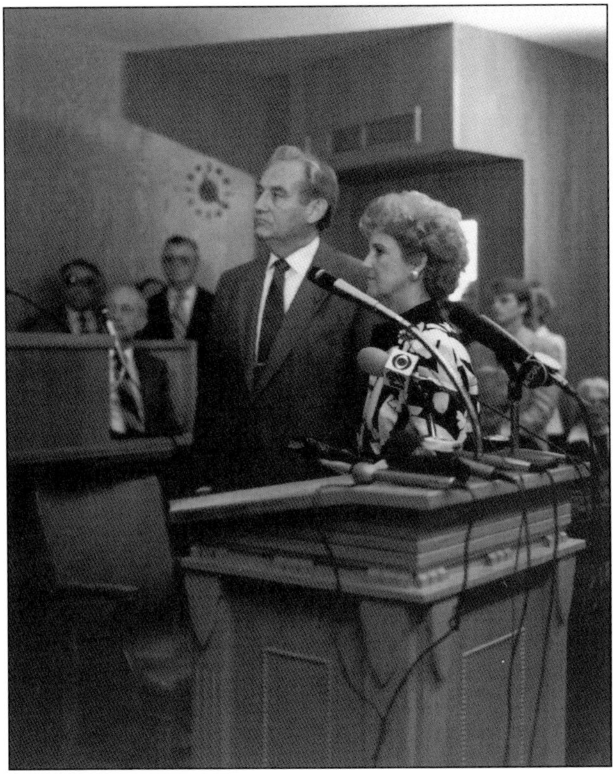

Sam B. Hall Jr. was born in Marshall in 1924 and devoted all of his life to the betterment of his community. He was a graduate of East Texas Baptist University and Waco University. After serving in the U.S. Air Force, he returned to Marshall to practice law. He was elected five times to serve the people in the Congress of the United States. President Ronald Reagan nominated him as a federal judge for the Eastern District of Texas. He served in this capacity until his death in 1994. The Sam B. Hall Federal Courthouse in Marshall was named in his honor. Pictured here are Sam B. and Madelaine Hall.

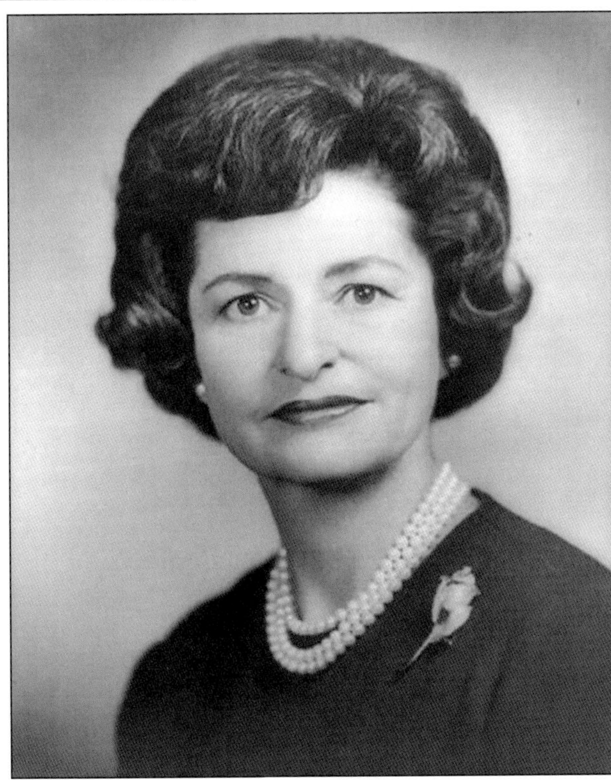

Lady Bird Johnson assumed the role of First Lady when her husband, Lyndon B. Johnson became president of the United States in 1953. She was born on December 22, 1912, in her family plantation home near Marshall. She lived in Atlanta for a time after her mother died, but then she returned to East Texas to attend school, and in 1928, she graduated from Marshall High School, third in her class. Her service as first lady was noted for her gracious manner. In 1977, she received the Medal of Freedom Award from President Ford. In 1988, President Reagan presented her with the Congressional Gold Medal.

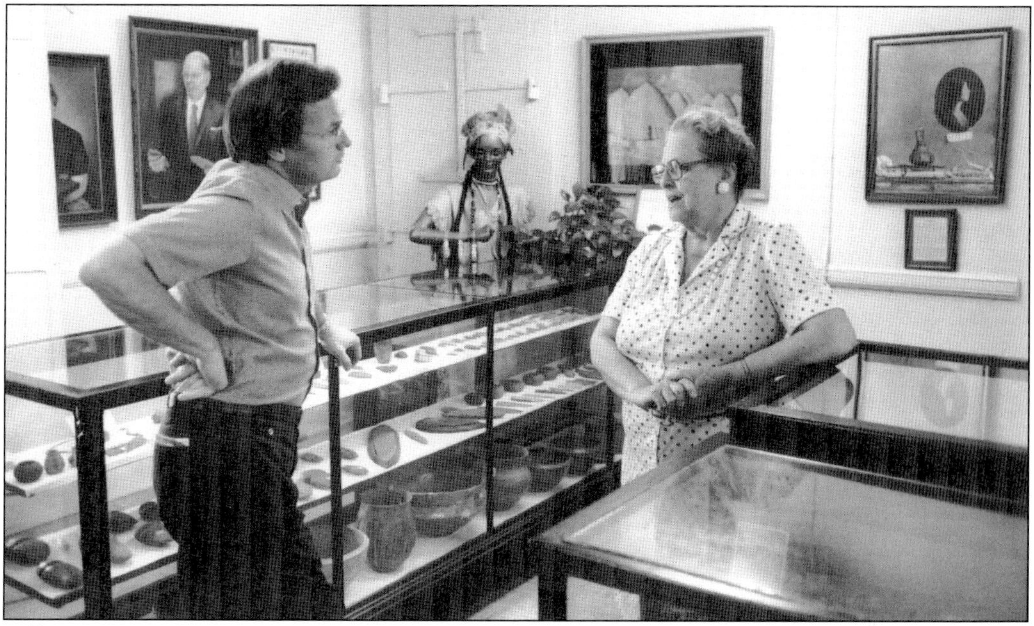

Bill Moyers was born on June 5, 1934, in Hugo, Oklahoma. He moved to Marshall and graduated from Marshall High School. He completed a journalism degree at North Texas State University and also received a degree from Southwestern Baptist Theological Seminary in Fort Worth, Texas. Moyers was press secretary to Pres. Lyndon Johnson. He was deputy director of the Peace Corps and served as a presidential assistant and in many others roles during his career. He is shown in this photograph with Inez Hatley Hughes who served for more than 25 years as curator for the Harrison County Historical Museum.

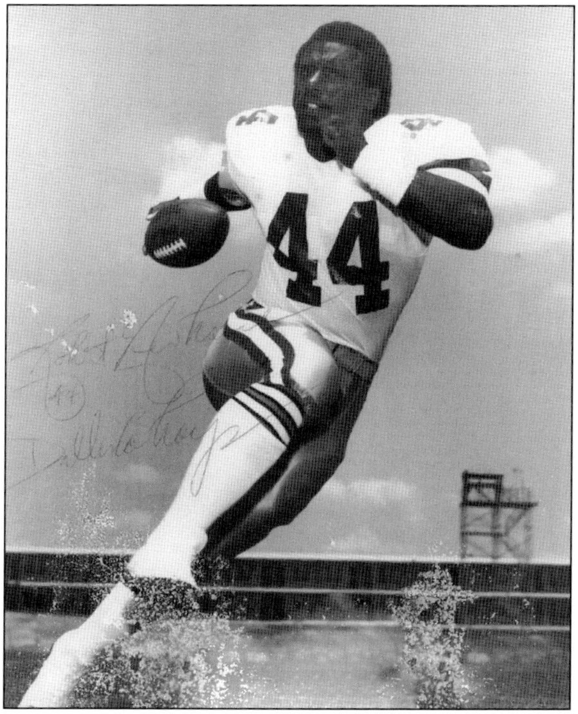

Harrison County native Robert Newhouse was a fullback with the Dallas Cowboys of the National Football League from 1972 to 1983. He ended his collegiate career at the University of Houston as all-time leading rusher. He symbolized the NFL during the 1970s with his hard-nosed approach to playing football. He is remembered for tossing a touchdown pass for the final score in the Cowboy's Super Bowl XII win.

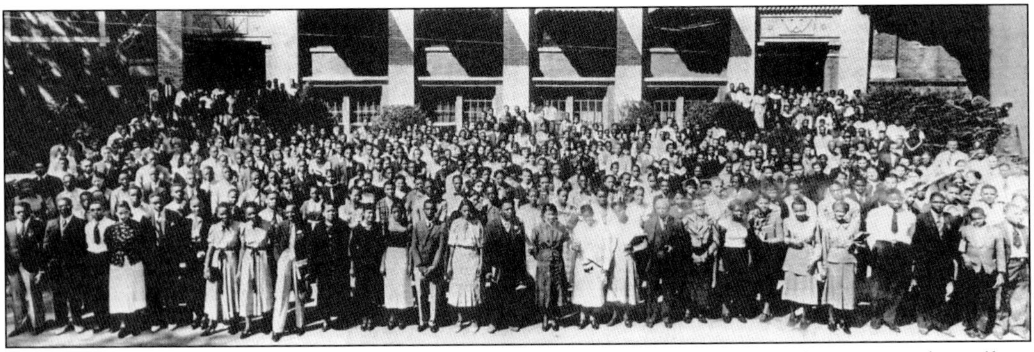

Matthew W. Dogan served as president of Wiley College for 45 years. During his tenure, the college became known nationwide for the excellent quality of its education. This photograph shows Dogan and students in front of the administration building of Wiley College in the 1940s.

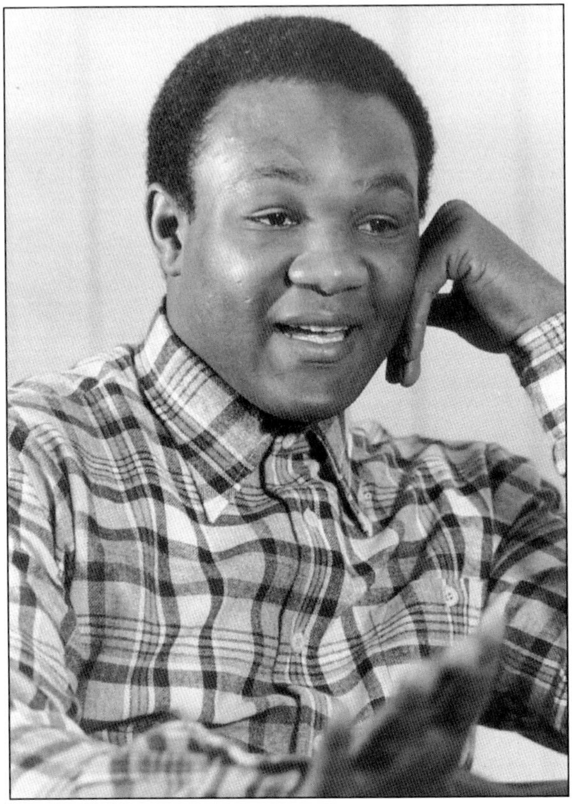

George Foreman was born in Marshall in 1949. After moving to Houston, young Foreman found himself in trouble with the law. He credits Job Corps, his counselor, and boxing coach with saving him from prison. Foreman won a boxing gold medal in the 1968 Olympics. In 1973, he became world heavyweight champion. He again fought for the championship in 1994 and became the oldest fighter ever to win the title.

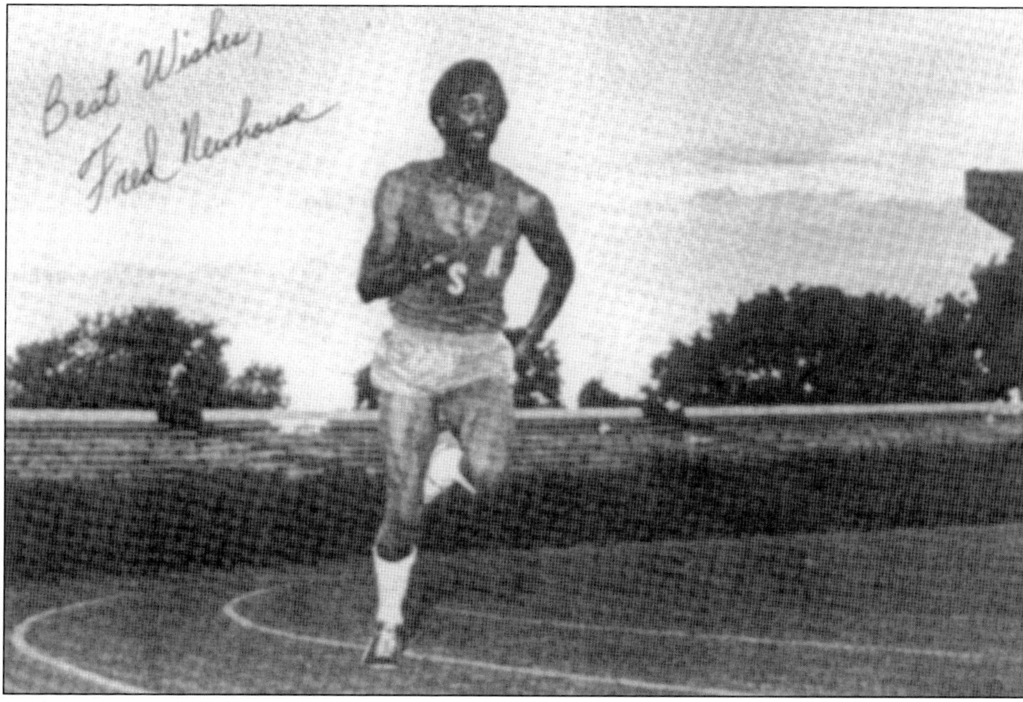

Fred Newhouse is recognized as one of the fastest sprinters in the world today. He was first recognized in 1970 when he broke the world record for the 440-yard dash with an astounding 45.6-second performance. He participated in the Pan American games in Columbia in 1971, collecting both a gold and silver medal. The same performance was repeated in the 1976 Summer Olympics in Montreal. He has been selected for seven All-American teams and has represented the United States in numerous competitions.

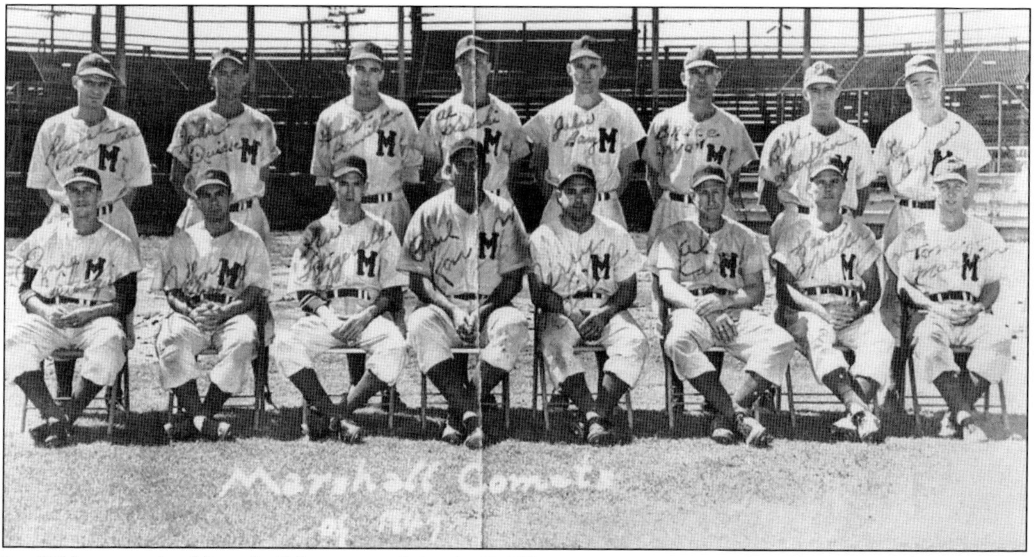

In 1910, organized baseball began in Marshall. Their semipro team, the Blues, won the semipro championship. According to Ernest Berglund, admission fees to these early games were collected by passing the hat. Baseball was suspended during World War II. In 1947, Marshall had a professional baseball team named the Comets, pictured here. They were a part of the Lone Star League.

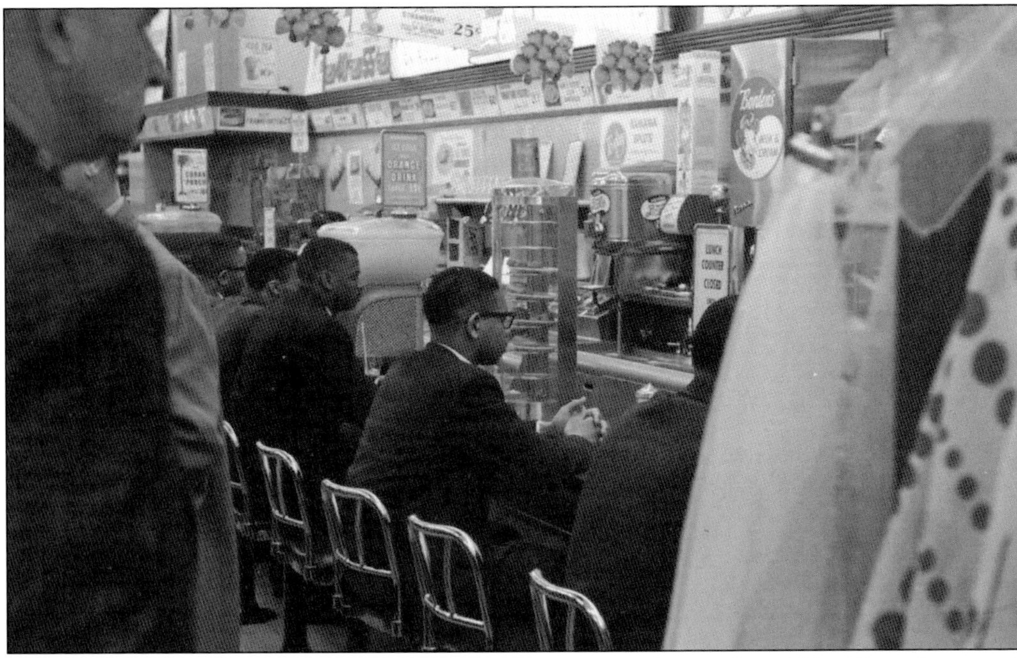

Marshall had several peaceful civil rights demonstrations during the 1950s. This photograph shows one that was held at Woolworth Department Store's lunch counter.

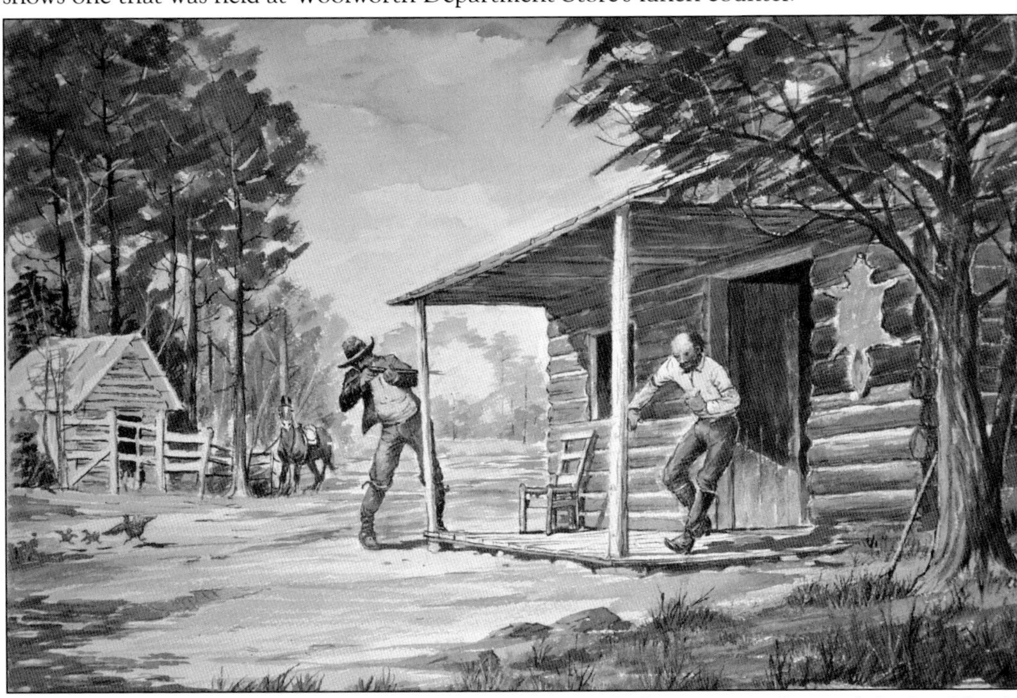

Peter Whetstone is regarded as a major benefactor of Marshall, Texas. He donated the land for the courthouse, a church, and school, and he supported many positive things for the community. In 1830, he came to Texas with his wife, Dicy, and their children. His contemporaries described him as a man of "great originality." He was involved in the Regulator-Moderator War, which occurred in Marshall. It was because of this that he was killed in his own home on November 9, 1843.

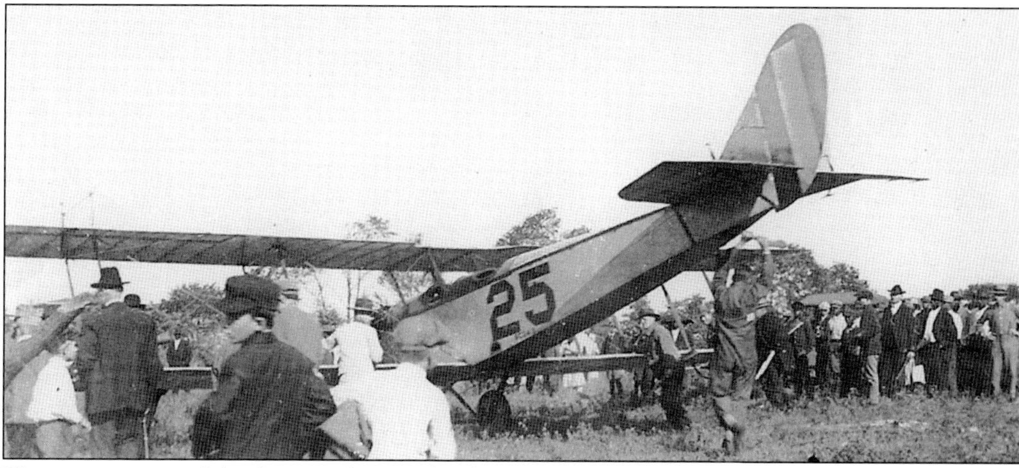

This is a picture of the first airplane to land in Marshall. No information is available about the date or place. Note the large number of people that attended the event.

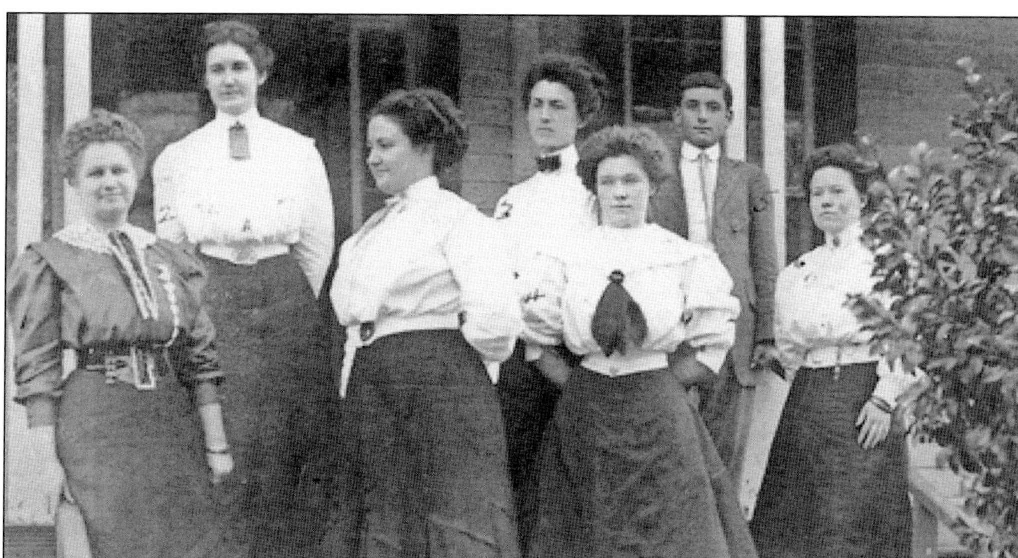
Pictured here on January 22, 1911, are Julia Shamburger (second from left) and students in one of her classes. Shamburger founded the Shamburger Select School.

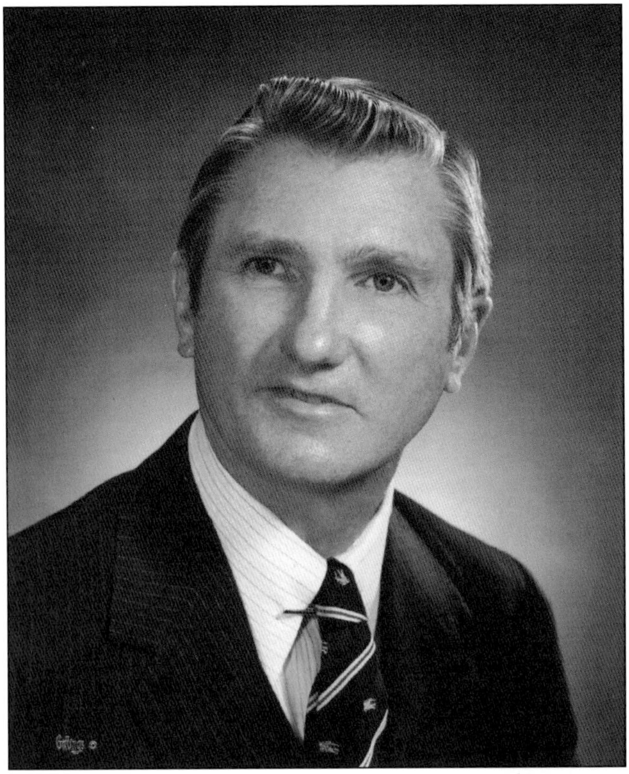

As chair of the Courthouse Preservation Council of Harrison County, Franklin Jones Jr. led the effort to preserve the 1901 historic Harrison County Courthouse in Marshall. His love of Marshall and Harrison County history was evidenced through a major contribution to the Harrison County Historical Museum. Jones was the third generation of his family to practice law in Marshall.

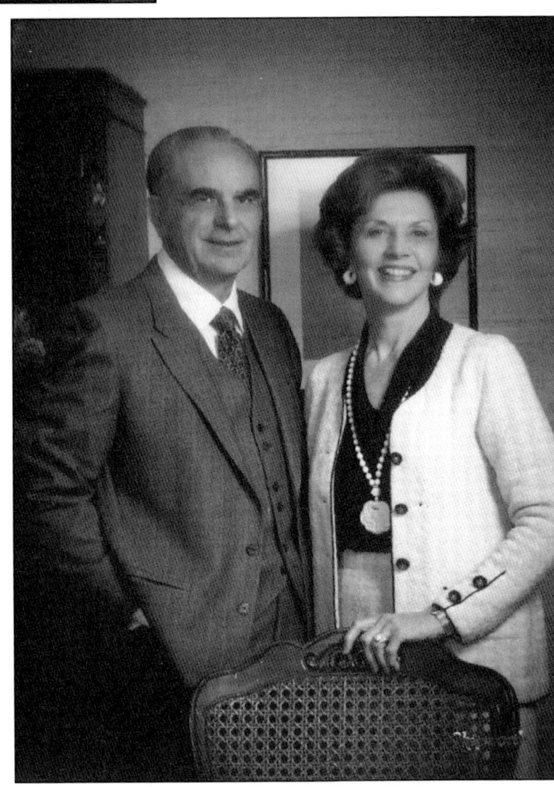

Throughout its history, Marshall has benefitted greatly from the generosity of its citizens. Quinton and Mildred Carlile are philanthropists who have stepped forward to make Marshall better. Marshall's Michelson Museum of Art and the beautifully restored 1901 Harrison County Courthouse are possible because of their generosity.

Rebecca Buard (right) was recognized as an outstanding educator and historian. Buard received a bachelor of science degree from Bishop College and an master's degree from Southern California University. She taught in several places, including a Rosenwald School in the High Ridge Community, Pemberton High School, and Wiley College. The Buard History Trail is named in her honor.

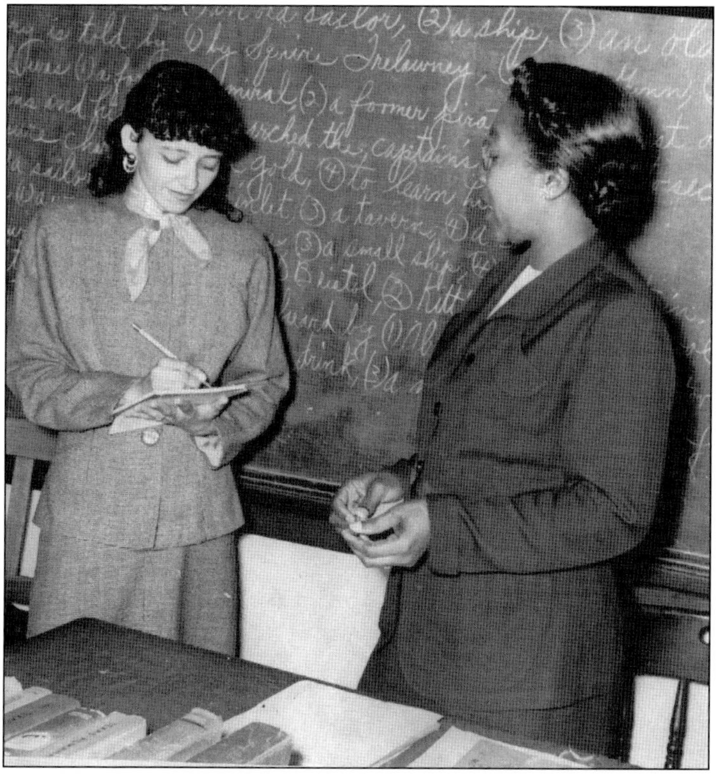

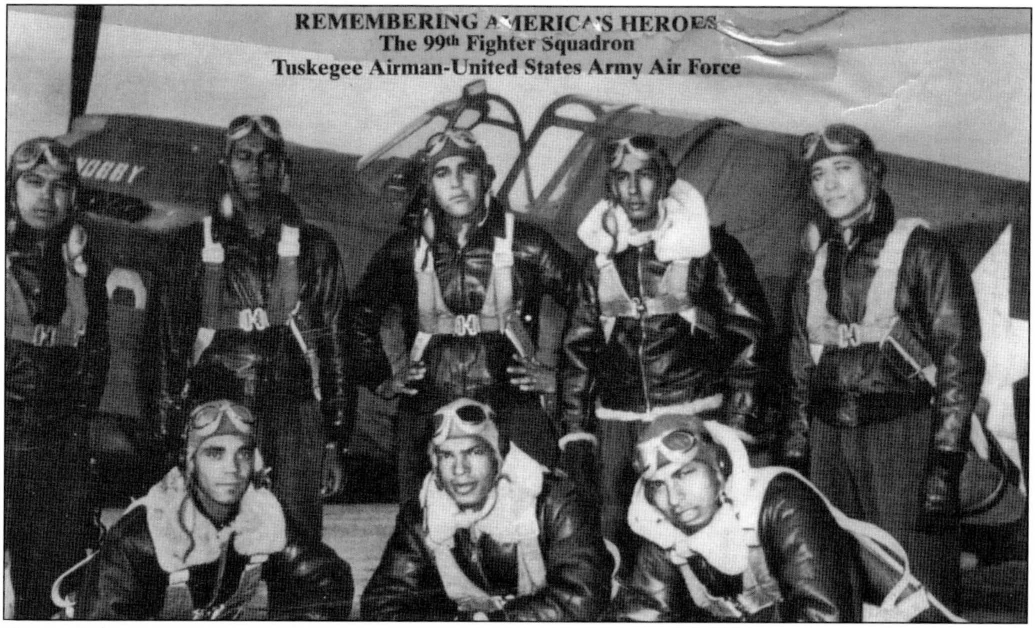

One of the most respected fighter groups in World War II was the Tuskegee Airmen. These were dedicated young men determined to serve their country. Marshall had four men who were members of this group: Mac Hopkins (flight instructor), Charlie Johnson (flight officer), Fred Weathersby (flight crew), and Romeo M. Williams (2nd lieutenant, pilot.) Williams is on the back row, fourth from the left.

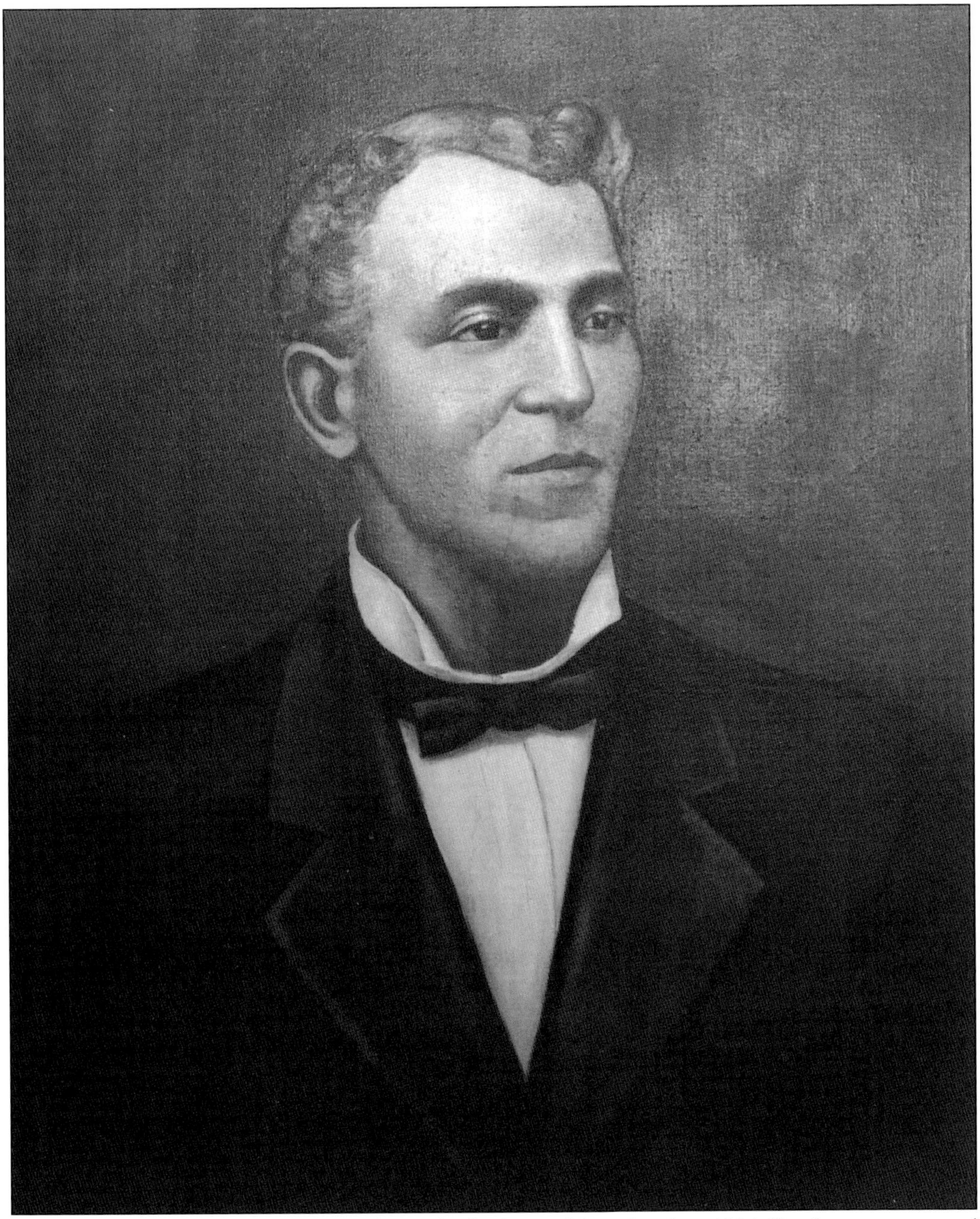

Prof. H. B. Pemberton Sr. established Marshall's first public school in 1894. Pemberton arranged a loan for Central School. The African American community repaid the loan. In 1925, Central moved to a new building on Rosborough Springs Road. In 1941, it was renamed Pemberton High School in honor of its founder. Pemberton was the first college graduate of Wiley College in 1888.

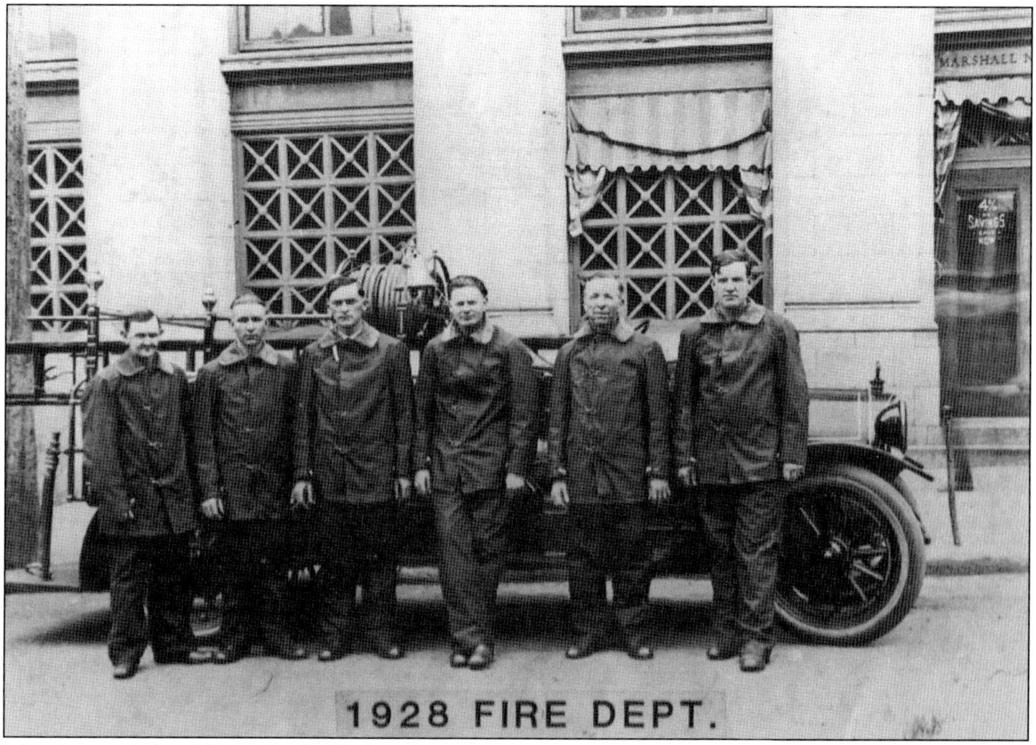

Members of the 1928 Marshall Fire Department pose in front of their equipment. An early important advantage for the growth of cities was the public service organizations like a fire department and police department.

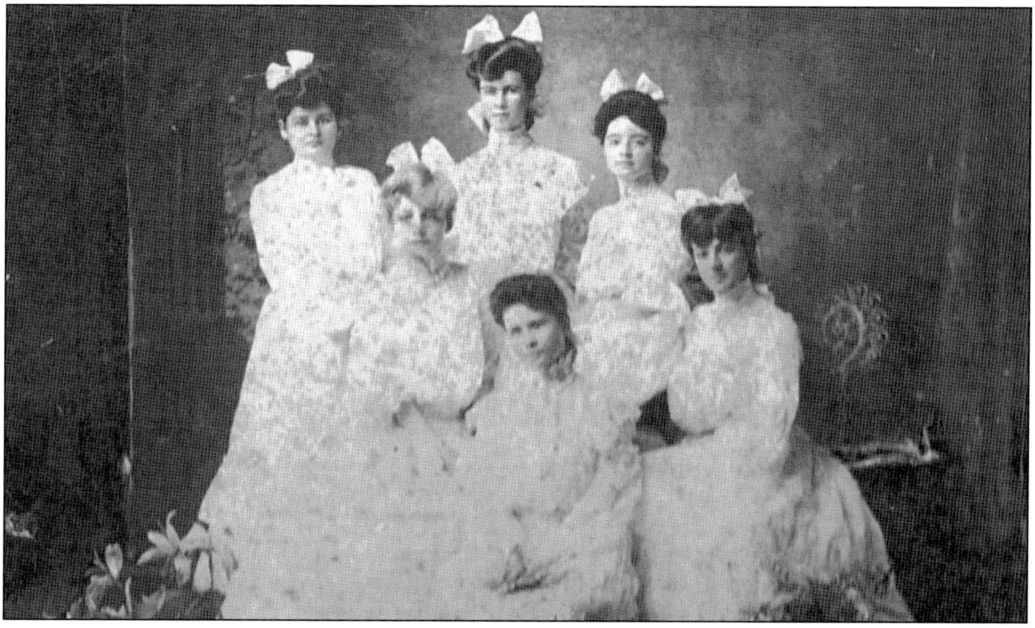

These young ladies are students in the Marshall Masonic Female Institute, which was established in Marshall by Masonic Lodge No. 22 in 1843. For many years, this was the only school in Marshall that young women attended.

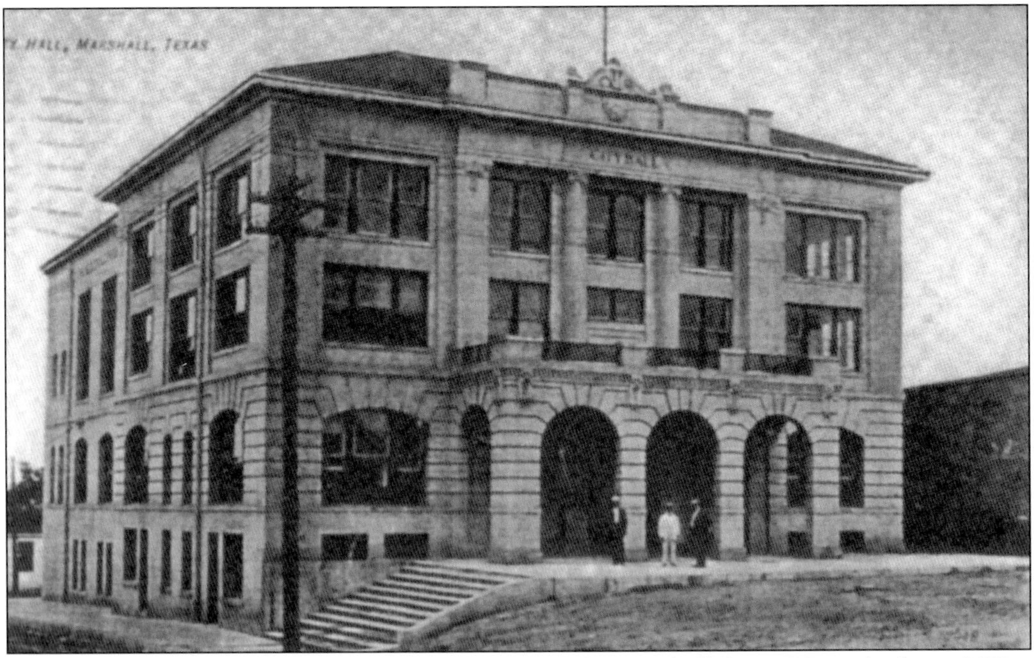

In 1907, Marshall erected a city hall on the site where the Marshall Opera House had stood. This building burned in 1923. Erected in its place was the 1930 Marshall City Hall. It is still in use today, although not as a city hall. It houses the offices of the Harrison County Historical Museum.

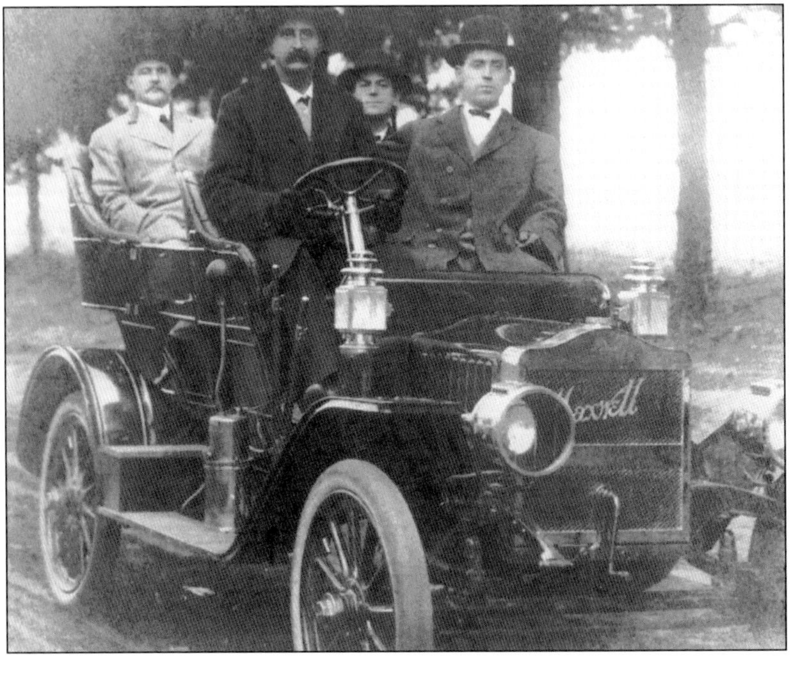

Judge H. T. Lyttleton is shown here driving his 1909 Maxwell. The passengers with him are not identified. Cars were beginning to be seen more frequently on the streets of Marshall.

Ten

The Bright and Shining Future of Marshall

This has been a whirlwind tour of Marshall, hopefully one that preserves the past for readers. Old and young alike may learn of the rich heritage that makes Marshall the special place that it is today. The past is intertwined with principles that have contributed to the greatness of the United States, but what about the future? What lies ahead?

In 1879, "A Pen Picture of the City of Marshall and Harrison County," published by the *Tri-Weekly Herald,* described Marshall as a place that is "picturesque and charming" with "broad streets" and "charming residences, in which modern architectural taste is conspicuous." The author further states that the "views from the courthouse and railway headquarters are very fine." And finally, "There are very few towns in Texas that present so many picturesque scenes." This statement is as true now as it was when it was written. That is not an accident. Why is Marshall today still picturesque and charming and full of personality and optimism?

Attention has been paid by Marshall leadership to revitalization of neighborhoods. In 2001, the Marshall City Commission adopted an historic neighborhood preservation plan to assist declining neighborhoods in revitalizing themselves through the formation of neighborhood associations. Two very active associations, New Town and East End, are leading the way in revitalization efforts.

Economic development remains a continuing force in Marshall and Harrison County. There has been a concerted effort to reverse the trend to abandon downtown Marshall and to instead focus on capitalizing on its beauty and uniqueness. Much of the leadership for this comes from Marshall's Main Street Program, a downtown revitalization program of the National Trust for Historic Preservation. Marshall is benefitting from the Sam B. Hall Federal Court, which is located in Marshall. Efforts go beyond the city limits and expand into the county. In 2009, the land once home to Longhorn Ordnance Works was designated by the Texas Parks and Wildlife to be a wildlife reserve.

Historic preservation is a viable part of the economic growth of Marshall. From its historic, carefully preserved courthouse, to its lovely old homes and stunning display of flags that are visible next to the school administration building, Marshall exhibits pride in its past and optimism for the future. This optimism shines with enthusiasm, as Marshall becomes a "Wonderland of Lights" each Christmas season.

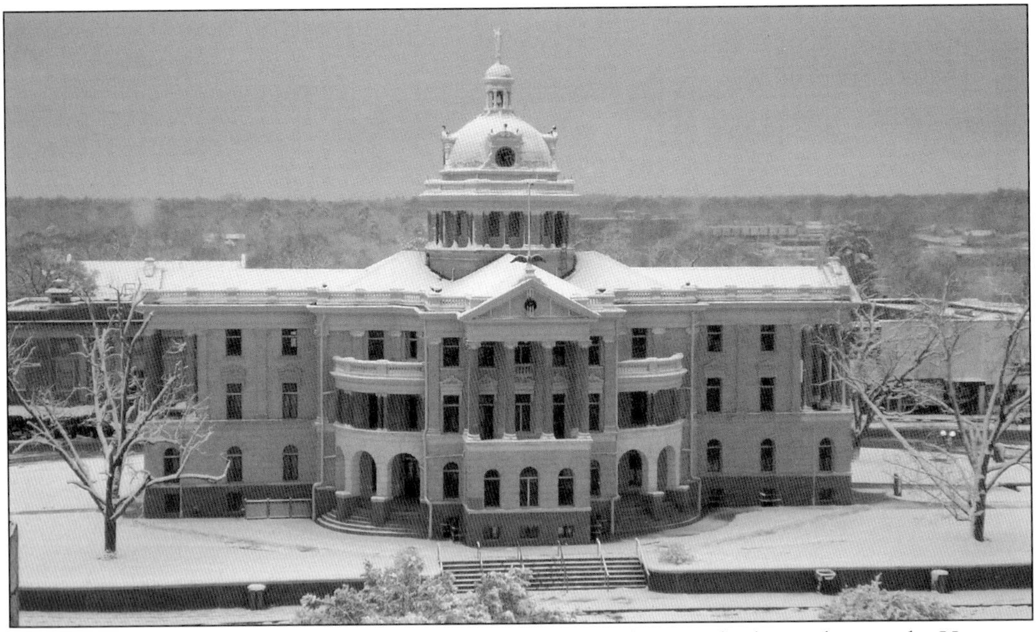

A shining tribute to the future of Marshall is the 1901 courthouse, which now houses the Harrison County Historical Museum and the county judge and commissioners court. This photograph, taken from the top of the Capitol One Bank, shows the courthouse in the snow that fell in 2010. (Courtesy of Elaine Sutton.)

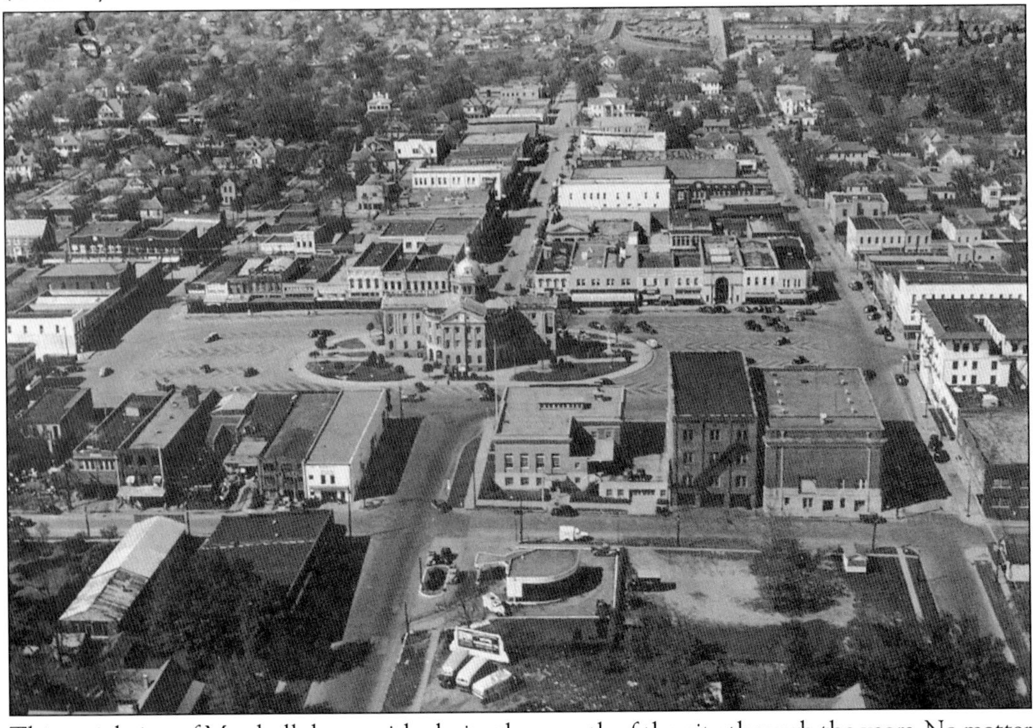

This aerial view of Marshall shows with clarity the growth of the city through the years. No matter the angle from which a photograph is taken, the courthouse is still the center of attention and the hub around which the community operates.

This historic old home, the Allen House, was built by Walter Monyrcue Allen. In 1842, he married Eliza Ann Handley. He pastored several churches and finally they moved to Marshall. In 1878, they completed this home at 610 North Washington Street. The home was purchased by the Harrison County Historical Society in 1976 and completely restored to serve as an important reminder of the days of antebellum homes throughout the South.

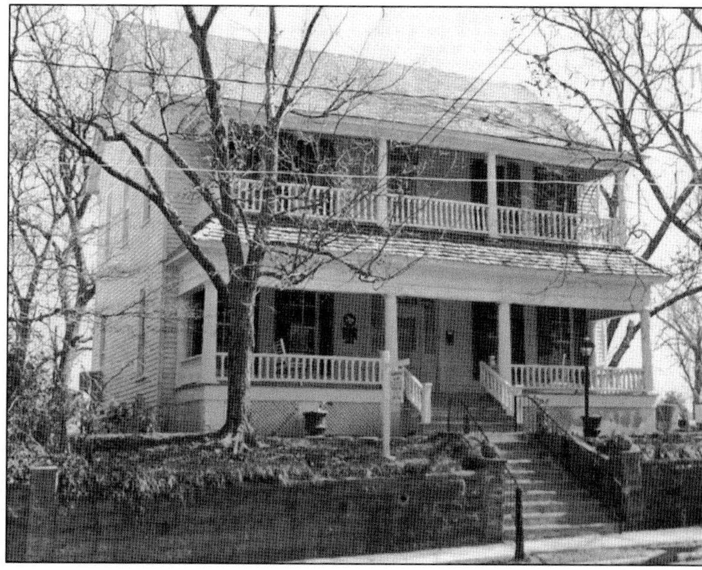

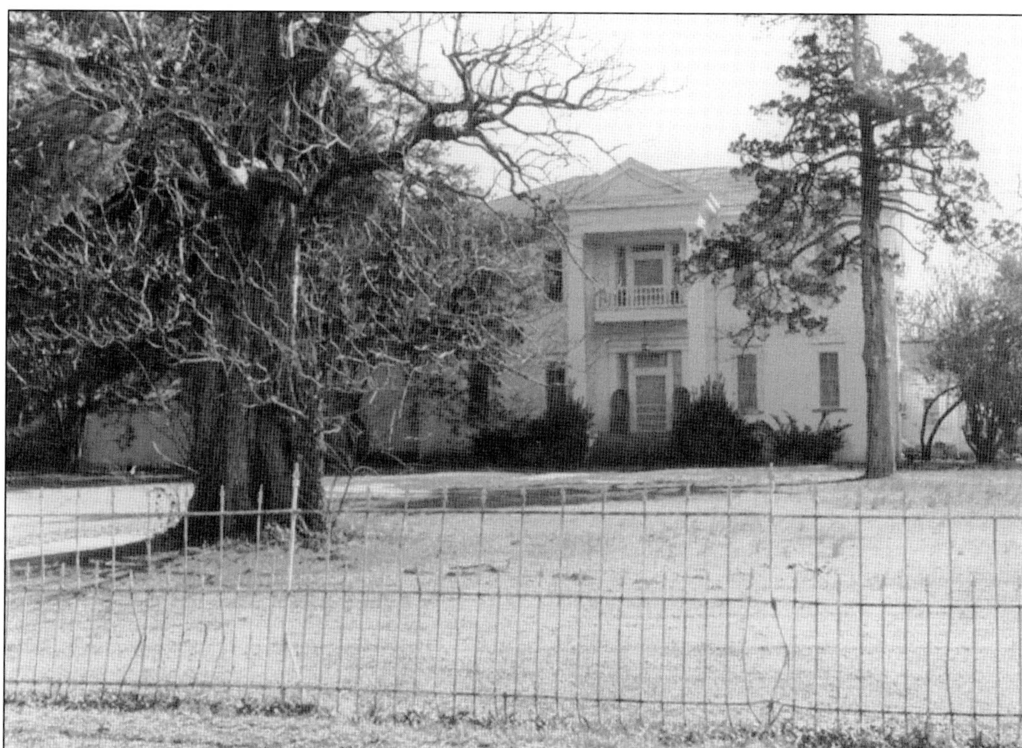

In 1843, Milt Andrews built this grand home on his cotton plantation near Karnack. T.J. Taylor purchased the home in 1902. In 1912, Taylor's daughter Claudia (called Lady Bird) was born at the home. Lady Bird lived there until 1928 when she left to continue her education. She married Lyndon B. Johnson and became First Lady of the United States.

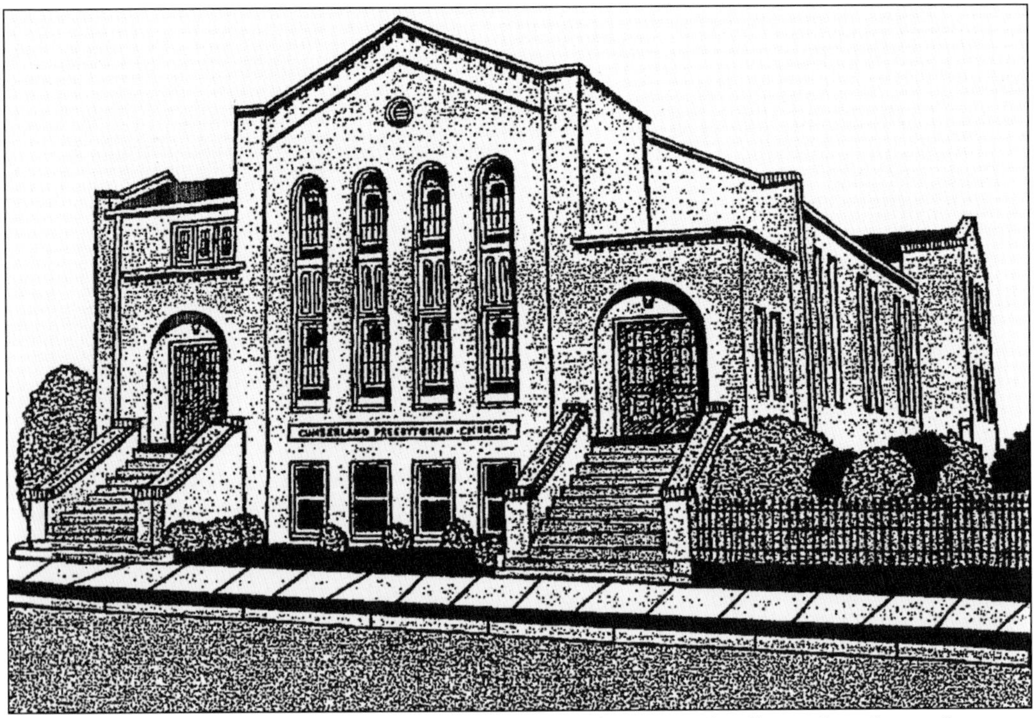

The Cumberland Presbyterian Church was renovated in 1932 and still stands today at the same site where it was built originally (corner of East Grand and North Washington Streets.) It is still in use as a church today, but not as Cumberland Presbyterian. (Drawing by Richard Magrill.)

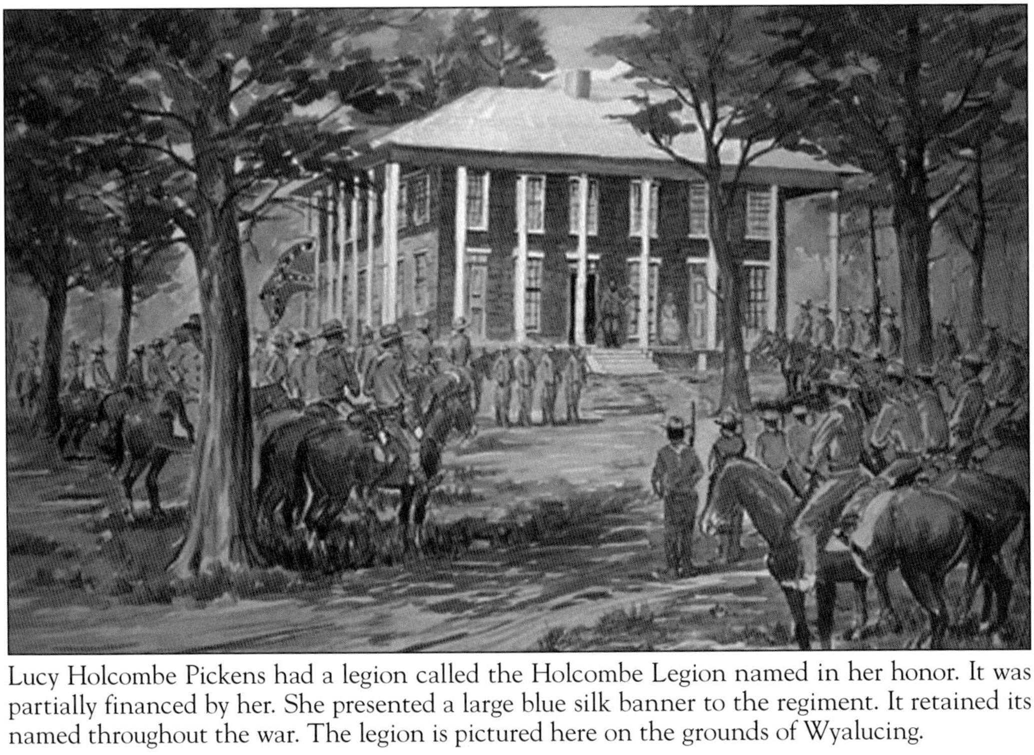

Lucy Holcombe Pickens had a legion called the Holcombe Legion named in her honor. It was partially financed by her. She presented a large blue silk banner to the regiment. It retained its named throughout the war. The legion is pictured here on the grounds of Wyalucing.

Marshall's historic neighborhoods give the city its distinct identity. From East End to Northside; Rainey to Gregg; Belmont to Baptist Hill; New Town to West End; and Sunny South to Yankee Stadium, these neighborhoods portray the growth and development of the city. This is the Dr. O. M. Heartsill home in the East End neighborhood, which lies east of Alamo Boulevard and extends north and south from East Houston Street.

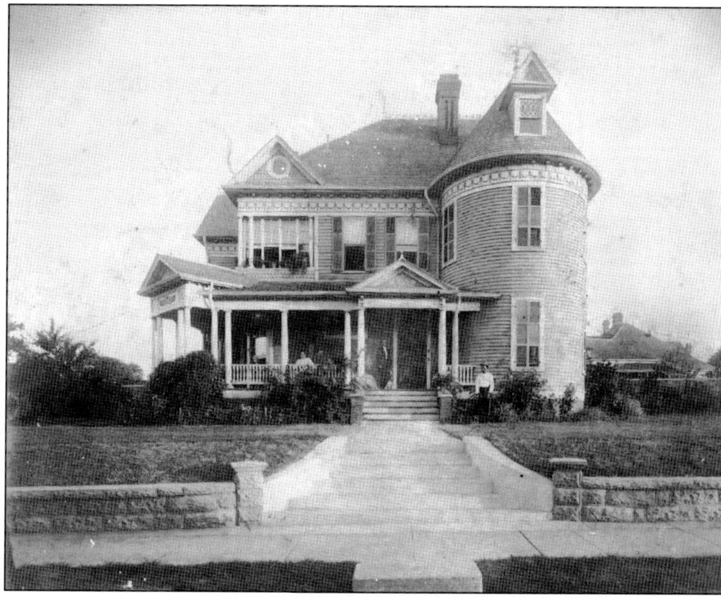

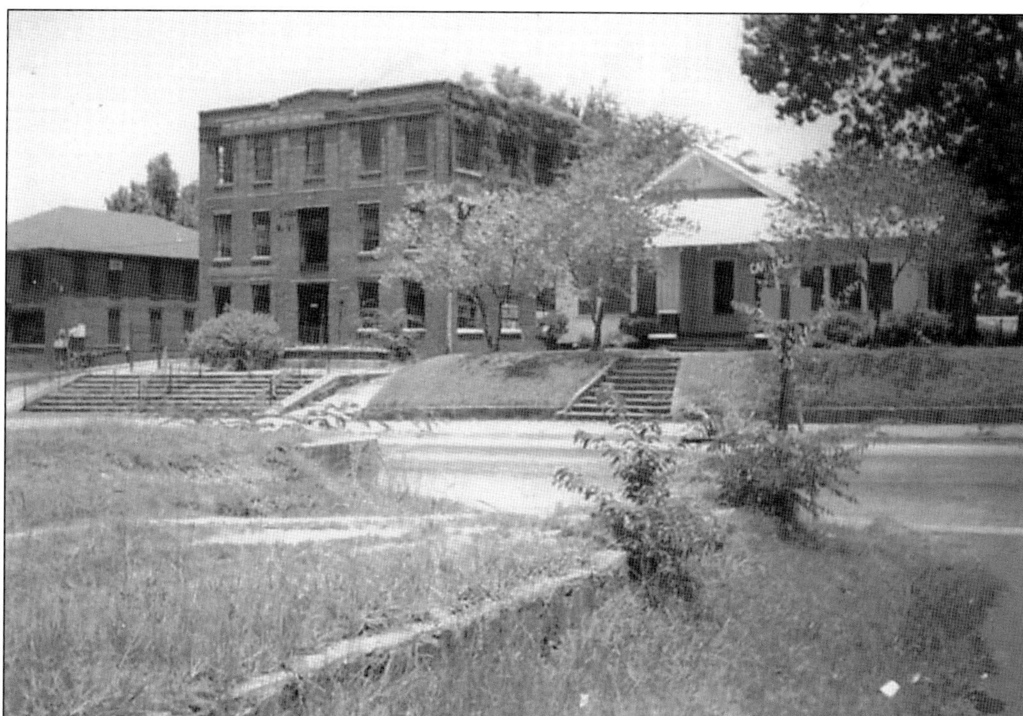

Marshall's "Historic Preservation Plan" states that the city's historic neighborhoods "give the city character and image unlike any other place." New Town is one of these historic neighborhoods. Developed about 1910 around Wiley College, it was a self-sufficient neighborhood with grocery stores, restaurants, medical offices, and funeral homes. Sheppard's Sanatarium, a hospital founded in 1925 for African Americans, is the three-story brick building in this photograph.

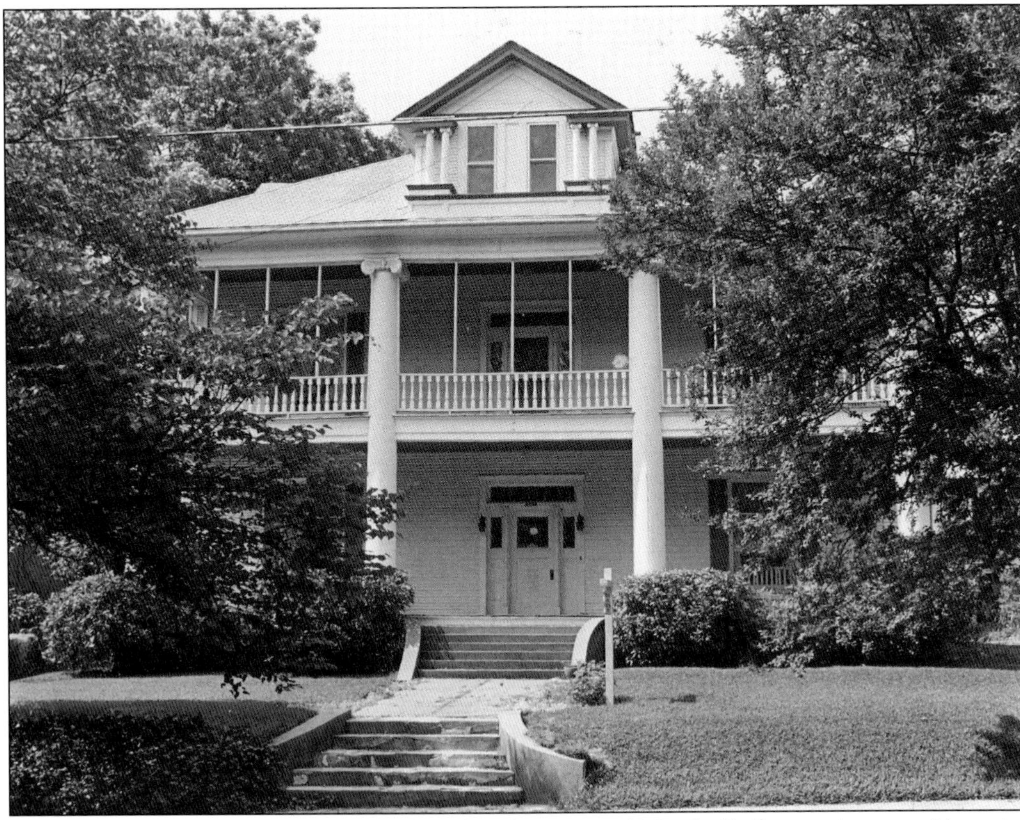

Marshall's historic neighborhoods define the character of Marshall. Queen Anne or Victorian styles of architecture dominate the building environment in both the East End and West End historic neighborhoods. This house, called "The Columns," is in the West End neighborhood that is west of Grove Street and lies between West Houston Street and West Grand Avenue.

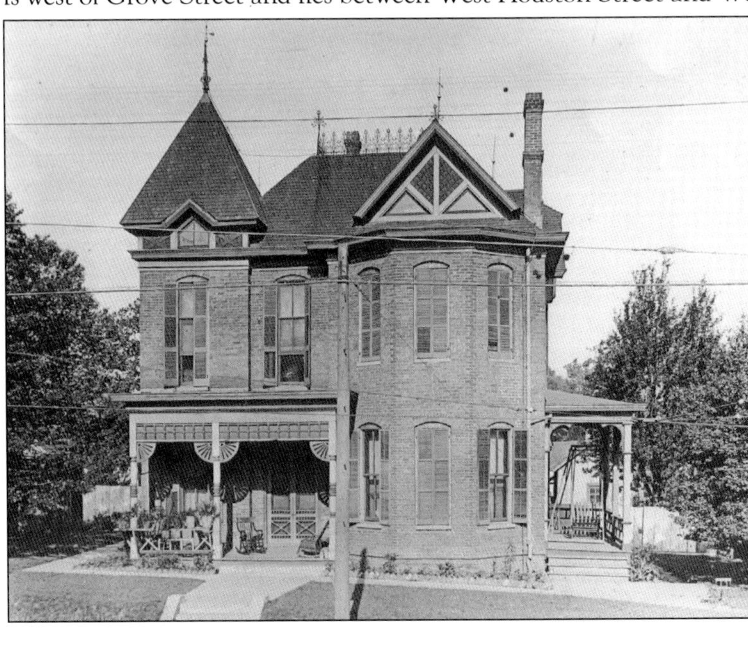

The Ginocchio home is in the Ginocchio Historic District. The district was added to the National Register of Historic Places in 1974.

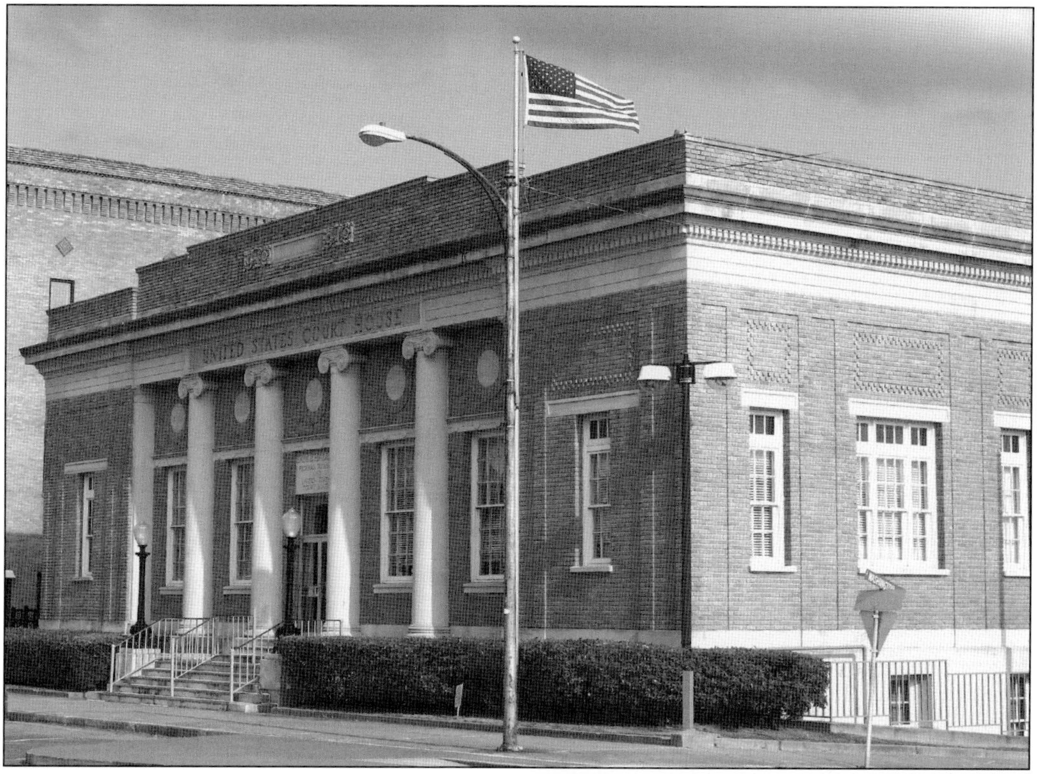

This building, formerly the Marshall Post Office, is now the Sam B. Hall Jr. Federal Courthouse. It was named for a longtime public servant who represented the people of this area in the U.S. Congress and later as a district judge in Texas. Cases heard in this court involve patents. It is an extremely busy court and brings in many cases to be tried in Marshall.

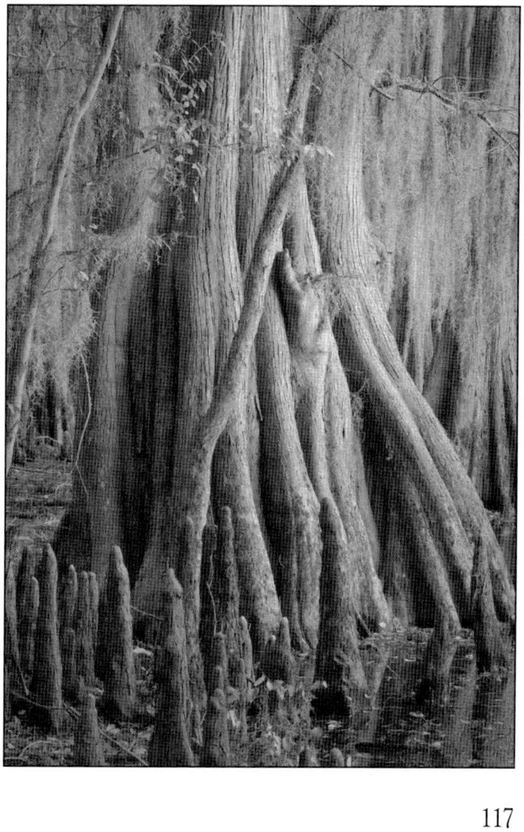

The Caddo Lake National Wildlife Refuge is located near the sleepy little town of Karnack, the girlhood home of first lady and wildflower conservationist Lady Bird Johnson. The refuge consists of over 7,000 acres, including one of the best examples of old growth hardwood bottomland forests in the state of Texas. The refuge offers a wetlands center, an equestrian Wildlife Observation Trail and Auto Tour, and many opportunities for wildlife viewing and photography. Admission is free. (Courtesy of John Johannson of Tyler.)

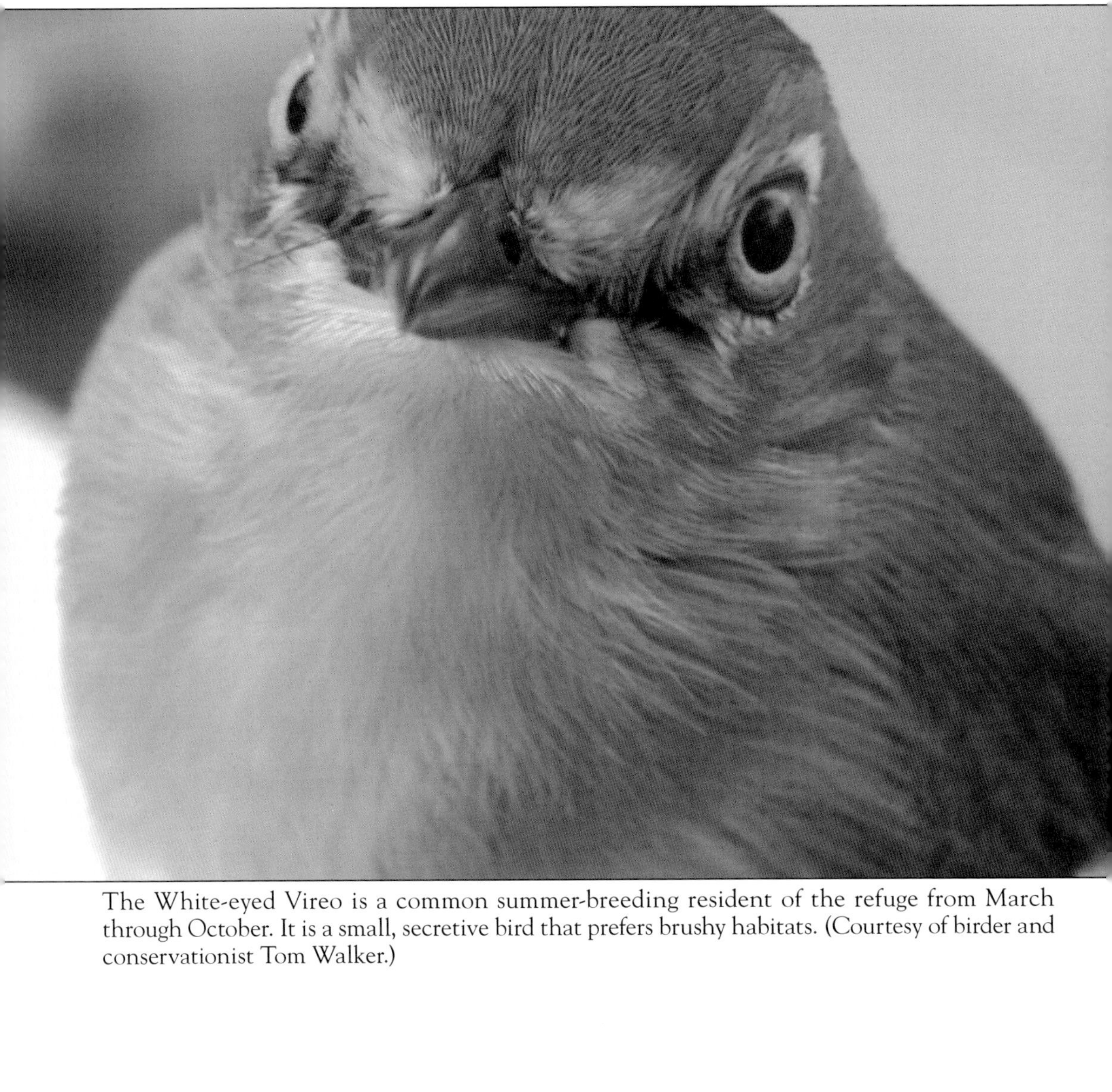

The White-eyed Vireo is a common summer-breeding resident of the refuge from March through October. It is a small, secretive bird that prefers brushy habitats. (Courtesy of birder and conservationist Tom Walker.)

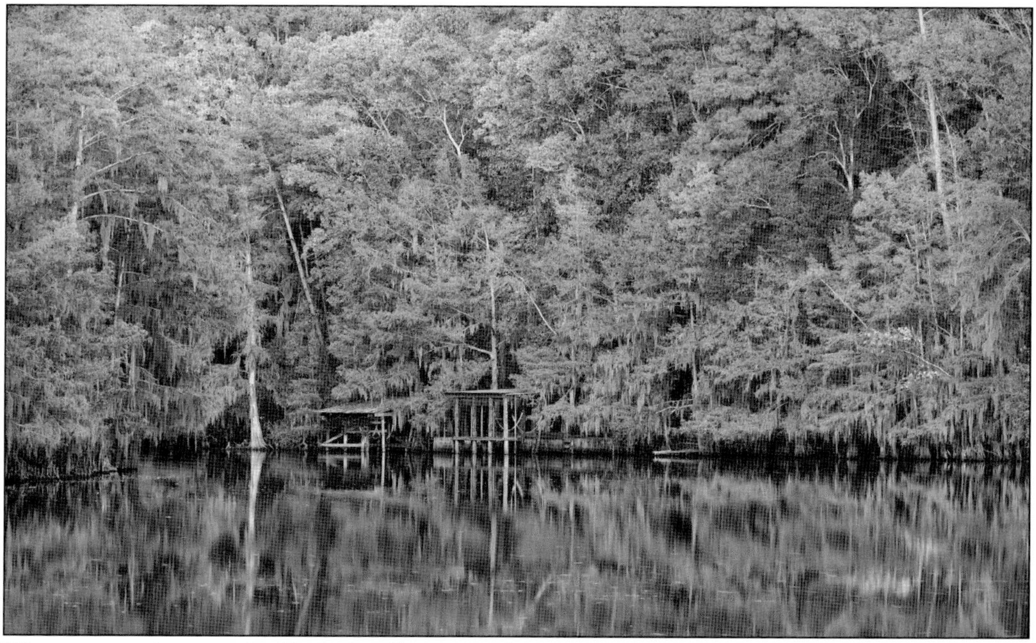

This scene taken on Caddo Lake illustrates the type of plants and other vegetation that are found there. This fishing camp is another reason why visitors love the area. It is these items that make the area an ideal site for the newly formed Caddo Lake Wildlife Refuge. (Courtesy of John Johannson of Tyler.)

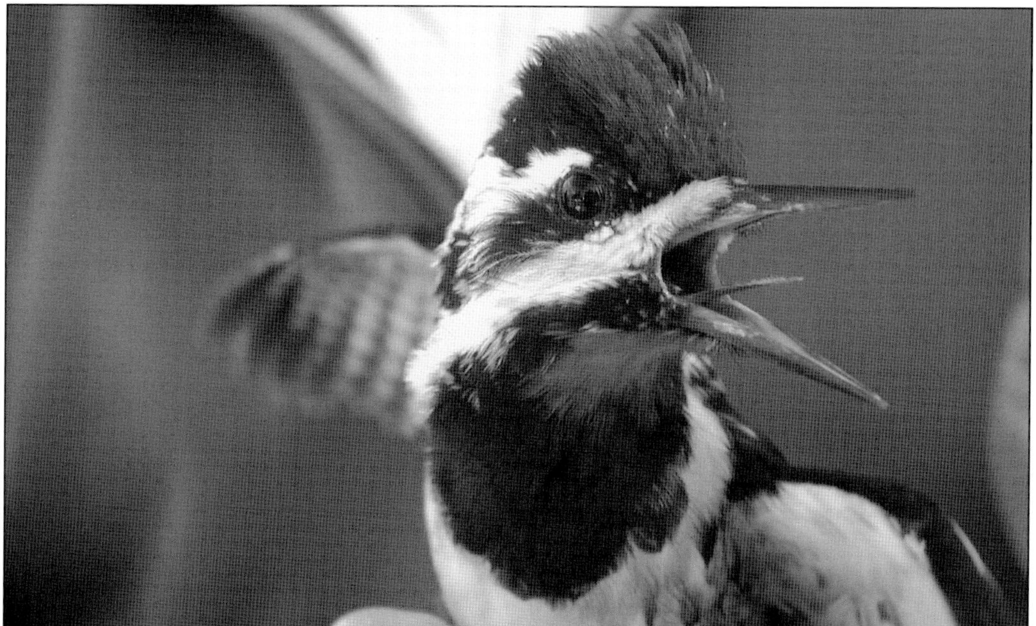

This bird is but one example of the wide variety of birds and other wildlife present in the Caddo Lake Wildlife Refuge. Cypress and other trees are also found in abundance in this area. The variety of vegetation makes the spot ideal for photographers and other nature lovers. (Courtesy of birder and conservationist Tom Walker.)

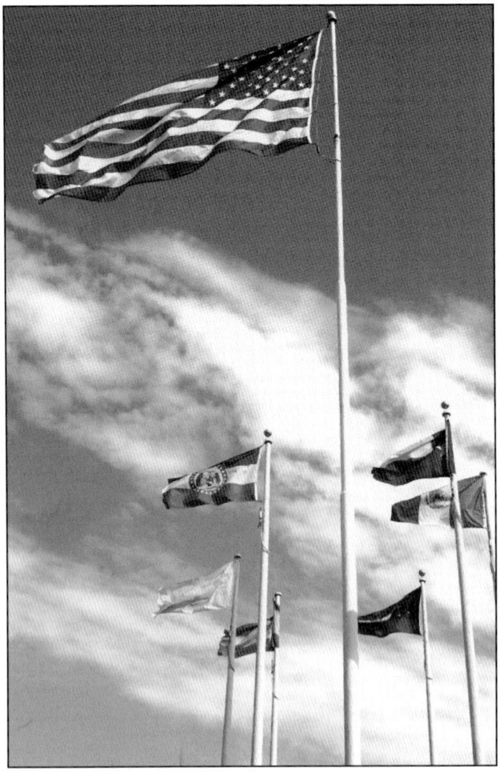

This impressive display of flags, which have flown over Marshall, stands today at the intersection of Highways 43 and 79. The display was erected with memorial gifts in 1984 and was among the final projects completed by Pat Smith-Gasperson during her last days as superintendent in 1994. (Courtesy of Ben Hughes.)

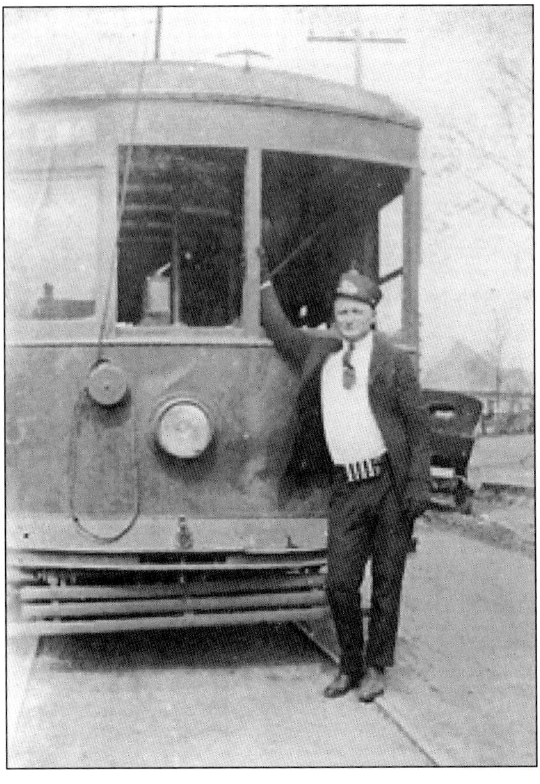

Transportation played a major role in the growth of Marshall, from the railroads of the 19th century to the construction of Interstate 20 in the 20th century. Streetcars served the city during its early days. In 1913, there were five streetcars running in Marshall. The streetcar ran from the Capitol Hotel to the depot. The service was discontinued as cars became more plentiful. Pictured here is a streetcar conductor Edgar Davis in 1923. Good transportation systems are still important to the growth of cities. Marshall leaders continue the efforts of the city's early leaders to have excellent transportation systems serving Marshall.

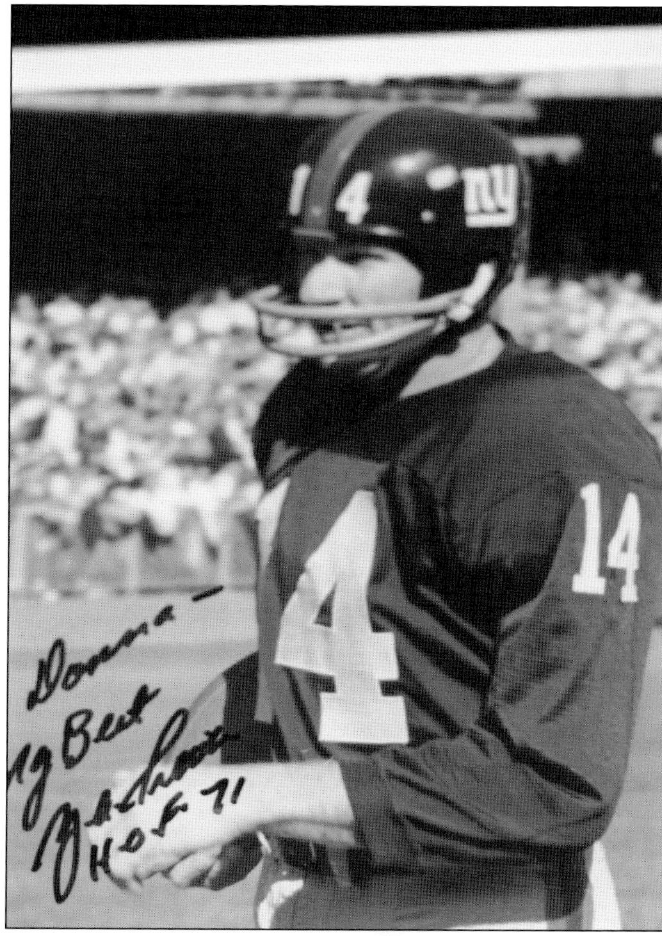

Y. A Tittle was born in Marshall on October 24, 1926. He played college football at Louisiana State University, and his pro football career began with the Baltimore Colts in 1948. In 1950, he joined the San Francisco 49ers. Later he was traded to the New York Giants where he set a record by throwing 36 touchdown passes in one season. In 1971, Tittle was inducted into the Pro Football Hall of Fame. (Courtesy of Matt and Donna Burns.)

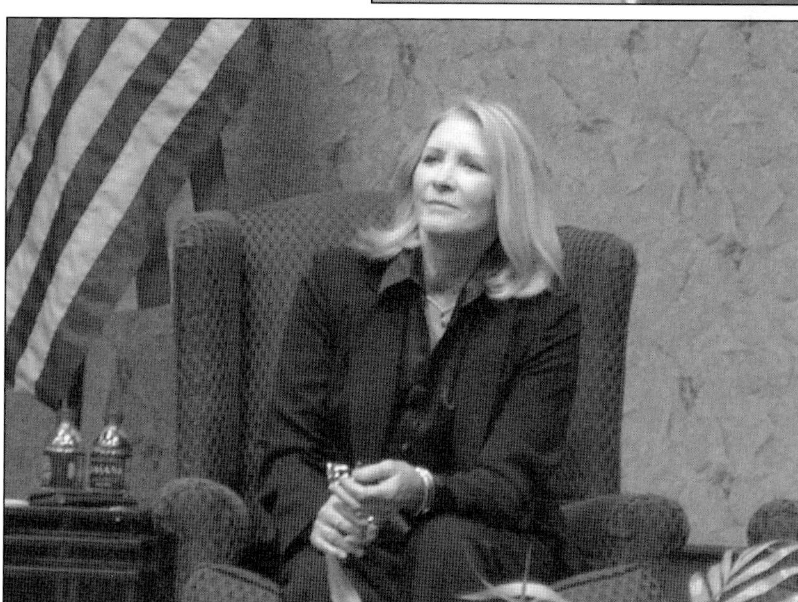

Susan Howard, well known for her starring role in the television production *Dallas*, lived much of her early life in Marshall. She is a graduate of Marshall High School, and she attended the University of Texas before going to Hollywood to begin her acting career. She and her husband live near Austin.

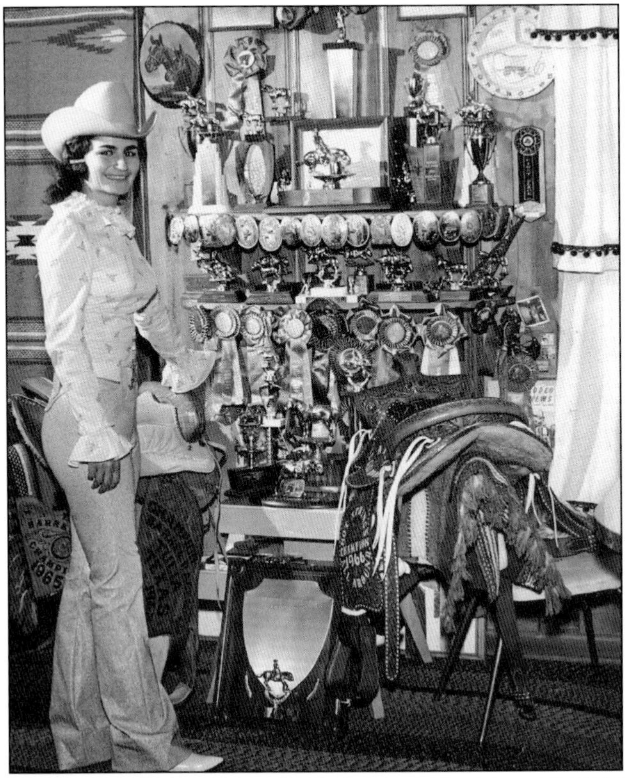

Harrison County's Martha Josey won an Olympic Gold Medal as a member of the 1988 U.S. Olympics equestrian team. She won world barrel racing championships for four decades beginning in 1968. Josey, along with her husband, R. F. Josey, trained thousands of young horse riders at their clinics and schools held on the ranch east of Marshall. They host the internationally known annual Josey Junior Championship Barrel Race.

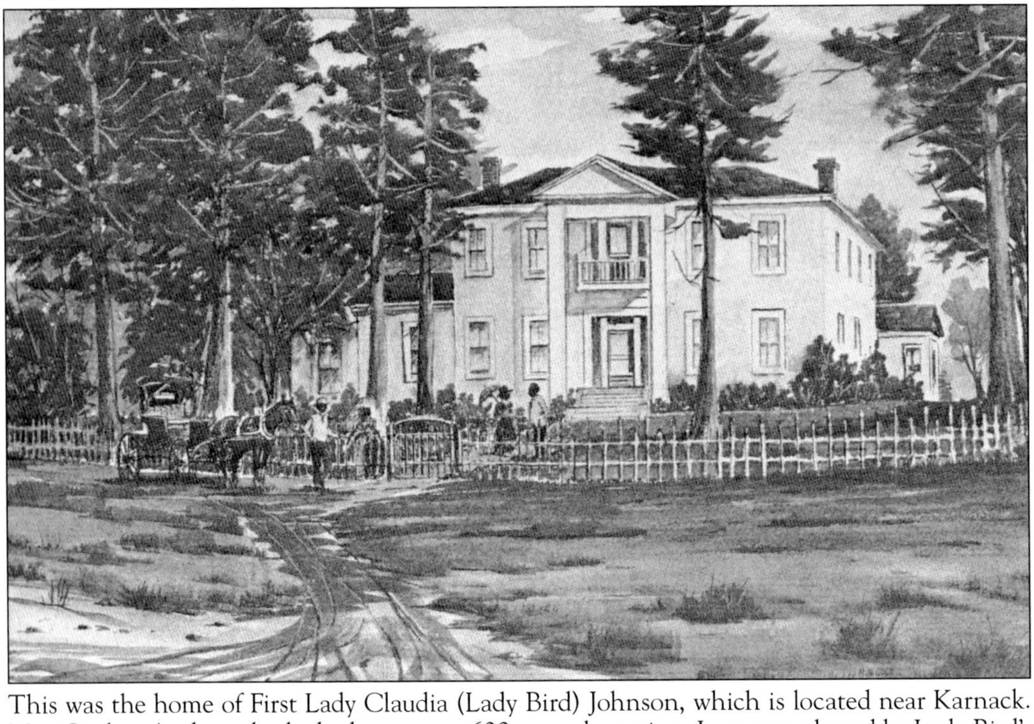

This was the home of First Lady Claudia (Lady Bird) Johnson, which is located near Karnack. Maj. Cephas Andrews built the home on a 600-acre plantation. It was purchased by Lady Bird's father, T. J. Taylor, in the 1900s.

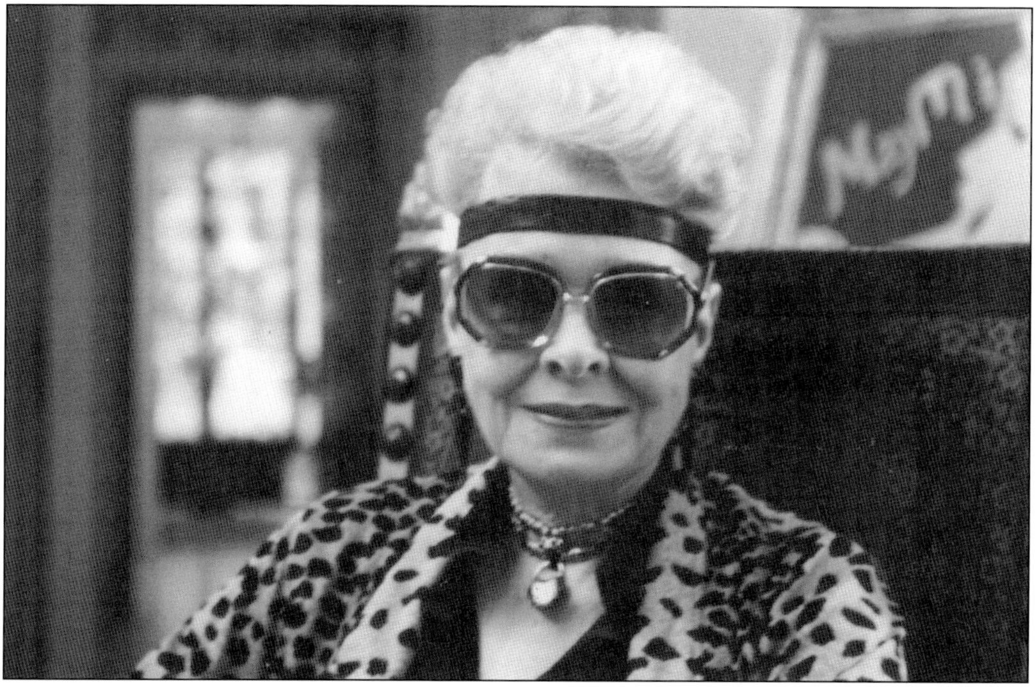

Marshall's Wonderland of Lights began when former Marshall resident Wendy Russell Reves gave a challenge gift. The result was the ever-expanding Wonderland of Lights. Reves has continued her interest in Marshall and has played a major role in the founding of the Michelson Museum of Art.

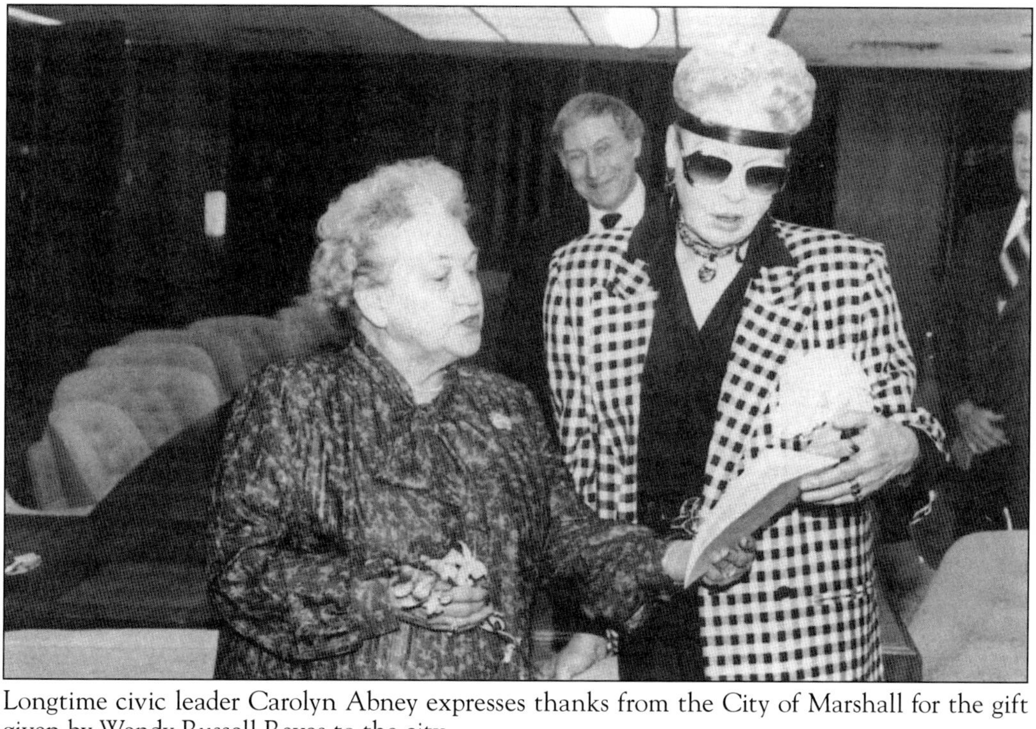

Longtime civic leader Carolyn Abney expresses thanks from the City of Marshall for the gift given by Wendy Russell Reves to the city.

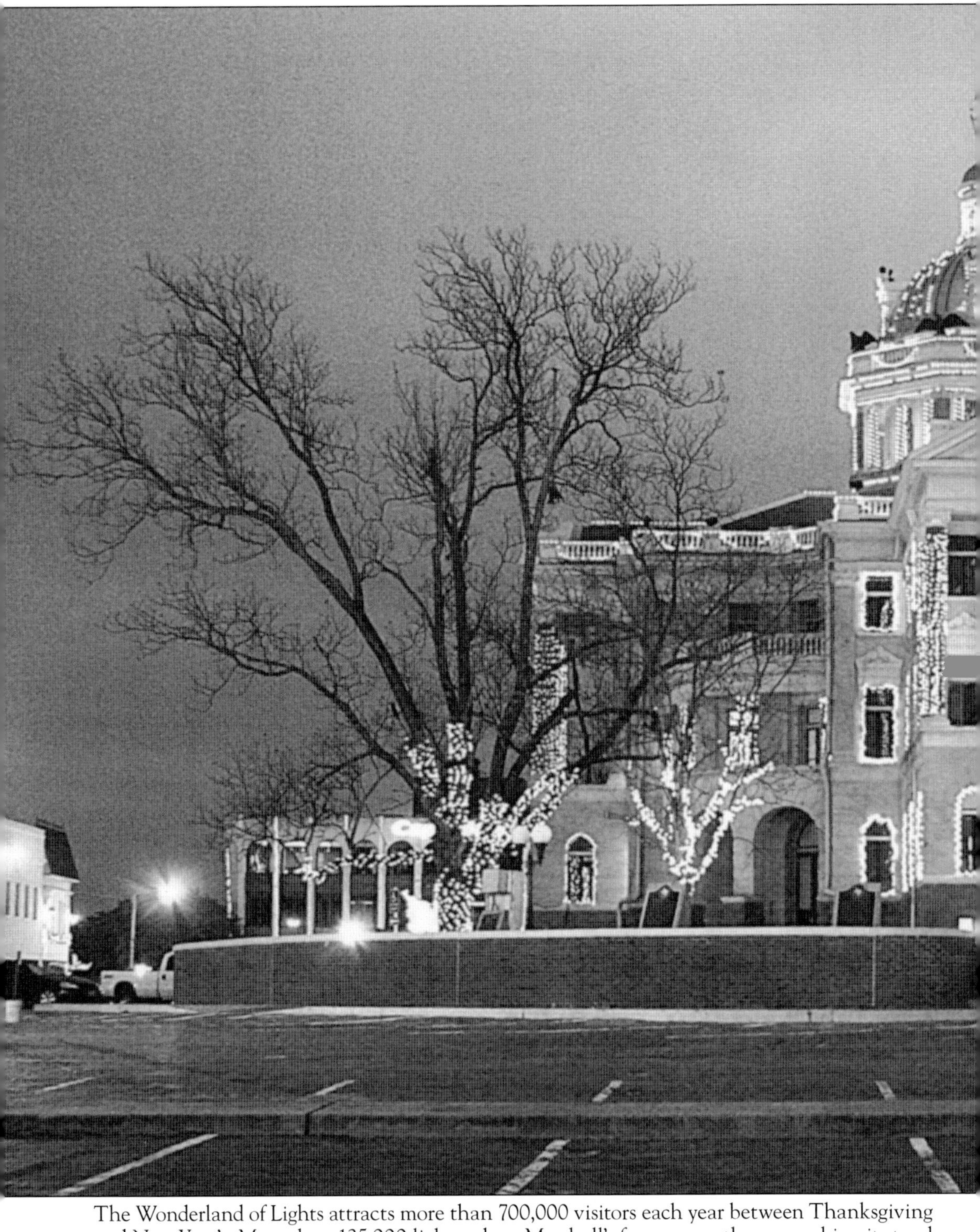

The Wonderland of Lights attracts more than 700,000 visitors each year between Thanksgiving and New Year's. More than 125,000 lights adorn Marshall's former courthouse, making it stand out as a reminder of the rich and colorful history of Marshall and of the vision that Marshall has

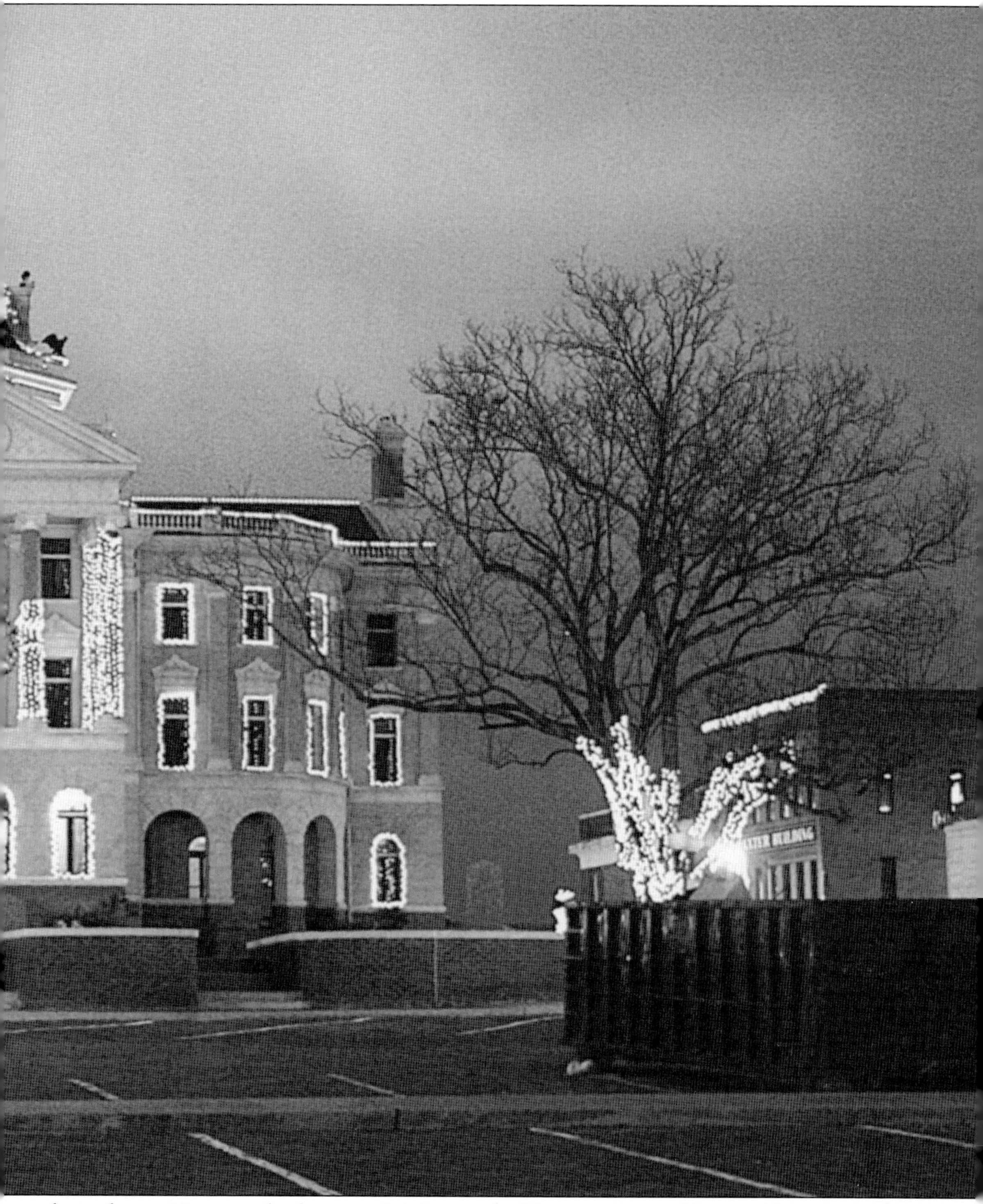

for its future. Now completely restored, it houses the Harrison County Historical Museum and the county judge and county commissioners. (Courtesy of Ben Hughes.)

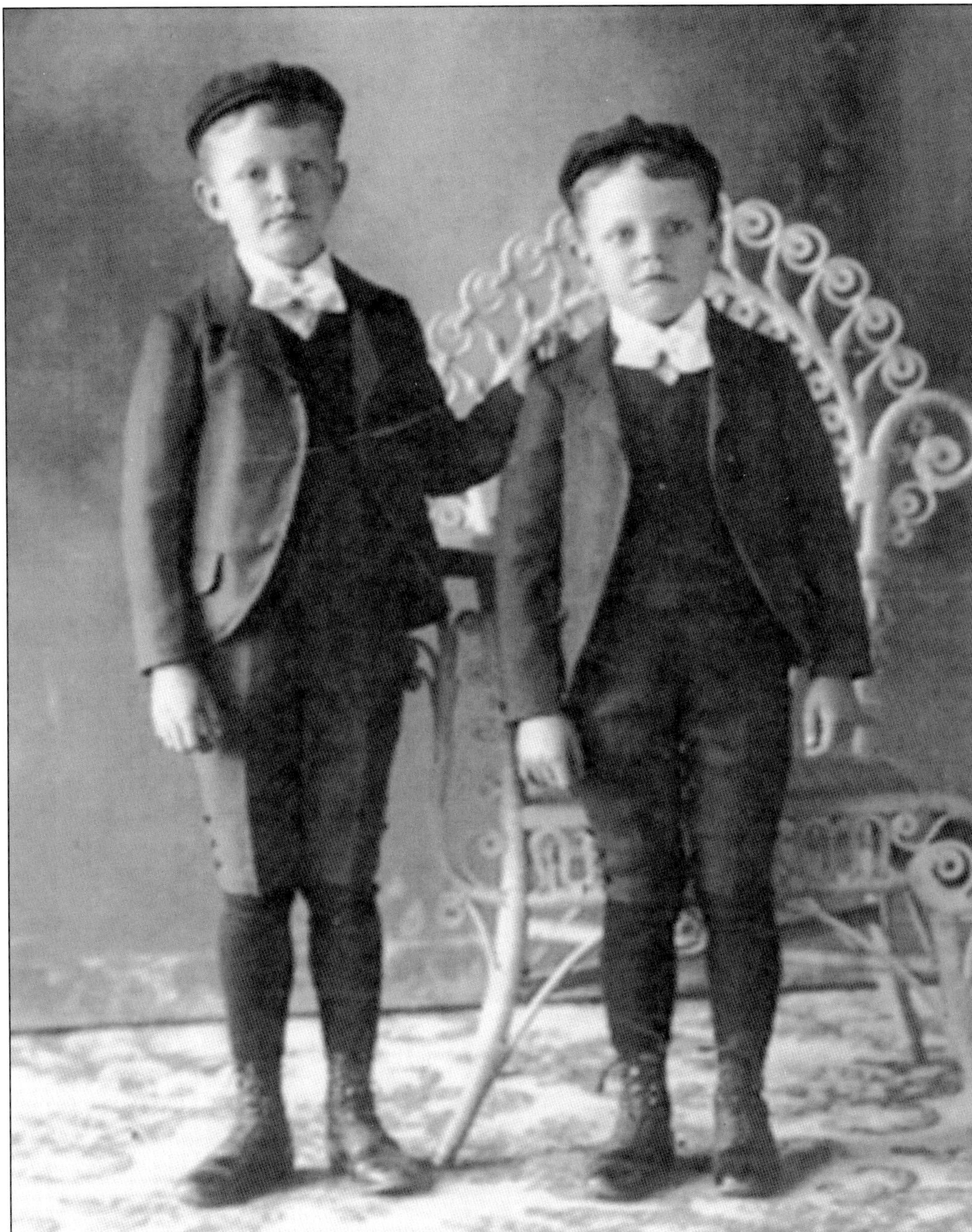

So ends this whirlwind history of Marshall, Texas. It seems appropriate to end it with a photograph of young people because that is where Marshall's hope lies. These two young men in knee pants are unidentified in this photograph, which was found in the Harrison County Museum. They do not need a name to remind us of what everyone knows. The hope for the United States of America lies in the young people who will be charged with guiding it in the future. How much more wisely they will be able to guide if they have a solid foundation of their heritage. It is our hope that this book will help to inform and strengthen citizens of Marshall as they press forward to a new and brighter tomorrow!

BIBLIOGRAPHY

Berglund, Ernest. *History of Marshall.* Austin: Steck Company, 1948.
Bolton, Herbert Eugene. *Texas in the Middle Eighteenth Century.* Austin: University of Texas Press, 1915.
Hackney, Vivian H. *Historical Hallmarks of Marshall.* Marshall National Bank: Marshall, 1964.
"Marshall." *Handbook of Texas* online. July 2009.
Marshall News Messenger. *Pictorial History of Marshall. Marshall:* News Messenger. 1980.
Peacock, Howard. "Marshall: City with Star Quality." *Texas Highways Magazine* (October 1996): 40–48.
Plummer, Edward R. *Historic Marshall Revisited.* Marshall. 1988.
Rickard, J. A., and Maurine Bullock. *Your Texas History.* Austin: Benson Publishing, 1962

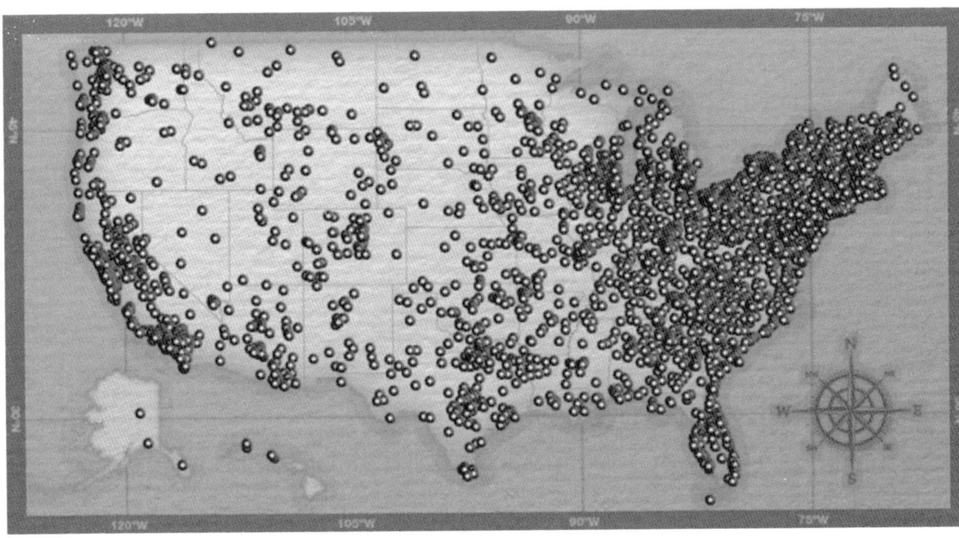